MW01030117

A PERSIAN
AT THE COURT OF
KING GEORGE
1809-10

To the memory of Effat Samiian,
Mirza Abul Hassan Khan's
great-great-great-grand-daughter

and for his many descendants
all over the world

A PERSIAN
AT THE COURT OF
KING GEORGE
1809-10

THE JOURNAL OF MIRZA ABUL HASSAN KHAN
TRANSLATED AND EDITED BY MARGARET MORRIS CLOAKE
INTRODUCTION BY DENIS WRIGHT

> . . . that which would afford the most amuse-
> ment, would be the publication of his own jour-
> nal, which he regularly kept, during his absence
> from Persia; and which on his return there, was
> read with great avidity by his own countrymen.
>
> JAMES MORIER

BARRIE & JENKINS
LONDON

First published in Great Britain in 1988 by
Barrie & Jenkins Ltd
289 Westbourne Grove, London W11 2QA
Copyright © Margaret Morris Cloake 1988

British Library Cataloguing in Publication Data
Khan, Mirza Abul Hassan
 A Persian at the court of King George: the
 journal of Mirza Abul Hassan Khan, 1809-10.
 1. Great Britain. Persian diplomatic
 service, 1809-1810. Biographies
 I. Title   II. Cloake, Margaret Morris
 327.2'092'4

ISBN 0-7126-2105-9

CONTENTS

FOREWORD

F ROM THE EARLY SEVENTEENTH CENTURY, when Queen
Elizabeth I granted a charter to the merchants of the East
India Company to trade in the East, Englishmen have visited
Persia. Some went as merchants, some as soldiers, some as diplo-
mats. Many were servants of the East India Company. More often
than not they recorded their impressions – in words and in pictures –
of Persia and its peoples. They described the exotic and despotic
Shahs of Persia, and the routes to their courts: at Qazvin, Isfahan,
Shiraz and finally at Tehran. Some made valuable architectural and
archaeological notes and drawings. There is no dearth of books by
English travellers to Persia.

Persian travellers to England, on the other hand, were few indeed
before the twentieth century,[1] and fewer still were those who wrote
of their experiences. *The Book of Wonders* – the London journal kept
by the Persian Ambassador Mirza Abul Hassan Khan Shirazi[2] in
1809-10 – is only the fourth such early account by a Persian of a
journey to England to be translated into English. Among the four it
is the second in order of date.[3]

Abul Hassan's journey was diplomatic – his mission was to secure
the ratification of an Anglo-Persian Treaty – and he writes that he
kept a journal in the hope that it would be of use to future ambassadors.

On the diplomatic side, Abul Hassan records his meetings with
Government Ministers and East India Company officials and his
endless frustration and distress over the incomprehensible (to him)

delays in the ratification process. But the journal also provides a foreigner's personal and privileged view of English mores and manners in the year before George III lapsed into his final madness and the Prince of Wales assumed the Regency. Unlike the memoirs of this period written by European or American visitors to England, Abul Hassan's journal records the impressions of a foreigner quite unused to European ways – an intelligent, observant and cultured man brought face to face with a different civilization.

Abul Hassan may have chafed at being kept waiting in London for eight months while Ministers and Privy Councillors debated each clause of his Treaty, but he was not bored. Sir Gore Ouseley, who was his official host in London, filled his days with riding, calls, sightseeing and shopping, and his evenings with parties and the Opera. Abul Hassan was naturally curious, and he recorded sights and statistics with equal delight.

He must also have enjoyed finding himself the toast of London. Charles Lamb wrote in a letter in January 1810, 'The Persian Ambassador is the principal thing talked of now.'[4] The Persian Ambassador – the first to visit the capital in almost 200 years – was thirty-four years old, tall, dark and very handsome (as can be seen in the Lawrence and Beechey portraits), and he wore superb robes and turbans of silk and brocade; the smart hostesses of London bombarded him with invitations and the newspapers reported his every move. He was specially cultivated and befriended by Mrs Perceval, the wife of the Prime Minister; and he fell in love with the Foreign Secretary's niece.

His popularity was heightened by his wit, and he was lucky enough to have James Morier almost constantly at his side to translate his quick repartee and impromptu verses with equal wit. Years later, however, Abul Hassan was less than pleased to recognize himself as the model for Mirza Firouz, the Persian Ambassador in Morier's famous satire of Persian life, *The Adventures of Hajji Baba of Ispahan*, which was published in 1824. We do not know if he ever saw its sequel, *Hajji Baba of Ispahan in England* (1828), but he would certainly have recognized his own journal as its inspiration.

The mission completed, Abul Hassan returned to Tehran with Sir Gore Ouseley, newly appointed British Ambassador to Persia, and James Morier, Secretary to the Embassy. Fath Ali Shah was pleased: he rewarded his Envoy with the title of Khan and his Envoy's book with the title of *Heirat-nameh (The Book of Wonders)*.

Abul Hassan's own copy of the journal has disappeared, but contemporary copies were made for circulation at the Persian Court, and later copies were made from these – it is impossible to know how many. One is kept in the library of the Iranian Parliament and there is a greatly abridged version in the British Library.[5] Another copy, with the poetry omitted, appeared at auction in London in 1981. The copy I have used for this translation belonged to Abul Hassan's great-great-great-granddaughter, Mrs Effat Samiian. An outstanding teacher, Mrs Samiian was a woman as charming as she was capable. Sadly, she did not live to see the English translation of her distinguished ancestor's journal in print. She died in Tehran in 1985.

Mrs Samiian's copy of the journal is a 371-page undecorated manuscript in the clear *nastaliq* of a nineteenth-century scribe.[6] Abul Hassan begins with his departure from Tehran and includes both the outward journey – overland to Smyrna (Izmir) and thence by ship to Plymouth (7 May to 25 November 1809) – and the return journey – by ship from Portsmouth (18 July 1810) via Rio de Janeiro. The journal breaks off in Rio on 16 September 1810; but it was another five and a half months before they finally reached Bushire on 1 March 1811.

The London section of the journal comprises 276 pages; but there are two unexplained gaps in the narrative which the scribe has noted as 'missing': the periods 13-31 December (including Abul Hassan's first audience with King George III) and 16-22 March. Oliver Hoare very kindly allowed me to copy the passages covering these periods in the manuscript copy of the journal which he acquired at the 1981 auction for his Ahuan Islamic Art Gallery in London. I am very grateful to him.

The original London journal is about twice the length of the selection from it presented here. The passages omitted are mainly of two kinds: lengthy descriptions of English customs and institutions, often containing a lot of financial and other statistics, which Abul Hassan had included in his desire to make his journal a useful guide for the Persian Court and for future ambassadors; and repetitive and trival accounts of parties attended, conversations of no great interest and frequent visits to the Opera. Many of the short verses which he quoted or composed have also been omitted.

I am grateful for help and information from Zia Bayandour, Gordon Calvert, Mariam Emamy, Christopher Gandy, Dr Ernst Grube and Dr Eleanor Sims. Dr Alice Wemyss Cunnack and Bernard Bevan were generous with information about their ancestor James Morier; and B W Robinson kindly elucidated some problems concerning the Marquis Wellesley's portrait of Fath Ali Shah.

I spent many fruitful hours in the Public Record Office, the British Library, the BL Newspaper Library and the India Office Library. The Hertfordshire Record Office and the Morden Public Library also answered particular questions. At the National Army Museum I am grateful to the Director, William Reid, and to David Smurthwaite and Dr Peter Boyden.

There are four people to whom I wish to express special thanks. I must first mention my dear friend Guity Fallah, another of Mirza Abul Hassan Khan's great-great-great-granddaughters, who spent long hours helping me with the intricacies of nineteenth-century Persian. My heartfelt thanks to Guity and to her husband, Dr Abbas Fallah: their interest and assistance was ever constant and constructive.

Sir Denis Wright is well known as a former British Ambassador to Iran and as the author of many books about that country. The last, *The Persians Amongst the English*, contains a chapter on 'The Envoy

Extraordinary'. I count myself privileged to have been able to profit from his deep knowledge of Iran's history and culture. I am most grateful to him for his interest and encouragement and for agreeing to write the Introduction which sets the scene for the Persian Ambassador's arrival in London.

And last, but certainly not least, I thank my husband John Cloake. It may be thought that his greatest contribution to *The Book of Wonders* was to rival James Morier by rendering Abul Hassan's verses into English. But he was also able to help me in matters of architecture and genealogy. Above all I thank him for his continuing interest and good humour during the years I have spent with the Persian Ambassador.

MMC

[1] See Denis Wright, *The Persians Amongst the English*, I B Tauris, London, 1985.

[2] Persian names and titles need some explanation. Until the 1920s there were no surnames, but some individuals denoted their place of origin by a suffix after their given name: *Shirazi* in the case of Abul Hassan and his family. *Mirza* used as a suffix denoted a 'Prince' (as in Abbas Mirza, Crown Prince of Persia); but as a prefix (as in Mirza Abul Hassan) it denoted a scribe, a secretary or an educated man. *Khan* was a hereditary or tribal title, but was also sometimes bestowed by the Shah for service to the State. Abul Hassan was not given the title until after his return to Tehran in 1811, so in London in 1809-10 he was known as Mirza Abul Hassan. During his second mission to London, in 1819, he was known as Mirza Abul Hassan Khan. He did not use his family name.

[3] Abu Taleb Khan, *The Travels of Mirza Abu Taleb Khan in Asia, Africa, and Europe during the years 1799, 1800, 1801, 1802, and 1803*, 2 vols, Longman, London, 1810. Written by himself in the Persian language, translated by Charles Stewart, MAS.

HRH Najaf Koolee Meerza (son of Prince Firman Firman, Grandson of HM Fathali Shah, the late Emperor of Persia), *Journal of a Residence in England, and of a Journey from and to Syria* [in 1836], translated by Assad Y Kayat, Printed for Private Circulation Only, London, undated.

Nasr ud-Din Shah, *Diary of HM the Shah of Persia*, translated by J W Redhouse, John Murray, London, 1874. [The diary includes an account of the Shah's visit to England from 19 June to 5 July 1873.]

[4] *The letters of Charles Lamb,* ed E V Lucas, vol II, p. 90. Dent and Methuen, London, 1935.

[5] BL Add 23546.

[6] It is apparent that the dates of many of the entries in Mrs Samiian's manuscript have been inserted later by another hand and that some of these are incorrect. Abul Hassan's popularity with the press has made it possible to identify the exact dates of many of the incidents he describes; in some cases this has meant correcting the date given in the manuscript or a minor rearrangement of the order of the entries. At times, especially in the month of March, the impression is that the scribe was working from unbound sheets which he dropped on the floor and reassembled in haste!

INTRODUCTION

R ARELY HAS ANY FOREIGN VISITOR to England made such a
deep impression on London society so quickly as the Persian
Envoy, Mirza Abul Hassan Shirazi. He arrived in England
at the end of November 1809 charged with an important diplomatic
mission by the bearded and philoprogenitive Fath Ali Shah of
Persia. James Morier, who had accompanied him on the long land
and sea journey from Tehran and was to make unkindly fun of him
in his two Hajji Baba books, noted that 'the Meerza is the great lion
of all the Routs, and there is no entertainment given but what he is
the principal feature'; 'the women are quite mad about him, and
make as much interest to get an introduction to him as if it were the
Shah in person.'[1] His name regularly appeared in the social columns
of the daily papers. Parties were given in his honour by the Prince
and Princess of Wales, the Royal Dukes and other leaders of
London society. Yet, while constantly referred to as 'the Persian
Ambassador', he enjoyed no such status though, in order to justify
the extraordinary attention they paid him, the British Government
itself decided to entitle him 'Envoy Extraordinary and Minister
Plenipotentiary'.

During his eight months in London, the Mirza kept a journal in
which he recorded his day-to-day activities and impressions.
England was, as he recorded in his journal on 16 March 1810, 'a
country full of wonders'.

Yet though his manuscript journal is the first account of life in

13

England as seen through the eyes of a native of Persia[2] it has remained unpublished. Now, at long last, thanks to the diligence and persistence of Margaret Cloake, we have this lively English translation from the Persian, enriched by illustrations which add greatly to the understanding and enjoyment of the text.

Mirza Abul Hassan makes frequent mention in his journal of the East India Company and its directors, who wined and dined him and commissioned his full-length portrait for their Leadenhall Street Offices. This attention reflected the important position then occupied by the Honourable Company in Anglo-Persian relations. Since the early seventeenth century when the Company first began trading with Persia via India, it had enjoyed a commercial monopoly in the country. Also, until the arrival of Sir Harford Jones in Tehran in 1809 (described below) its agents or factors in Persia conducted such diplomatic or consular business as there was, there being no British ambassador or consul. By 1778, when the port of Bushire on the Persian Gulf became the Company's headquarters, its Resident there was the senior British representative in the country. He took his orders from the Governor of Bombay who, in turn, was responsible to the Governor-General in Calcutta. The authorities in London were content to leave Persian affairs in the Company's hands until seized with the country's strategic and political importance for the defence of India; thereafter, through much of the early nineteenth century, there was friction and rivalry between London and Calcutta over Persia.

The end of the eighteenth century marked an important turning point in the East India Company's relations, hitherto essentially commercial, with Persia. By this time the Company had, through its military victories over the French and local rulers, laid the foundations of its Indian Empire. This it now saw threatened, both by Zaman Shah of Afghanistan, who was in the habit of embarking annually on an invasion of the Punjab on the north-western fringe of the Company's territories; and by Napoleon Bonaparte, who had landed in Egypt in July 1798 and was thought to be planning an invasion of India through Turkey and Persia. In the face of these dangers the Company saw Persia as an important bastion in the defence of its Indian possessions. This caused it to send two missions in quick succession to the recently enthroned Qajar Shah, Fath Ali.

The first of these missions was inspired by Jonathan Duncan, the Governor of Bombay, who appointed a Persian exile in his employ, Mirza Mehdi Ali Khan, to be the Company's Resident at Bushire, from where he was to travel to Tehran and encourage the Shah to frustrate French (and Dutch) activities in his domains and attack Zaman Shah in his rear and so divert him from the Punjab.

Alarmed by the French threat to India, and without awaiting the results of Mehdi Ali Khan's mission, the Governor-General in Calcutta (the Marquis Wellesley, who would be Foreign Secretary by the time Abul Hassan reached London) decided in August 1799 to send one of the Company's up-and-coming young officers, the thirty-year-old Captain John Malcolm, to Tehran. His task was to negotiate both a political alliance and a commercial treaty. By January 1801 he had achieved both objectives. Under the terms of the political treaty the Shah undertook to attack Afghan territory, should that country invade India, and in the event of French forces landing on Persian territory to join with the British in expelling them. In return, the British were to supply the Shah with arms, should either the Afghans or the French attack Persia.

The size and splendour of the large retinue of British officers and Indian sepoys that accompanied Malcolm on this mission, together with the extravagant gifts in kind and gold he so liberally distributed, made a deep impression on the Persians – but not always a favourable one to judge by Abul Hassan's journal.

When, a few years later, the Russians attacked the Shah's Caucasian provinces he appealed in vain to the Government of India for help. Disappointed and already secretly in touch with the French, the Shah now concluded, in May 1807, the Treaty of Finkenstein with the French and agreed, in return for the promise of military assistance, to declare war on Britain, sever all political and commercial relations with her, and allow French troops the right of passage to India. Shortly afterwards a large French military and diplomatic mission under General Gardane arrived in Persia. Understandably the British, engaged in mortal war with France, were greatly alarmed. Both London and Calcutta decided to send missions to the Persian Court with the object of wrecking the French alliance and replacing it with a new Anglo-Persian treaty.

Sir Harford Jones, whose name occurs frequently in Abul Hassan's journal and who had twice visited Persia during his twenty years' service with the East India Company in Basra and Baghdad, was back in London lobbying hard to be posted to Tehran. The Foreign Office duly appointed him their Envoy. Meanwhile, in Calcutta, John Malcolm, who was also lobbying to be sent to Persia, was chosen by the Governor-General (Lord Minto) to go there as his representative. He was elevated to the rank of Brigadier-General for the occasion and set sail from Bombay in April 1808. Owing to various factors, including his own arrogant and minatory behaviour, Malcolm got no further than Bushire and returned empty-handed to Bombay, where Harford Jones was impatiently awaiting his return before himself sailing for Bushire.

By the time Jones reached Persia the tide had turned against the French who had done a deal with the Russians (the Treaty of Tilsit, July 1807) and had failed to honour their obligations under the Treaty of Finkenstein. Soon after his arrival in Tehran in March 1809 Harford Jones was thus able to secure the signature of what was termed a Preliminary Treaty of Friendship and Alliance under which the Shah declared previous treaties with any European power 'null and void', undertook not to allow passage to any European forces towards India nor to 'enter into any engagements inimical to his Majesty or pregnant with injury or disadvantage to the British territories in India'.[3] In return, should any European power invade

PLATE 1

'Stage-coaches resemble takht-i ravans.*' Engraved from a drawing by James Morier for his second book of* Travels.

PLATE 2

The Persian Ambassador (1810), by Sir
William Beechey.

Persia, he was promised a British force or, in lieu thereof, a subsidy, supplies of arms, and attachment of officers to help expel the enemy even if the British had already concluded peace with him. A definitive treaty with detailed provisions based on this preliminary document was to be drawn up. Mirza Abul Hassan, who had Court connections and had earlier spent some three years in exile in India,[4] where he saw something of the English, was now appointed by the Shah to go to England. There he was to secure the ratification of the Preliminary Treaty and negotiate details of the subsidy and other unsettled points for inclusion in a definitive treaty. He was also instructed to ask the British Government not to conclude peace with Russia ahead of Persia and to help secure the return of Tiflis and other lost Persian territory.

James Morier, of Harford Jones' staff, travelled with the Mirza and his Persian servants to London. There, though losing patience with the slowness of the negotiations, Abul Hassan achieved most of his objectives apart from those affecting Russia. The British, too, were pleased with his performance 'in promoting an alliance with Persia'[5] and, shortly before his departure, offered him a handsome pension for life 'so long as you shall lend your assistance to the British Ambassador in preserving the friendly relations between Great Britain and Persia'.[6] The suggestion had come originally from Sir Gore Ouseley who was attached to the Mirza as his *mehmandar* or escorting officer. Ouseley spoke Persian and struck up a warm friendship with Abul Hassan, who was delighted when he learned that Ouseley had been appointed Ambassador to Persia by the King.

Thanks to Ouseley's sponsorship, Abul Hassan had become a freemason in June 1810, the first Persian to do so in England. This and his acceptance of the East India Company's monthly pension are, even today, held against him by some of his own countrymen, who – with little or no justification – regard him as having sold himself to the English.

In July 1810 Ouseley and Abul Hassan sailed together with Lady Ouseley and the Ouseley's three-year-old daughter for Persia on HMS *Lion*. Ouseley and Abul Hassan remained good friends despite the long voyage and the crowding on board ship, which also carried the Mirza's eight servants, Ouseley's diplomatic staff and servants, and a cow to provide milk.

Harford Jones' success in negotiating the Preliminary Treaty after Malcolm's failure had not pleased the authorities in Calcutta. They were undoubtedly influenced by a jealous Malcolm, who had wanted to bring the Shah to heel by forcibly occupying Kharg Island in the Persian Gulf. Also they resented the treaty terms to which they had been committed without consultation by Jones. The Governor-General was so incensed by what he described as Jones' 'injudicious and unwarrantable proceedings' that he refused to honour his bills drawn on the Company and sent Malcolm (now a Major-General) back to Persia on a third mission with the aim of taking Jones' place and thus reasserting Calcutta's responsibility for Persian affairs. But Jones stood his ground and, by the time Malcolm reached the Shah's summer camp at Sultaniyeh in June 1810, had the satisfaction of informing him that Ouseley had been appointed Ambassador to Persia. Thus Malcolm's third mission also ended in failure. On the other hand Ouseley's appointment was, in a sense, a triumph for Abul Hassan (no admirer of Malcolm) who, because of the confusion in Tehran over Harford Jones' position, had been instructed by the Shah to ask 'that a full Ambassador should be sent to Iran in quality of resident Ambassador, whose powers should be recognized by the Government of India'.[7]

On the Mirza's return from London he was made a Khan by the Shah, who appears to have raised no objection to his receiving the monthly pension offered by the East India Company (the Company having written to the First Vizir about this proposal). But he was not allowed to rest on his laurels. Soon he was involved in peace negotiations with the Russians which resulted in the humiliating Treaty of

Gulestan (1813) under which Persia lost most of her Caucasian territories. Next he was sent to St Petersburg in an unsuccessful attempt to secure better terms from the Russians; from there in June 1816 he wrote a reproachful letter to Lord Castlereagh, the Foreign Secretary, complaining that the British Government had failed to give him the support promised by Ouseley.

The British obligations under the Definitive Treaty signed by Ouseley on 14 March 1812 had already been whittled down. The British Government declined to ratify this treaty and, now in alliance with Russia and no longer worried about a French threat to India, they insisted on adjustment of its terms. A final Treaty of Tehran was concluded by James Morier and Henry Ellis on 25 November 1814.

In May 1819 Abul Hassan returned to London on a second and much more difficult mission. Following the defeat of Napoleon and the conclusion of an alliance with the Russians the British no longer attached much importance to their Persian alliance. The Mirza spent ten months in London and once again attracted much social and popular attention, the more so as this time he was accompanied by a mysterious young female, known as 'the fair Circassian', allegedly bought in the Constantinople slave market. Her arrival aroused great curiosity, particularly among Abul Hassan's old female friends. But diplomatically his visit was not a success. He failed to rekindle British interest in his country and returned to Tehran with little to show for his efforts apart from some satisfaction over arms deliveries.

Abul Hassan never again returned to England. Back in Tehran he acted as adviser to the Shah on foreign affairs and in 1824 became Persia's first Foreign Minister, a post he held until Fath Ali Shah's death ten years later. He was Foreign Minister again from 1840 until his death in 1846. He played a helpful role in the Anglo-Persian negotiations that resulted in the commercial treaty of 1841. The British, who fondly nicknamed him 'Old Fatty', regarded him as a good friend. Visitors enjoyed calling on him, when he would delight them with such expressions as 'God bless me!' and 'Pon my honour'.[8] The last British visitor on record as having seen him noted that he was 'a fat jolly old fellow, always laughing, and still speaks a little of his broken English. He said he should very much like to go back again were he not too old.'[9]

Denis Wright

[1] James Morier to Sir Harford Jones, 27 January and 10 March 1810 (NLW, Kentchurch Court papers 9574 and 9576).

[2] Abu Taleb Khan, whose memoirs were published in 1810 (see Foreword, note 3), although regarding himself as a Persian, was born and lived in India.

[3] The Anglo-Persian treaties are found in C U Aitchison BCS, *A Collection of Treaties, Engagements, and Sanads relating to India and Neighbouring Countries*, vol X, Superintendent of Government Printing, India, Calcutta 1892.

[4] Abul Hassan's early life and family history help to explain his agitation in London when delays prevented him from accomplishing his mission as speedily as the Shah had commanded.

He was born in Shiraz in 1776, son of Mirza Mohammad Ali, a Minister of Nadir Shah (1736-47) and later of Karim Khan Zand (1759-79). His mother's brother, Haji Ibrahim, was for a generation the most influential Minister in Iran. He helped to put Aqa Mohammad, the first Qajar ruler, on the throne and became his First Vizir. On Aqa Mohammad's death (1792), he assured the succession of Fath Ali Shah. Abul Hassan married one of Haji Ibrahim's daughters; among his brothers-in-law were a son of Fath Ali Shah and the *Amin od-Doleh*, the Second Vizir.

The family experienced not only power and Royal favour, but also Royal displeasure. Abul Hassan's father was saved from being burned alive only by the timely assassination of Nadir Shah. Haji Ibrahim was killed (1801), in a vat of boiling oil, by order of Fath Ali Shah, who feared his power; and almost the whole family was exterminated. Abul Hassan, then Governor of Shushtar, was imprisoned and sentenced to death, but saved by a last minute reprieve. Fearing the Shah's continued wrath, he fled the country, travelling to Mecca and then to Calcutta. He stayed about two and a half years in India, returning to Persia only on receipt of a Royal decree assuring him of Fath Ali Shah's forgiveness and favour. (A fuller account of Abul Hassan's early life is given in *Morier* I, pp. 220-3.)

[5] The Secret Committee of the East India Company to the Governor-General in Council, 7 July 1810 (PRO FO 60/118).

[6] The Chairman of the East India Company to Abul Hassan, 7 July 1810 (PRO FO 60/118).

[7] From Abul Hassan's List of Requests to the Marquis Wellesley (IO L/PS/3/3, Appendix 19).

[8] J. B. Fraser, *Narrative of a Journey into Khorasan in the Years 1821 and 1822*, Longman, London, 1824, p. 152.

[9] W. R. Holmes, *Sketches on the Shores of the Caspian*, Richard Bentley, London, 1845, p. 366.

NOVEMBER

1809

Saturday, 25-Wednesday, 29 November

SHIP NEWS Plymouth, November 26. Arrived the Formidable, *from Gibraltar, with a convoy: the latter are gone up Channel. A Persian Ambassador, with dispatches of importance for Government, arrived in the* Formidable. . . .

(*The Times*, 29 November)

IN GREAT GOOD SPIRITS the crew brought the ship into Plymouth Harbour, which is one of the ports of England. Anchor was dropped and Captain Fayerman struck the sails. Although the season was winter, and there was rain and snow, the distant view of the city looked like a paradise to rival the Garden of Eden. We saw a beautiful green field with trees to shame the palm-groves of paradise. Sweet-singing birds warbled the psalms of David and Christian melodies refreshed our souls. And by this beautiful field there rose a hill, high as the hopes of lovers, with graceful trees spaced no further apart than their height, their branches arm-in-arm like affectionate brothers.

The Captain hoisted some flags – a signal which the English call 'telegraph' – and which, on a clear day, carries the news of a ship's arrival at Plymouth to London in twenty-five minutes. I was amazed to hear this and thought: What exaggeration! How is it possible to send messages to the capital, which they say is 300 'miles' away,[1] in such a short time?

The Captain explained that at night messages are sent by means of lights; during the day by flags. On arrival in a port, the ship hoists flags which are seen through telescopes on land; the message is then relayed to London via observation towers which cover the distance at one-mile intervals.

Because the King has decreed that no one, not even the King himself, may leave a ship for four days after arrival at an English port, we had to wait on board. But the sight of the flowers and trees on the

24

hillside by the harbour consoled me and my friends and servants.

During the waiting period, the General of Plymouth Harbour sent some of his relations and city dignitaries to the ship with presents. They conveyed his apologies for the delay and sought to entertain us. A group of musicians and dancers – young boys and pretty girls – also came on board and performed throughout the day and evening.

Later, while talking to the Captain, I asked why the passengers and crew were not yet allowed ashore. He explained that there can hardly be a single ship without at least one person on board who is ill or suffering from a fever. As a precaution, for fear lest the sick person should communicate disease to the inhabitants of the town, disembarkation is not permitted until the sick have recovered in the ship's hospital.

We were in the middle of this conversation when a crowd of women rushed on board. With bewitching guile and seductive glances they captured the hearts of the seamen. Each one chose a woman and, embracing her, carried her off to his quarters – followed by the hearts of certain deprived Iranians! Sounds of the seamen's carousing and love-making reached even to the ebony wheel of heaven and the din of their music and singing so excited my comrades that they were overcome by a desire to worship the vine.

Amazed by the scene, I asked Captain Fayerman to explain what was happening. He said it was simply a matter of prudent foresight – if these harlots were not allowed to relieve the crew of their money, to empty their pockets as clean as a glutton his plate, the shipowners might be faced with a severe shortage of labour for the next voyage!

The Captain has his home in the port, so he arranged for various gifts to be sent to me with apologies for our delay. Surprisingly, no one who came on board to call on us was allowed to disembark before the four days – which the English call 'quarantine' – had passed.

Newspapers were sent to us on board. It seems that about 100,000 newspapers are printed and sold every day in England. How extraordinary that today's newspapers will have no value tomorrow – except as toilet paper! Every day a new paper is required. Through the newspapers, the people are able to learn of events soon after they occur; and when husbands travel to Hind and Rum and Farang,[2] their wives in England buy such newspapers and send them to their husbands, either directly or through their ambassadors.

Listening to all this, I had a thought and said to Mr Morier:[3]

> *Let tomorrow bring what may –*
> *A new 'news' comes with each new day.*

Captain Fayerman and our companions all laughed and cried, 'Well said!' And so we passed the day talking about newspapers. And our fourth day in harbour came to an end.

---

[1] Plymouth-London: about 211 miles by road; about 190 miles as the crow flies.

[2] Hind and Rum and Farang: India, the Ottoman Empire (from its foundation Constantinople was called the eastern 'Rome') and Europe (from 'the Franks').

[3] James Justinian Morier (1780?-1849) was born in Smyrna. As Secretary to Sir Harford Jones' mission to Persia, he accompanied the Persian Ambassador to London with the Provisional Treaty. In London, he served as Abul Hassan's interpreter and lived with him in Mansfield Street. Back in Persia he served as Sir Gore Ouseley's Secretary and then as Minister Plenipotentiary *ad interim* in 1814-15. Subsequently, except for an appointment as a Special Commissioner to Mexico in 1824-6, Morier devoted himself to writing travel books and novels.

Thursday, 30 November

THIS MORNING THE wind of good fortune blew over the horizon and a General, accompanied by an assembly of soldiers and civilians, came out to greet us with ceremony appropriate to a General or a Governor; vessels of all sizes were drawn up along the shore of that vast ocean. I left the ship with Captain Fayerman and we rode in a four-horse carriage the short distance to a flower-strewn green. Ships fired their cannon; and the soldiers and civilians lined up on all sides, ceremonially putting their hands to their brows – their customary way of showing respect. Their handsome faces won our hearts. Each unit was headed by a band: the thunder of drum and fife and bugle filled the heavens, and our hearts were touched.

At the moment of our arrival on shore, the soldiers lowered their flags and I asked Mr Morier for the reason. He explained that when members of the Royal Family visit the port the flags are lowered as a sign of respect; and the like honour was due to the high rank of the Envoy of the Padeshah of Iran.

After passing through some open country, we entered the city of Plymouth and saw long, straight streets without twist or turn, smooth as marble, with houses of four and five storeys, all alike. The lower storeys are built of stone; the walls and roofs are carved and painted with figures of men and women, of fairy-like creatures, of birds and beasts. I felt there could be few more pleasing cities in the whole of Farang.

After driving through several streets, we reached our lodging, the *Dar-ol-Omara*, the Abode of Princes, specially built for Generals and Government ministers. Its walls are high enough to touch the Milky Way, its foundations securely anchored to the back of the Bull-Fish of the World. In praise of the house itself, suffice it to say that it is a fitting abode for an envoy from the Sultan of Sultans. I was settled in the upper storey of the building and from here I could observe the gardens of the port and the countryside planted with many kinds of cypress and pine trees. It was so pleasant that I quite forgot the storms at sea.

I had been resting for a time when a great General[1] called on me, accompanied by other Generals and their ladies, who were sumptuously attired and fragrantly perfumed. Each one brought a gift of welcome, opening the doors of friendship. The visitors consumed a variety of dishes, colourful sherbets and kebabs.

The season was winter: the night lasted for eighteen hours and the day only six. But it was so dark during the day with heavy rain and snow and fog that even those six hours could be called night. The sun never showed itself and one could hardly distinguish between night and day. I felt sad and depressed in my exile. Nonetheless, many nobles and distinguished men of the port (which numbers 12,000 families) called at my residence; there was not a moment when there were less than 2000 [sic] men and women in the house, curious to look upon the visage and beard of a native of Iran. They were a happy lot and sang songs.

And so we spent the day admiring the beauty of the English[2] ladies, all in lavish attire, who came in droves to visit us and pay us compliments. Laughing, and biting the finger of astonishment, they talked among themselves and flirted deliciously, stealing our hearts.

And so ended another day.

[1] The Governor of Plymouth Fort was General William Howe (1729-1814), 5th Viscount Howe.

[2] 'Farangi' (Frank) in the text: Abul Hassan sometimes writes 'English', so I have used it for the English throughout, and left 'Farangi' to mean a European of unspecified nationality.

DECEMBER

1809

Friday, 1 December

THE DAY DAWNED and the sun, ornament of the universe, drew its golden rays from the horizon's scabbard. The Governor of Plymouth, who is a General, came to call on me with the Admiral of the Dockyard[1] (that is, the factory for building ships), several officers and Captain Fayerman. They were all accompanied, as is their custom, by their wives. After the exchange of official courtesies, the sweet-tongued ladies showed great kindness; Mrs Fayerman in particular excelled in amiability.

Then the great General said: 'True to my word, I want to take you to visit the Dockyard, for shipbuilding is the major industry of this port.' We all mounted horses; and, as a mark of respect, my horse led the others. After passing through several streets, we reached the lofty entrance to the factory. Truly, it is a wondrous place. We saw a vast number of tall beams; storerooms full of hemp (which is similar to silk fibre); warehouses loaded with huge planks, box upon box of nails, stacks of iron sheets, and heaps of heavy-link chain – all the equipment and tools of shipbuilding were neatly arranged and stored. There were huge furnaces with double-headed bellows for the manufacture of iron plate and chain.

I asked the General for information about the enormous factory. He said that the beams and hemp come from Russia and the New World. He explained further that hemp is better than silk for anchor-rope, stronger even than metal chain in salty sea water. He also explained that the tall beams are used for making ships' masts. The building of warships, large and small, is continually under way; and in addition to this factory there are several others, even larger, which have been established in other ports at the King's command. Night and day, the work of shipbuilding never ceases. At present there are 1333 warships of various sizes; and every year some 100 new warships are built here and in other ports to replace old ships or those sunk or captured by the enemy.

Later I asked about stage-coaches: these resemble *takht-i ravan* and are drawn by two or from four to ten horses. He said that the distance between Plymouth and London is 250 miles (or 70 Iranian *farsakhs*). By coach the distance is covered in two days. Halting places for the coaches are found every ten miles along the highways. The road surface is smoother than the breast of a beautiful woman:

> *From purest pearl in morning mist enfolded*
> *The contour of my lady's breast was moulded.*

The ten-mile coaching inns are staffed and furnished with regal carpets and plates of gold and silver. Immediately upon their arrival, travellers are served with a choice of food and drink at nicely arranged tables. After a meal or refreshments the journey is continued with fresh horses. The passengers pay for these services and the money is used to maintain the roads and coaches, which occupies much of the innkeepers' time.

Mr Morier sent five of my servants on ahead to London in a fast-travelling coach.

> *One of the public coaches was hired to convey his servants to London;*
> *and when four of them had got inside, having seated themselves cross-*
> *legged, they would not allow that there could be room for more,*
> *although the coach was calculated to take six. They armed themselves*
> *from head to foot with pistols, swords, and each a musket in his hand,*
> *as if they were about to make a journey in their own country; and thus*
> *encumbered, notwithstanding every assurance that nothing could hap-*
> *pen to them, they got into the coach.*

(*Morier* II, *Appendix, p. 401*)

31

Saturday, 2 December

AFTER ALL OUR PREPARATIONS were made for the journey to London, the capital city, the Governor of Plymouth, Captain Fayerman and several Generals came to bid us farewell. I climbed into a four-horse carriage with Mr Morier, the son of Sir Harford Jones[1] and some attendants. The rest of the party got into other carriages and we set off on our journey. The landscape was smooth and flat and, although it was winter, it was as green as the slopes of Mount Alvand. The cheerful conversation of my travelling companions banished the memory of stormy seas from my heart and, truly, I so enjoyed coach travel that the delights of those days are never to be forgotten.

One of the wonders of the journey was a warm-water spring on the outskirts of Bath, which was crowded with people. The greenery of Bath resembles Mazanderan; the houses are built of white stone.

I asked Mr Morier about the throng of people and he explained that the spring is a manifestation of the power of Almighty Providence. Around it are built baths of various sizes and water is brought from it to them in stone conduits. The spring waters are endowed with special curative properties and the people we saw were invalids brought from all over England. Some are made to drink the waters; others to bathe in them. Then, God willing, they are cured.

After visiting the spring and the baths, we drove towards the city. A wide river flows through the middle of the town and over the river is a sturdy bridge. The streets are well laid out with houses and many churches, of differing design, but all built of white stone. Small rivulets flow down both sides of the street. The city is as beautiful as a flower-garden and the visit delighted me.

---

[1] On their departure from Tehran, Abul Hassan mentions Howel Jones, Sir Harford Jones' natural son, who had apparently accompanied his father to Tehran and was travelling to England with Abul Hassan and Mr Morier.

PLATE 3

King George III. From the studio of Alan Ramsey
(1713-84).

PLATE 4

*A View of Westminster Bridge and Lambeth Palace
(1821), drawn and engraved by Robert Havell.*

Sunday, 3 December

ON SUNDAY, which is the Christian Friday, there are crowds of men and women in the streets. Outside the door of one building two comely women were dispensing water to the passers-by; and I, too, was given a cup.

As there was a church in the neighbourhood, I went to see how the English worship. Priests and monks stood in a semi-circle singing Christian songs. I was captivated by the pretty women and children who stood hand in hand with bowed heads – according to their manner of worship – so that their ringlets fell forward over their shoulders. When they saw me they curtsied respectfully and gave me flowers, pleased that I had visited their church.

Monday, 4 December[1]

His Excellency and suite, together with those appointed to receive him, arrived at Demezy's, Hartford-bridge, on Monday afternoon, where he was received by one of the Under Secretaries of State, and several gentlemen belonging to the Foreign Office, and a sumptuous entertainment was prepared for him. His Excellency appeared highly pleased with the attention shown him; he slept there, and every possible accommodation was made for him the house could afford.

(*The London Chronicle*, 7 December)

I WAS MET WITH DUE CEREMONY by Mr Vaughan[2] and Mr Arbuthnot, brother of Mr Arbuthnot, a Deputy Minister.[3] They were extremely kind and courteous and had brought from London a special coach provided by his Majesty's Government. We spent the night, friends together, talking and praising the buildings of Bath and the goodness and beauty of the folk of that region.

---

[1] Abul Hassan does not mention Hartford Bridge in the journal; the entry for 3 December continues as if he met Mr Vaughan and Mr Arbuthnot in Bath. I have presumed a separate day on the basis of the *London Chronicle* item of 7 December and a further report on 23 December which states: 'Mr Vaughan, the Marquis Wellesley's Secretary, met the Persian Ambassador at the inn at Hartford Bridge.'

[2] The diplomatist Charles Richard Vaughan (1774-1849), knighted in 1833.

[3] Charles Arbuthnot (1767-1850) was a Joint Secretary at the Treasury 1809-23.

Tuesday, 5 December

On Tuesday, his Excellency and suite, and also those appointed to attend him, arrived at a house, prepared by Government for his reception, in Mansfield-street.

(*The London Chronicle*, 7 December)

I IN THE SPECIAL COACH, and my companions in theirs, travelled with the speed of lightning towards London. We came to a great river, greater even than the Shatt al-Arab,[1] and over its width loomed a mountain as tall as Demavand.[2] On closer observation this turned out to be a bridge built by some master of technology with great ingenuity. Its columns and arches rivalled those of the Tagh-i Khosrow,[3] and we saw that ships could easily pass under them. We crossed the bridge, and in the distance the city came into view. Then, suddenly, rain fell from the clouds, darkening the bright day, and we felt no inclination to move from our seats.

The fast coach stopped at a magnificent house[4] and the sentries standing at the door ran forward, removing their hats as a sign of respect. As they say: 'Alight, the honour is mine but the house is thine.' We entered a porch with lofty columns and found ourselves in a palace. Truly it is a wondrous house: one sitting-room is hung with tall mirrors to reflect the trees and mountain slopes of the surrounding countryside. We delighted in making a tour of the splendid edifice; but the army of sleep made a surprise attack on the army of consciousness and we were forced to take some rest.

I opened my eyes to banquet tables lavishly laid with every kind of delicacy: a variety of roast meats, preserves and confections. Each of my companions had been given a place at table appropriate to his rank, and behind each one an agile servant with the face of a *houri* stood in attendance.

I was truly vexed that there had been no *isteqbal*, no official welcome, from the inhabitants of the city, because of the severe rain.

35

Nonetheless, my grief and sorrow were dissipated by the riches of the banquet – and the evening passed happily.

> *[Mirza Abul Hassan] grew very anxious as we proceeded, and seemed to be looking out for an Istakball, or a deputation headed by some man of distinction, which, after the manner of his own country, he expected would be sent to meet him. In vain we assured him that no disrespect was intended, and that our modes of doing honour to Ambassadors were different from those of Persia: our excuses seemed only to grieve him the more; and although to a foreigner the interest of the road greatly increased as we approached the city, yet he requested to have both the glasses of the carriage drawn up, for he said that he did not understand the nature of such an entry, which appeared to him more like smuggling a bale of goods into town, than the reception of a public envoy. . . .*

(Morier II, Appendix, p. 402)

[1] The Shatt al-Arab: the union of the Tigris and Euphrates rivers, before it empties into the Persian Gulf.

[2] Demavand: the 18,000-feet-high cone-shaped mountain visible to the north of Tehran.

[3] Tagh-i Khosrow (the Arch of Khosrow, the name of several Sasanian kings): the great ruined fourth-century AD arch of Ctesiphon, on the Tigris, south-east of Baghdad. If Abul Hassan and his party did in fact spend the night at Hartford Bridge, about thirty-six miles south-west of London on the A30 road, the comparison of the famous Sasanian arch is probably to Staines Bridge! This route is south of the more direct Bath Road which Morier informed the Foreign Office they would take in a letter from Plymouth, dated 25 November (PRO FO 60/2).

[4] 9 Mansfield Street in Marylebone, an Adam house with a fine entrance. It was the London home of Colonel Henry Malcolm of Lingfield, Surrey.

Wednesday, 6 December

THIS MORNING Mr Morier and my other travelling companions came to greet me in my new residence. They told me that today, by Royal decree, the Marquis Wellesley[1] was appointed Minister for Foreign Affairs: his responsibilities include the making and breaking of treaties of friendship with other countries. That greatest of great ministers, Councillor[2] and Secretary of State, pillar among pillars of the nation, is a former Governor of Calcutta (which is the chief city of India) and has lately been charged by the King with an embassy to Spain. He returned to the capital only a few days ago. Endowed with every gift, the Marquis Wellesley is well versed in the literature of Hind, Rum and Farang, and is fluent in the idioms of Arabic, Turkish and Persian. Never before in England, indeed in the whole world, has there been a well-born minister of such tact and authority, such a paragon of perfection.

Mr Morier said to me: 'The King has appointed Sir Gore Ouseley,[3] a gentleman of high station, a Baronet (that is to say, a nobleman of high rank), to be your host, your *mehmandar*. But as his house is outside London, some distance away, he was unable to wait upon you last night. He begged me to carry out in his stead any wishes your Excellency might have.'

At this moment Lord Radstock,[4] the husband of Mr Morier's maternal aunt, came to call on me. And while we were becoming acquainted, it was announced that Sir Gore Ouseley, Bart, had arrived at the house. When my eye fell upon him, I had the feeling that I had known him for years. 'A friend knows the voice of a friend.'

When he pronounced the official courtesies on behalf of the King and Prime Minister, he spoke so eloquently that my heart was touched and my spirits utterly transformed. I was made conscious of his high rank and authority and I felt as if I were conversing with an

Iranian friend. Then, with flattering words and a sweet tongue, he told me he had been appointed by the King to act as my host. His Persian is so fluent that I doubted he was truly an Englishman! I thought to myself:

> *He was the dearest soul, so I was told.*
> *I saw him – and it's true, a thousandfold.*

While talking together it became apparent that not only does he know Persian; he is also familiar with the languages of Hind, Rum and Bengal, of France, Italy and Greece. And so learned is he about all religions that each sect considers him one of their own and conceals none of its mysteries from him. I thought to myself: What if God would make it his destiny to be Ambassador to Iran; what if the King of England, because of my friendship with the man, would appoint him to the Court of the Sultan of Sultans (may God perpetuate his reign) in order to maintain and strengthen the ties between our two Governments?

Sir Gore Ouseley offered so many apologies on behalf of the King and the Prime Minister that I became quite embarrassed. Thereafter I felt no desire for the companionship of anyone else. It is the good fortune of His Majesty the Shahanshah, the Hope of the Incomparable God the Creator, that such a man has become my companion, to make my days content.

I learned that the King had today, as is his custom every Wednesday, travelled in state from Windsor, some six *farsakhs* away, to hold a Council at his magnificent Palace in London,[5] which his Ministers and Councillors are required to attend. Each one takes his place according to rank and the current business of the Kingdom is deliberated. Today, the seals of the Minister for Foreign Affairs, a position of the highest rank, were bestowed on the Marquis Wellesley.

Because of the cold and the dark, our gathering was lit by a blaze of candles in crystal chandeliers and candelabra of gold and silver. The eye was dazzled by the reflection of light in the mirrors, which greatly increased their brilliance. Yet again I pondered on the wonders of the universe and the marvels of science.

The King's Deputy Master of the Ceremonies[6] came to call on me. When I remarked on the use of so many thousands of candles during the day, he said we would not see the sun for another four months!

[1] Richard Colley Wellesley (1760-1842), 1st Baron Mornington and 1st Marquis Wellesley. Governor-General of India, 1787-1805; Foreign Secretary, December 1809 to January 1812; Lord Lieutenant of Ireland, 1821-8 and 1833-4. Elder brother of the Duke of Wellington.

[2] Councillor: Abul Hassan uses this term presumably to denote members of the Privy Council, but also virtually synonymously with Minister.

[3] Sir Gore Ouseley (1770-1844), 1st Baronet, was the second son of Captain Ralph Ouseley of Limerick. In India, 1787-1805, he engaged in commerce and studied languages and literature. At Lucknow he held the appointment of Major-Commandant to the Nawab Vizir of Oudh. He was Abul Hassan's official host in London and Ambassador to Persia 1810-14. He devoted his retirement to the study of Oriental texts and was a founder of the Royal Asiatic Society in 1823.

[4] Admiral William Waldegrave (1753-1825), 1st Baron Radstock, was the younger son of the 3rd Earl Waldegrave. He married in 1785 Cornelia van Lennep, daughter of the Dutch Consul-General at Smyrna. Her sister Clara married Isaac Morier and was James Morier's mother.

[5] The King used the Queen's House (Buckingham House) on official occasions; but the Royal Family lived mostly at Windsor.

[6] Robert Chester (1768-1848) was later knighted and served as Master of the Ceremonies to George III, George IV and William IV.

Thursday, 7 December

The Persian Ambassador cannot stir out of doors until he has delivered his credentials to his Majesty at his Court.

(*The Times*, 15 December)

MR MORIER TOLD ME he had been to call on the East India Company: they are extremely displeased with the conduct of Lord Minto[1] towards Sir Harford Jones,[2] especially in view of the Royal favour shown towards his Excellency by his Majesty the Shahanshah. As regards myself, they are completely satisfied: my papers have been delivered to the Palace.[3]

Towards evening Sir Gore Ouseley arrived. He told me that his family arrived in town today, so he may now devote himself with an easy heart to acting as my companion and sympathetic support. 'It is no secret,' he said, 'that a *mehmandar*, like a powerful minister, may authorize expenses for an ambassador from the time of his arrival and throughout his stay in the capital.' And so, said he:

We are at your service; what is your command?

I replied: '*Alhamdolillah valmenah!* Thanks to God's grace and the bounty of the Government of his Majesty the Shahanshah, I come well stocked with provisions, and lack no necessities. So, it is a matter for your discretion. However, I would be pleased to have live animals and game birds for my servants to slaughter, as well as rice and other dry cereals. Otherwise, I lack for nothing.'

While we were talking, a note was delivered from the Master of the Ceremonies asking for a translation of the *farman* from the Sultan of Iran to King George III. I said: 'Your Ambassador in Iran has already translated it and sent a copy to the Prime Minister. For my part, it is impossible for me to unseal the *farman* except to deliver it into the hands of the English King at his Court, as is fitting and proper between governments.'

Sir Gore Ouseley replied: 'As you were to carry the original, Sir Harford Jones sent only a summary copy of its contents to the Prime Minister – so you must not blame the Ministers.'

I was indeed angry; but, bowing to the *farman*, from which all justice flows, I removed the seals from the casket and fully acquainted him with its contents, penned with the customary eloquence. After perusing the letter, he reproached Sir Harford Jones exceedingly for his inaccurate reporting.[4]

I announced that I would be patient for no more than four days: on the fifth I must meet with the English King to carry out my mission of good will.

Sir Gore Ouseley answered: 'But, my dear friend, you must understand English customs. The Ambassador from Istanbul[5] has been waiting for three months now; and envoys from other countries – from India and Africa, as well as from Russia and other countries of Europe – are finding it more or less impossible to secure an audience. You are not yet rested from the rigours of the voyage. You have not even left the house to visit the city or walk in the pleasure-gardens of London.'

'But,' I insisted, 'until I have seen your King, I shall not set foot outside this house.'[6]

[1] Gilbert Elliott (1751-1814), 1st Earl of Minto, was Governor-General of India 1807-13. The conflict between Lord Minto and Sir Harford Jones is discussed in the Introduction, pp. 13-21.

[2] Sir Harford Jones (Brydges) (1764-1847), 1st Baronet, was assistant and then Factor of the East India Company in Basra 1793-4; the Company's Resident in Baghdad 1798-1806; Envoy Plenipotentiary to Persia 1809-11. He assumed the additional name of Brydges on inheriting property from his maternal grandmother in 1826. Author of *An Account of the Transactions of His Majesty's Mission to the Court of Persia, in the Years 1807-11*, 2 vols, James Bohn, London, 1834.

³ Throughout the journal, Abul Hassan writes of the *Daftar-i Shah*, the Royal Office. I have used 'Palace' or 'Foreign Office' according to the context.

⁴ In his Despatch No. 10, Sir Harford Jones referred to Abul Hassan as *chargé d'affaires*; in his translation of the Shah's letter, he left the Persian word *vakeel* (representative). In his own translation of the letter, Ouseley used the title of minister. (All three documents are in PRO FO 60/2.) The question of title was important because only an ambassador was accorded a public audience of the King. In the event, Abul Hassan's audience on 20 December was private; but he was shown unusual distinction in the protocol arrangements. Although the press and the public always referred to him as the 'Persian Ambassador', he was recognized by the English Government as Envoy Extraordinary and Minister Plenipotentiary (see Wellesley's letter to the King, 11 December 1809, BL Add. 34285, f.200).

⁵ Istanbul: Abul Hassan uses the Persian and Turkish *Islambul*, rather than 'Constantinople' used by the English.

⁶ Ouseley's report to Lord Wellesley on this day's conversation with Abul Hassan contains the following paragraph: 'Your Lordship is so perfectly well acquainted with the disposition of the Asiatics, and the indirect & ingenious artifices they [employ] to arrive at the object of their wishes, that it would be presuming as well as superfluous in me to offer any opinion as to the [degree] of importance to be attached to H. Excellency's remarks' (PRO FO 60/2). (I have guessed at the words in square brackets, which have been lost in the PRO binding.)

Friday, 8 December

ARLY THIS MORNING Mr Morier came to see me. He told me that he had been summoned by the Prime Minister, who had said to him: 'Why is the Iranian Ambassador so insistent upon being presented to the King? He is not yet rested from the fatigues of his journey; and the Ministers have not yet met in Council. Do not allow him to become anxious.'

This disturbed me and I spoke sharply: 'If I am to understand that the King does not exercise the ultimate authority in London, I shall not fail to make this known to the Shah of Iran; I have no desire to find myself the object of his Royal wrath because of my prolonged absence. It is on this account that I am anxious.'

At this point Sir Gore Ouseley arrived to say that my wishes had been made clear to the Prime Minister – thank God! – and that my mission could now proceed to everyone's satisfaction. I felt re-assured by having his support in these discussions.

In the evening musicians were summoned, and the gates of music and song were opened to a company of gentlemen which included Lord Radstock. He presented me with several signed drawings and an English book.

I spent the evening with a happy heart.

Saturday, 9 December

IN THE MORNING my *mehmandar* arrived with Lord Teign-mouth,[1] who is known in India as Sir John Shore, and who was for some time Governor-General of that country. He is thoroughly acquainted with the history and language of Iran, and when he spoke I was astounded by the extent of his knowledge of Iranian scholars and sages. I took great pleasure in his company.

It then happened that letters arrived from the *Motamad od-Doleh*[2] and the *Amin od-Doleh*.[3] After I had read them, Sir Gore Ouseley asked if he might also look at them. When he saw that the letters directed me to hasten my return, he sank the head of attention into the collar of reflection and spoke in whispers to Mr Morier for some time. Finally, I told them their whispering had gone on long enough.

I said to Sir Gore Ouseley: 'If you are discussing Sir Harford Jones' remarks about me, that is one thing. But if it concerns my Padeshah's letter – the first Royal epistle to reach London and England from Iran – in which the Qibleh of the Universe addresses the King of England as his dear and illustrious Brother, then due honour and respect should not be forgotten.' As always, he apologized gracefully.

Day turned to evening. That night I was seized with so debilitating a fever that I understood nothing of the conversation, the music or the dancing of the young people.

---

[1] John Shore (1751-1834), 1st Baron Teignmouth, was Governor-General of India 1793-8.

[2] *Motamad od-Doleh* ('Trusted of the State') was the title held at this time by the First Vizir (Prime Minister) of Iran, Mirza Mohammad Shafi Mazanderani.

[3] *Amin od-Doleh* ('Trustee of the State') was the title of the Second Vizir (Minister of Finance), Haji Mohammad Hosein Khan, who was Abul Hassan's brother-in-law.

Sunday, 10 December

THE DAY DAWNED and an affectionate note arrived from my friend and companion, Sir Gore Ouseley, in which he said that 'since today is Sunday and a holiday for us, I am deprived of the pleasure of the company of my distinguished and true friend. The Foreign Office is closed today; but tomorrow, which is Monday, the Foreign Minister will call on you to discuss your audience with the King.' The letter ended with salutations.

Then there arrived a present of fruit from Mr Vaughan, who had taken part in my *isteqbal* on the first day. My companions partook of it, but I was too ill to dare delight in it.

Mr Vaughan himself came to see me. He said: 'The King has ordered me to accompany Mr Wellesley,[1] brother of the Marquis Wellesley, who is to be Ambassador to Spain. I am to be the Second Gentleman. We leave tomorrow.[2] He told me that Lord Wellington,[3] another brother of the Marquis Wellesley, commands 20,000 soldiers in Spain and Portugal.

Every day news from Europe has but one theme: the agreement of a marriage between France and the daughter of Austria.[4]

After he left, I took to my bed in a state of fever and tightness of heart, and slept until morning.

---

[1] Henry Wellesley (1773-1847), later 1st Baron Cowley, succeeded his brother, the Marquis Wellesley, as Ambassador to Spain.

[2] *The Times*, 29 January, reported that 'Mr Henry Wellesley and Mr Vaughan sailed for Cadiz yesterday.'

[3] Lieutenant-General Arthur Wellesley (1769-1852), 1st Viscount (later 1st Duke of) Wellington.

[4] Napoleon's marriage to Josephine was dissolved in December 1809. He married the Archduchess Marie-Louise, daughter of the Emperor of Austria, in April 1810.

45

Monday, 11 December

The Marquis Wellesley has this day visited the Persian Minister, although that attention cannot be claimed by any European Minister below the rank of Ambassador.

(Letter from the Marquis Wellesley to the King, 11 December)[1]

TODAY I WOKE EARLY from sleep, before dawn, and in the customary manner I prayed to God.

I was reclining on a cushion when Sir Gore Ouseley appeared at my side with a handsome, dark-eyed youth of fourteen years, the son of the Minister.[2] Sir Gore Ouseley was telling me that as a mark of respect I should personally welcome the Foreign Minister at the door of my palace and escort him in, when we heard the commotion of his arrival. I acted according to Sir Gore Ouseley's advice and showed the Minister to his place. I flung open the doors of hospitality and coffee was offered to the assembly. He raised the cup to his lips, but did not drink. And since it is not the custom here to offer the *qalian* with coffee, sweets and fruit were served.

The officials who accompanied the Minister were all of handsome mien; they wore ceremonial dress and were perfumed as if to appear before their King. It is an established practice that the King's Government rewards distinguished service to the Crown with decorations which differ in appearance according to the importance of the service rendered. Most dukes and lords, etc., have such decorations – some fashioned in the shape of the sun and some like stars – shining things, which they wear fixed to their chests. Sir Gore Ouseley explained that the Minister had been awarded such an emblem and raised to the office of Governor-General of India at the time of the conquest of the Indian States, the killing of Tippu Sultan and the subjugation of the Marathas. Some years ago he despatched Malcolm[3] to the Court of the Qibleh of the Universe (may the

46

angels watch over him) to request the Sultan of Iran to send an army against Herat in order to depose the ruler Zaman Shah.[+] He said: 'The Minister honours you with his visit as a mark of great respect and gratitude to the Sultan of Iran as well as to your own high rank.'

One of his brothers, Mr Wellesley, is a 'padre' of the large church known as St Paul's. Another is Lord Wellington, Commander of the Army in Spain. Yet another is Mr Wellesley-Pole, who is Secretary for Ireland. And his youngest brother is an ambassador, soon to leave for Spain. He has three sons and two daughters, all handsome and talented. All the brothers, like the wise Minister, are members of the Council and able administrators. Most of the family are pillars of the Government, respected for their wisdom and for their good counsel.

The Minister said: 'I am sorry that you did not come to this country in the good season, for now the world-illuminating sun has turned its face from the city, and the day is perceived as dark night.'

In reply, I indicated his decoration – which looks like a sun embossed with the Royal Seal – and said:

> *If London's dark, as the sun won't shine*
> *Come, stand on the roof, my Lord, with thine.*

Sir Gore Ouseley translated into English. The Minister was well pleased and said, 'Bravo!'

As we conversed, I recognized him and recalled that I had met this peerless Minister some years previously in Calcutta, where I had been made aware of his achievements. So I communicated the messages of the Qibleh of the Universe to that wise man's ear. I spoke briefly of Lord Minto's letter dismissing Sir Harford Jones. And I also expressed my deep appreciation for all the trouble Mr Morier had gone to on my behalf during our journey to London.

In reply he said: 'As for Mr Morier, it is his good fortune to have served you, for he has gained in reputation thereby.' He continued: 'Your mission will be accomplished, God willing, and every effort will be made to ensure its success. Today I shall convey your request to the King that when he comes to the city we may conduct you to his presence and fulfil all that you desire.' He spoke of Malcolm's praise of me and, turning towards his companions, praised me exceedingly himself. Then he rose from his chair, recommended me with much eloquence to Sir Gore Ouseley, and returned to his home.

And so ended another day – but that night I grew restless from homesickness and high fever:

> *O Lord, what can I do? The night returns –*
> *And with the night, once more my fever burns.*

[1] BL Add.37285, f.200.

[2] Henry Wellesley (1794-1866), the Foreign Secretary's brilliant youngest son and future Principal of New Inn Hall, Oxford, was not quite sixteen.

[3] Colonel (later Major-General Sir) John Malcolm (1769-1833), Governor of Bombay 1827-30. His three missions to Persia are discussed in the Introduction, pp. 15-18.

[4] The ambitions of Zaman Shah, ruler of Afghanistan 1793-1800, were the original cause of co-operation between Britain and Iran. See the Introduction, pp. 14-15.

PLATE 5

Sir Gore Ouseley, Bart, engraved after the painting by Samuel Drummond for The European Magazine and London Review, *July 1810, which had an article about his appointment as Ambassador to Persia. Ouseley was Abul Hassan's official host in London.*

PLATE 6

PLATE 7

Plate 6: A View of St James's Park (1813)
engraved by Franz Joseph Manskirch.

Plate 7: East India House, Leadenhall Street (1802)

Tuesday, 12 December

THE SUN ROSE from the world's horizon and early in the morning Sir Gore Ouseley came to see me with several gentlemen and a handsome young lord from Ireland, the Marquis of Sligo.[1] They performed the courtesies of respect and friendship according to their own customs.

After a time, Sir Gore Ouseley begged to be excused as he had to go to the Palace to see if the date of my audience with the King had been fixed. Saying that he would return, he entrusted me to my friends and took his leave. From depression and high fever, I sought my own bed; and no matter how much my companions talked in order to distract me, I still felt weak and weary.

At the end of the day, Sir Gore Ouseley returned to say: 'It has been arranged that on Wednesday of next week, when the King comes to the capital, the Ministers will conduct you to the King's presence to deliver your letter as is fitting and proper.'

I said: 'In my state of indisposition, each day passes like a year – I have not the patience to wait nine days. It is pointless for me to see the King in this condition. I know I must return the call of the Foreign Secretary; but after I visit him to deliver my credentials, I shall turn my face from London and return home.'

Then Mr Morier said that his Excellency Mirza Mohammad Shafi, the *Motamad od-Doleh*, First Vizir of Iran, had told Sir Harford Jones that he intends to send a courier daily to London with despatches.

In reply, I said: 'I take this to mean that the Iranian ministers have agreed that whatever he wants and requests will be accomplished; his wishes are met as if he were nominated as a fourth minister in Iran; his credentials from the King are interpreted as the King purposed – and in word and deed he is the King's representative. But what was right and what was wrong in the interpretation of my own titles has become obvious to the English leaders. In any case, this conversation is pointless and does not advance the cause of my embassy. I will not stay in this city one minute longer.'

Speaking in Persian, Sir Gore Ouseley apologized and said: 'Try to compose yourself – do not act hastily in this business. The King's health is poor and his great age makes it difficult for him to travel, so allowances must be made. Tomorrow the Prime Minister, who is the Deputy of the Kingdom, and the support of the pillars of government, will come to see you.'

This discussion took us up to dinner, when a jovial company gathered for a party organized in much the same manner as previously described.

> *Wishing to keep his Excellency the Persian Envoy in good spirits . . .*
> *I went to dine with him this Evening in company with Lord Radstock,*
> *Captain Malcolm and Mr Forbes. After expressing the very great*
> *pleasure he felt in the honor Your Lordship yesterday conferred upon*
> *him, and the hopes of success which he consequently was induced to*
> *entertain, he asked me seriously if he was to be presented tomorrow –*
> *To which I replied that I knew that was impossible as His Majesty*
> *could not come in from Windsor sooner than Wednesday se'en-*
> *night. . . . He immediately got up from the table, ran upstairs, and*
> *returned with his Secret instructions from the King of Persia – with*
> *tears in his eyes he . . . said a private audience tomorrow, with the*
> *certainty of keeping his head on his shoulders, was all he wanted – for*
> *the most distinguished honors he could receive at any future day could*
> *never save his life – In short, my Lord, he said so much that I thought*
> *it my duty to get up at once from the table and come home.*
>
> (Letter from Sir Gore Ouseley to the Marquis Wellesley,
> 12 December)[2]

[1] Howe Peter Browne (1788-1845), 2nd Marquis of Sligo.

[2] BL Add.37285, f.204.

Wednesday, 13 December

Wednesday, all the King's Ministers, in full dress, paid their respects to the Persian Ambassador.

(The Times, 15 December)

A T NOON MY SERVANTS came running from all sides with the news of the Prime Minister's [1] arrival. I received him with the same courtesy I had shown the Marquis Wellesley and I conducted him personally to his place. After an exchange of suitable compliments, the doors of conversation were opened on both sides.

At one point I said that I was depressed and dispirited by the long wait to meet the King and the continual battle with my fate. Because of my illness I was extremely impatient for replies to my letters so that I might leave the city –

and take the road to Basrah and Baghdad.

The Minister heard me out politely and calmly and answered me in a friendly manner: 'You are not yet recovered from the hardships of your journey – please do not be anxious.' I told him it was impossible for me to wait and he said he regretted that, since it was clear that I was not happy with them, he must make a clean breast of things. He said: 'The King is ill.' 'But,' he went on, 'on Wednesday of next week his Majesty will come to the capital and your objectives will be attained as you wish.'

I then insisted that, in corroboration, I must have a letter in the hand of the peerless Minister, and bearing the English King's seal, to explain the delay in my obtaining an audience with the King. I made a convincing speech and pointed out that I had no other option.

After listening to me, the wise Minister reflected; and, turning to two of his trusted companions – two young and handsome brothers[2] – said something in English to the effect that the Ambassador of the

51

Shah of Iran was young, noble and learned, and that if this were not so, the Padeshah of Iran would not have honoured him with high office – his words are full of wisdom and truth. To me he said: 'Whatever shall be your desire, it shall be done.' Then he rose and hurried home.

And so ended another day.

[1] Spencer Perceval (1762-1812) was the seventh son of John Perceval, 2nd Earl of Egmont, by his second wife Catherine Compton. Tory MP for Northampton; Prime Minister from 4 October 1809 until his assassination on 11 May 1812.

[2] Dudley Ryder (1762-1847), 1st Earl of Harrowby, Minister without Portfolio 1809-12, and Richard Ryder, Home Secretary 1809-12, were brothers.

Thursday, 14 December

THIS MORNING Mr Dundas, the Minister for the Company,[1] came to see me in a spirit of friendship. He spoke of the Shah's great concern for the Afghan people and of the overthrow of their Government. He praised the people of Iran and criticized Lord Minto's behaviour towards Sir Harford Jones.

When Sir Gore Ouseley and his friends came to the house, he said: 'A remarkable thing happened today which has never occurred before. Red livery is reserved for the King and the Heir Apparent. Servants of the nobility are not allowed to wear red; even the servants of the other English princes, sons of the King, except for the Heir Apparent, do not dare to do so. But today red liveries have been delivered by the Government for the servants who have been engaged for your service.'[2]

Now he explained the reason for this honour done to me as follows: the Sultanate of Iran is an ancient one and, as our long history shows, it was the Sultans who wore the signet of Iran who were the founders of monarchy and the originators not only of law and order in the state, and of the rules of war and the treatment of prisoners, but also of benevolence towards their subjects. Therefore, other countries must show respect to the Padeshahs of Iran. Many distinguished ambassadors have come to London from Hind and Rum and Farang, from Turkestan and Russia and Africa; but none have been received with such esteem and respect.

---

[1] Robert Saunders Dundas (1771-1851), later 2nd Viscount Melville, was Tory MP for Edinburgh; President of the Board of Control of the East India Company 1809-12. The President enjoyed ministerial rank.

[2] *The Morning Post*, 20 December, described the state dress of the Persian Ambassador's servants as '. . . a scarlet coat, embroidered with two rows of deep gold lace; breeches and waistcoat of green and gold; hat, cocked with gold lace'.

Friday, 15 December

THIS MORNING Lord Teignmouth, accompanied by Lord Radstock and some other gentlemen, came to enquire about my health. They announced that this evening their wives, together with some other noble ladies, would come to visit me, to ease my homesickness with their sympathy and affection.

Therefore, crystal chandeliers and wax candles in forty[1] candelabra of crystal and gold and silver were lighted; and the reflection of their light on the panelled walls of my palace was truly wondrous. I was admiring the effect when the ladies entered, their faces radiant as the sun. With great courtesy, each one took a seat and with sweet tongue kindly enquired about my health.

It happened that among them was an Armenian lady from Shiraz. She is the wife of Mr Smith,[2] who has been serving in the port of Bushire, and she has come to London to learn English. Our eyes met and she was reminded of Shiraz – she recited these lines from Hafez:[3]

> *I remember the days when I lived at the end of your lane.*
> *Every time that I looked at your door my eyes shone once again,*
> *And I said to myself, 'Now I never will lack for a friend' –*
> *And we tried – how my heart and I tried! – but our efforts were in vain.*

The lady is very attractive, eloquent and sweet-spoken. I was deeply touched by the homesickness she feels in her exile.

And so ended another day.

---

[1] Iranians use the figure forty to express any large number of things.

[2] Nicolas Hankey Smith was British Resident at the Persian Gulf port of Bushire in 1795?-8, 1807-8 and 1809-10.

[3] Shams ud-Din Mohammad Hafez of Shiraz (died 1389) is the most famous of all Persian poets.

Saturday, 16 December

ARLY IN THE MORNING a note arrived from Sir Gore Ouseley to say that two important gentlemen, holding positions of high authority in the India Company, were coming to see me.

Mr Grant,[1] Chairman of the East India Company, and Mr Astell,[2] the Deputy Chairman, arrived with some other gentlemen. Their beaming faces brought the sun into the house. Each one was respectfully shown to a place of honour and the gates of friendship were opened to them.

I showed the letters from my honourable Ministers to the two Chairmen. I also reiterated, point by point, the dissatisfaction of the Qibleh of the Universe concerning their procrastination and negligence, Sir Harford Jones' mission, and Lord Minto's letter which was based on Malcolm's lies.

Mr Grant is a man of intellect and intelligence, with a thorough knowledge of Iranian history and geography. He expressed regret and said that ever since Lord Wellesley had strengthened the bonds of friendship between the Governments of the Shah of Iran and the King of England, and initiated an exchange of letters and Ambassadors, the East India Company had continued to exert its utmost efforts in support of a just and equitable Treaty of Friendship between the two Monarchs – and would continue to do so.

He then expressed shame and anger about Lord Minto's behaviour and said that, at the time of my arrival at the *Dar ol-Khalifeh*, the Abode of the Caliphs, Istanbul,[3] a formal letter of instructions had been sent to the Governor-General insisting that Sir Harford Jones' proposals should be acted upon, especially those concerning his Majesty's view on agitation among the Afghan tribes, and whatever else might be considered prudent for the strengthening of friendship between the two Governments.

He further expressed the opinion that if his Majesty the

Shahanshah were to build a few small warships to attack the Russians from the Black Sea, confounding that band of fiends, it would be better than a war on land. It was a thousand pities that our sea[4] is not connected with the Black Sea; then we should easily find the means to repel them.

[1] Charles Grant (1746-1823), MP for Inverness-shire 1802-18, Chairman of the Court of Directors of the East India Company in 1809-10 (and also in 1805-6 and 1815-16).

[2] William Astell (1774-1847), MP for Bridgewater, was a director of the East India Company for an unprecedented forty-seven years from 1800. He was Deputy Chairman of the Court of Directors in 1809-10 and Chairman in 1810-11.

[3] On the journey to London Abul Hassan and his party spent some weeks in Constantinople before embarking from Smyrna on 7 September 1809. See *Morier I*, pp. 362-6.

[4] The Caspian Sea.

Monday, 18 December

OUT OF AFFECTION FOR ME, Lord Radstock came to the house with a few friends. He expressed the hope that, after my audience with the King and the presentation of the Shahanshah's letter, I should visit his house to see his paintings of beautiful women. I told him that I was not at liberty to promise, but that if the Minister for Foreign Affairs agreed, and would take the trouble to come himself, then I should also come.

Sir Gore Ouseley then joined the company. We talked of many things until the conversation touched on the titles of the English nobility. I asked for some details. He said that next in line to the King is the Prince of Wales, which means the heir to the throne. the King has seven sons, each distinguished by a title of honour. They are all called Duke and also Prince, except for the heir to the throne, who is called Prince of Wales. Second is the Duke of York; third is the Duke of Clarence; fourth is the Duke of Kent; fifth is the Duke of Cumberland; sixth is the Duke of Sussex; and seventh is the Duke of Cambridge. The King's daughters are called Princess.

Sir Gore Ouseley was so eloquent and sympathetic about my sad and heavy heart, the result of my fever and illness, that I spent much time talking to him. I was astonished to find so much erudition in one man, and I asked him what and where he had studied. He said he had studied Persian for some time with masters of the language at Lucknow.

Tuesday, 19 December

TODAY MY HEALTH was back to normal and my fever was now gone.

Sir Gore Ouseley said: 'It has been arranged that a Royal coach will be sent for you to ride in tomorrow. When you reach the entrance to the Palace, one of the King's sons, accompanied by many noblemen and soldiers, will meet you and conduct you to the presence of the King with honour and respect.'

'But,' I said, 'until I receive a letter written in the Minister's hand and with the King's seal, detailing the facts of the King's illness and advanced years and the long distance from the Royal residence to the capital, I will not set foot in the coach. On the first day, Mr Perceval, the Prime Minister, promised to write a letter under the King's seal, explaining that the delay in my audience in no way reflected on the Shah's Majesty, but was necessitated by the reasons stated. Unless my request is granted, my situation is impossible.'

Sir Gore Ouseley then went out to explain the situation to the Prime Minister, who agreed to write the letter and to sign it himself – its truth attested by the seal of the exalted King of England.

Wednesday, 20 December

THE KING'S MASTER of the Ceremonies, accompanied by a troop of soldiers and officials of the English Court, brought the special coach – drawn by six bay horses in matching harness – to the entrance of my house. Sir Gore Ouseley also arrived, having just left the Prime Minister; he brought the good news that the letter had been written. 'Thank God!' he said and, composing himself, mounted the coach. Four of my own attendants also got in and we set off for the Palace.[1]

The streets were lined on all sides with men and women; and from the splendid palaces where beautiful, sunny-faced girls were sitting to watch, came whistles and shouts of 'Hurrah! Hurrah!' I asked the meaning of this uproar and of the word 'hurrah'. I was told it is a word used by the English in moments of joy and happiness: when an ambassador goes to meet the King, all the people shout 'Hurrah!' as a mark of honour and respect.

Snow began to fall heavily, pitching a white tent over the streets and avenues and house-tops, delaying our arrival at the Palace.

Finally we reached a spacious square with colonnades. Nearby, at one side of the square, was a vast pool; and massive trees were planted – like worshippers with arms raised in prayer. Streams of water ran in channels. Truly, it was a marvellous sight![2]

The coach stopped at the door of the Palace and I and my companions got out and entered the building. From all sides officials of the King's Government greeted me with courtesy. I was conducted to a waiting-room on the ground floor; and, finding the room unpleasant, I asked the reason for the delay. The Minister for Foreign Affairs came in and said that the King was being robed and we must wait a little. 'The letter explaining the delay in your audience is ready sealed,' he said; and, reaching into his breast pocket, he drew it out and handed it to me. Then he left us, returning after a while to say the time had come. Sir Gore Ouseley and I followed him up to the first floor of the building.

We entered a small gilded room where the King was standing alone.[3] I did not recognize him, and Sir Gore Ouseley said: 'My dear friend, this is the King.' After carrying out the formalities due to so great and powerful a monarch, I took his Majesty the Shah's letter – in its gold case – and placed it myself in the hands of the English King. The King received the letter with great respect and handed it to the Prime Minister.

The King did me the honour of enquiring after his Majesty the Shahanshah's health, and of expressing his appreciation for his assistance in the overthrow of Zaman Shah's Government.

I replied: 'The Shah has done everything required by his affection and friendship for you: in return, he asks that – just as you helped the Sultan of Turkey to liberate Egypt from the armies of the French – you will do even better now and assist in liberating the city of Tiflis from Russian occupation. This would further strengthen our amity and friendship.'

When I spoke of Lord Minto's unworthy conduct, the King grew angry and said that any servant of his who caused annoyance to the exalted Shah of Iran was useless and should be rebuked. As to the request regarding the Russians, he would do his best; and, God willing, as a result of the firm friendship between our two governments, the enemy would be repulsed – assuredly their expulsion from Tiflis would be even more successful than the Egyptian affair.

After this, he spoke in English to the Prime Minister, praising me with compliments worthy of a King: 'Until today we have seen no ambassador from any monarch so young and so learned: it betokens the good fortune of the Government and the great glory of the Shah of Iran.' The King praised Sir Gore Ouseley's Persian highly, and gave us leave to depart with eloquent instructions to my *mehmandar*. On leaving the Audience Chamber, we met a group of Nobles in Court Dress waiting to enter. My companions and I then mounted the carriage provided for us and went home.

His Excellency returned to his house, where the crowd was so extremely great, that it was impossible for his Majesty's footmen to get from the carriage, to open the carriage door, and knock at the house door; and had it not been for the vigilance of the Bow-street patrole, it would have been impossible to clear the door-way. The populace gave his Excellency three cheers again, upon his leaving the carriage.

(The Morning Post, 21 December)

On his Excellency's return to Mansfield-street, he invited Sir Gore Ouseley and Mr Morier to partake of an entertainment, called in the Persian language a Pillau; *it was composed of rice and fowls stewed together with spices; the dish was prepared in the same way as* marinaded *chickens. This Noble Personage is extremely abstemious in his diet; his only beverage is* orgeat, *and occasionally a glass of wine.*

(The Morning Post, 21 December)

[1] Buckingham Palace was known at this time as Buckingham House, the Queen's House or the Queen's Palace.

[2] Abul Hassan must be referring to the canal in St James's Park and the rows of trees planted on either side.

[3] Although, on 11 December, the King had agreed to a public entrance, Wellesley wrote on 17 December 'that it has been found impracticable to make the necessary preparations for the Public Entrance of the Persian Envoy previously to Wednesday next'. As Abul Hassan was so anxious to present the Shah's letter, a private audience was arranged. See *Aspinall/Geo.* III, V, p. 472.

Thursday, 21 December

THIS MORNING I WENT OUT with my friends in the carriage to see the sights of London. Splendid houses line both sides of the street. They all look alike; the name of the owner is painted on each door. I saw no humble dwellings, only fine houses of four storeys. The first storey is built of stone and the other three of brick and stucco. The ceilings are decorated with gold and azure; and the walls are covered with designs of wild beasts and birds, *divs* and *peris*. The windows are glazed with matching panes. Stables and carriage-houses are conveniently placed behind each house. When we reached the centre of the city, a bridge of massive stones came into view which spans a river like the one at Baghdad. Words fail to describe it![1] After crossing the bridge, we came to a street with shops built to the requirements of the various trades. Outside the shops there are signs. If anyone wants to buy something, the shopkeeper opens the door for him; and then the customer, without bargaining, makes his selection, pays for it and returns to his carriage. Because of the cold weather, as well as for fear of thieves, drunkards and madmen, shop doors are kept shut, except to allow customers to enter. Both sides of the market street are closed off by nicely carved balustrades to prevent horse-riders from crossing on to the pedestrian pavement.

Above the entrance to each house, large round glass lanterns are suspended from iron hooks. One man is responsible for cleaning the glass of the lamps; another looks after the wick and the oil; and at sunset a third comes with a ladder and sparking torch – in the twinkling of an eye the lamps are lit. The owners of the houses pay the lamplighters a monthly wage which enables them to live comfortably. It is truly amazing that in winter it is so dark in this city that the sun is invisible and lamps must be lighted day and night. Indeed, the eye is dazzled and no one need carry a hand-lantern even when going out in the evening.

Every man, whether of high or low estate, wears a watch in his waistcoat pocket; and everything he does – eating or drinking, or keeping appointments – is regulated by time. Factories (and bakeries) and livery stables all have fixed hours of work which are strictly adhered to; and each one has a large clock fixed to the wall which strikes the hours.

Servants do not disturb their masters' privacy until summoned.[2]

These are only a very few of the customs of the inhabitants of London. They are recorded here because it is my hope that this journal will prove to be a useful guide for future ambassadors.

[1] The entry for 23 December identifies this as Westminster Bridge.

[2] *Lord Radstock's Letter* of 10 January 1810 (see Bibliography) reports of Abul Hassan 'that among the many of our customs which he approved, he admired none more than that, of not suffering the servants to remain in the room when they were not wanted'.

Friday, 22 December

SIR GORE OUSELEY came to the house with some English gentlemen. After an exchange of courtesies, we talked of many things and then of the war with the Russians. I explained that my only reason for enduring the hardships of ocean and desert was to discharge promptly and successfully the mission entrusted to me by his Majesty the Shah as his ambassador to the English King. So spending my time sight-seeing in London only increased my discontent. I urged them to make every effort to repulse the Russians, to deliver Tiflis, and to expedite my return. Sir Gore Ouseley asked me to be patient until the end of winter when, God willing, my mission would meet with the desired success.

I got into the carriage with Mr Morier. After driving around the square, we came to Lord Radstock's house,[1] where we had been invited for the evening. We entered his splendid palace, and found that Sir Gore Ouseley was also there. The house is decorated with many paintings on canvas. I asked about them and was told that they are the works of Old Masters, any one of which might sell for some 4000 *tomans*. They are as much desired as if they were wealth and riches in themselves. Some people have spent as much as 100,000 *tomans* to decorate their palaces with Old Masters, even paying as much as 10,000 *tomans* for one painting. I found all of this very strange.

I was surprised that Lord Radstock's daughters did not appear and that all the ladies in the assembly were old. Finally, I said to my friends: 'I am tired of talking to old ladies – I want to go home! Our host refuses to let us meet his daughters and only wants to show off his old and lifeless paintings. He is like one of them himself! He spends so much money for the pleasure of gazing upon these ancient painted faces, it seems he also prefers them in the flesh, and has therefore invited me to meet them. But my own tastes are different!'

PLATE 8

Fath Ali Shah, by Mirza Baba. This is the
portrait sent by the Shah to the Marquis Wellesley.

PLATE 9

The King's Theatre, Stage and Auditorium. This
theatre, also known as the Italian Opera House,
was much frequented by Abul Hassan. Aquatint by
Pugin and Rowlandson for Ackermann's
Micrcosm of London, *1808-10.*

It was explained to me that throughout the year, and especially during the long winter evenings, these older ladies and gentlemen meet in each other's drawing-rooms or go to the theatre together. Young men and pretty girls attend dances. There is some sense in this for, while dancing and talking together, they may develop an affection which may result in their marrying someone of a suitable background.

At last, Sir Gore Ouseley persuaded our host to summon his daughters. When the girls joined the party, they were accompanied by a lady who sang for the guests with such feeling that our hearts were touched. No one in London, or in the whole of England, can be more accomplished than she in the art of music.

When the evening came to an end, I left the party and went home.

<hr />

[1] Lord Radstock lived at 10 Portland Place, the site now occupied by Broadcasting House. The grandest street of eighteenth-century London, Portland Place was laid out by James and Robert Adam about 1778 and named after the Duke of Portland.

Saturday, 23 December

SIR GORE OUSELEY and I left the house to take a look at London. We strolled through the streets until we came to Westminster Bridge. We left the bridge and went to Sir Gore Ouseley's house[1] to rest. His wife[2] was very ill and I prayed to the Lord God for her recovery. He showed me every kindness. His sweet little two-year-old daughter was frightened by my large and bearded figure; and as I calmed her fears the heartache of my exile was eased.

---

[1] Ouseley writes to Wellesley from 15 Park Lane as well as from 15 Savile Row; but Boyle's *Court and Country Guide* for April 1810 gives the Savile Row address.

[2] Ouseley married in 1806 Harriet Georgina, daughter of John Whitelock.

Sunday, 24 December

AT SUN-UP THIS MORNING, Sir Gore Ouseley, Lord Radstock and some other gentlemen accompanied the Ambassador from Istanbul to my house. While talking, the Ambassador said that he had been in London for seven years. He also pointed out that he had been to see me twice and that I had not yet returned his calls.[1]

I then told Sir Gore Ouseley that, since I was commanded by his Most Noble Majesty the Shahanshah not to remain in London for more than forty days, he should call on the Minister for Foreign Affairs to settle my business. He told me that the Minister had said yesterday that he intends to call on me tomorrow evening; but that since returning from his embassy in Spain he has been busy putting his affairs in order and it has not been possible to see him.

Today the bad weather and the anguish of exile made me lose control of the reins of my patience.

---

[1] *Lord Radstock's Letter* of 10 January 1810 mentions an earlier occasion when 'the Turkish Ambassador paid him a visit. "What are you about?" cries the Turk. "I am writing English!" "Writing English! why you have scarcely been here three days, whilst I have been in England seven years, and know not a syllable of the language, or how to form even a single letter."' James Morier gave Abul Hassan an English lesson every day.

Monday, 25 December

THIS MORNING A messenger brought a note from Sir Gore Ouseley to say that Lord Wellesley had forgotten that today is one of their holidays and that it would not be possible for him to visit me. He would see me tomorrow night.

In reply I wrote: 'Such an excuse is unacceptable: it makes me wonder what the Minister is trying to hide. They are well aware that my desire is to strengthen relations between our two Governments by whatever means are most correct and expeditious, so that I may be permitted to depart; and that replies to my ministers' letters should be written and despatched.'

When Sir Gore Ouseley received my note, he became agitated and came to the house himself with profuse apologies. He raised the question of financial assistance for the war with Russia. He asked me for an *ashrafi* (a gold coin with the image of the Shah) looked at it, and then returned it.

Then he said: 'Tomorrow night after dinner we shall go to see the Minister and then go to a theatre called the Opera – until you have seen it for yourself, you cannot imagine what it is like. On behalf of the Government, I have rented a good box for you for three months at 300 *tomans*.'

I replied that it would not be correct to go to a theatre from the Minister's house and that we should put off the theatre until another night. He agreed.

Tuesday, 26 December

AFTER DINNER I went with Sir Gore Ouseley and some lords to the house of the Foreign Minister.[1] When he was informed of our arrival, he sent his son and brother to greet me. They received me in the forecourt with due ceremony and escorted me into the Minister's house. It was magnificent: large mirrors and paintings from all over the world hung on all sides, and wax candles were lighted in gold and silver and crystal chandeliers; silk brocade curtains were draped around the doors and windows, and fine English carpets covered the floors; columns and doors were inlaid with ivory patterns which take years to make. The beauty of the place is a wonder of the world.

The peerless Minister showed me great respect and did everything possible to express friendship and kindness. While we spoke he was holding a beautiful manuscript copy of *Joseph and Zuleika* by Mullah Jami,[2] which had been given to the noble Lord by Colonel Malcolm on his return from Iran. He read some verses from the book and asked me to confirm their meaning.

After the formal exchange of courtesies, he took me and Sir Gore Ouseley into his private study, where he opened the doors of friendship and affection and showed extreme kindness. He said that the important object of my mission was in accordance with his own heart's desire, and that he would in no way neglect the matter.

I answered: 'Oh Minister, since your Ambassador was received in audience by the Ornament of the Country, his Majesty the Shah, and since consequently the wishes of the exalted King of England were gratified, especially in regard to stirring up trouble among Zaman Shah's Afghan tribes – now, in return, we need your friendship and help in liberating Tiflis and delivering it from the Russians. I have drunk bitter salt water from deserts and oceans; I have been alarmed by the strange cries of wild animals; I have crossed desolate country and raging oceans; and on several occasions

I almost lost my life in storms at sea – all so that I might now have the honour of talking with the great and highly placed Minister and of conveying to him the messages of his Majesty the Shah. Again I beg you to overcome any delay and to expedite my departure from London. It is true that if I were a lustful and pleasure-seeking man I would not wish to leave this city of beautiful buildings and beautiful women – this earthly paradise. But Sir Gore Ouseley and other noble friends will testify that, although Mr Morier has tried his utmost to persuade me to go out to parties with him, I have not accepted. Others have asked me to go to the theatre; but I have refused to go until I had the opportunity – today in private – to explain my wishes to you personally.'

The Minister concurred and told me that they wish to send an ambassador of distinction to Iran in order to strengthen the bonds of friendship between the exalted Padeshah of Iran and the King of England, as is fitting and proper. I pointed out to him that the customs of Iran differ from those of Europe: Iran is ruled directly by the Shah, the Shadow of God on Earth; and there is no council. The English Ambassador should be a man of quality and accomplishments and an excellent linguist – interpreters are useless.

The Minister told me that Lord Minto would be reprimanded by the King for having written that Sir Harford Jones was not the King's representative, and for attempting to dismiss him. Arrangements satisfactory to both countries would be made for the transfer of funds to Iran through the Company in neighbouring India. I replied that the Shah had ordered that we should make a written agreement of the amount to be transmitted through the Company, so that no servant of the English Government could act contrary to the agreement and the Minister's instructions regarding the transfer of funds. He asked me to be patient for four or five days until the councillors could meet to carry out my wishes.

Then my companions and I left the Minister's study and went to the floor below where a group of lords and gentlemen, including the

Minister's brother, who is Ambassador to Spain, awaited us. We sat down to eat at tables covered with a rare array of food and drink.

It happened that among the guests was a gentleman who had spent some time in India and had boasted to the Minister that he knew Persian, hoping to be honoured with the ambassadorship to Iran. My friends decided to test him and told him that if his claim to speak Persian were true, he should converse with the Ambassador from Iran. When he spoke, and it was apparent that he knew only a word or two of Persian, the guests made fun of him. He was ashamed and regretted his claim.

When we left the party, my companions tried to persuade me to go to the theatre; but I refused and we went home.

[1] Apsley House, Hyde Park Corner.

[2] Mullah Nur ud-Din Abdur-Rahman Jami (1414-92) was one of Iran's greatest poets, scholars and mystics.

Wednesday, 27 December

S IR GORE OUSELEY arrived to say that he had taken a draft
agreement based on my instructions to the Foreign Office
and had shown it to the Minister.[1]

My servants started to quarrel among themselves, and I was just
about to punish them when Sir Gore Ouseley stopped me. He said
that in this country the master does not have absolute power over his
servants – even in the case of the King of England. Laws exist for the
welfare and protection of all classes of people and are administered
in the King's name. If a master locks up his servant, the servant may
complain to a judge, and the judge may summon the master to pay a
fine. On hearing this, I begged him to forbid the English servants
from divulging these matters to my own servants: it would make my
work in this foreign land all the more difficult.

[1] A list of requests made by Abul Hassan to Lord Wellesley in the context of the
treaty may be found in IO L/PS/3/3, Appendix 19.

PLATE 10

The Great Hall of the Bank of England. Abul Hassan wrote that 'the Bank, with its vast organization of clerks, soldiers and labourers, is more impressive than the Court of a powerful Sultan.' Aquatint by Pugin and Rowlandson for Ackermann's Microcosm of London, *1808-10.*

PLATE 11

Queen Charlotte, from the studio of Allan Ramsay
(1713-84).

PLATE 12

The Grand Staircase at Buckingham House. Abul Hassan was much impressed by the trompe l'oeuil *painting of 'statues' on the ceiling cornice. Aquatint by J. Stephanoff for Pyne's* Royal Residences, *1819.*

PLATE 13

The Saloon at Covent Garden Theatre. At Covent Garden Abul Hassan saw a performance of King Lear *– revised to produce a happy ending! – followed by a Pantomime with the great clown Grimaldi. Caricature by Robert and George Cruickshank for Egan's* Real Life in London, *1820.*

Thursday, 28 December

BECAUSE I WAS FEELING bilious and sad, Sir Gore Ouseley took me out to a place called Hyde Park: it is a vast open field, which in spring becomes a flower-garden with green lawns two miles square. Paths surround it, where men and women may walk for pleasure and relaxation. Other paths are reserved for horse-riders and carriages.

It happened that my horse shied and I almost fell to the ground; but my *mehmandar* skilfully managed to control it. He said that tomorrow he would arrange for me to have a gentler mount. They have truly splendid horses in England; but it is a pity that they clip short their manes and tails.

We left the park and hurried home to find an assembly of lords and gentlemen, who had come with their wives to call on me. We talked together and the Armenian lady from Shiraz[1] and Mr Morier's sisters wiped the dust of exile from my care-worn face. A lady missionary – they are famous for their goodness and beauty – was among the guests. When her eye fell on my huge beard, she took fright and left the room.

---

[1] Mrs Nicolas Hankey Smith. See 15 December.

73

Friday, 29 December

MRS SMITH, THE Armenian lady from Shiraz, brought me a fine present of a sack of musk, but she did not stay.

Then Sir Gore Ouseley came in to say that today I must return the call of the Chairman of the India Company. We set out together and drove four miles out of London to a magnificent house – rarely have I seen a house so large.[1]

On our arrival we were greeted by several of the Company directors in sumptuous attire, who escorted us to the high entrance portico. Here a large group of gentlemen and distinguished English merchants, with about 1,000 soldiers, was gathered to honour me. Mr Grant, Chairman of the Company, came out of the house himself to greet me and conduct me with due ceremony into the reception.

The house has been decorated by master-craftsmen and, after the formal exchange of compliments, Mr Grant took me to see the library. It is a high-ceilinged room with cases built to hold books, which are beautifully painted in gold and azure. Above the bookcases, arched niches hold small book-chests; and in one part of the room the shelves hold neatly ranged books in Arabic and Persian. I noticed one small chest with particularly beautiful calligraphy on it, and I asked about it. Respectfully, he brought the chest down from its place and, bowing, he handed it to me. I too bowed respectfully, took it and opened it, and was thrilled to see the miraculous verses of the Qibleh of the Universe. Mr Grant told me that Colonel Malcolm had brought back this *divan* of the Shah's poetry, together with a magnificent portrait of him, which he would now show me.[2]

Having said this, he took my arm and led me upstairs to a high-ceilinged room whose magnificence can hardly be surpassed anywhere. The portrait was displayed on an easel at the entrance of the room. When I beheld the beauty of the Qibleh of the Universe, I bowed low until my head was level with his feet.

Then the Chairman took me to another place where the portraits of Shah Abbas's Ambassador[3] and several others were hanging. He told me he wished to have my portrait painted to hang beside that of the Ambassador of Shah Abbas.[4]

Truly, Mr Grant expressed so much esteem for me on behalf of the Company that I was highly gratified, especially as I obtained a firm promise from him regarding a Treaty of Friendship between our two Governments.

[1] East India House was in Leadenhall Street, in the middle of the City of London.

[2] This portrait of Fath Ali Shah was given by him to John Malcolm in 1800 as a gift for the Marquis Wellesley, who in 1806 presented it to the East India Company. Painted by Mirza Baba and signed by him 1213 AH (1798/9 AD).

[3] Naqd Ali Beg was Ambassador to London from Shah Abbas in 1623.

[4] The East India Company commissioned a full-length portrait of Abul Hassan from Sir William Beechey. See journal entry for 29 January for the first sitting.

Saturday, 30 December

King's theatre. Serious opera of Sidagero. *Music by Guglielmi, principal characters by Signor Tramezzani, Signora Collini, and Mme Calderini, & a favourite Divertissement, & also an entirely new Historical Ballet entitled* Pietro Il Grande *by Signor Rossi (Vestris, Moreau, Boisgirard, Mme Angiolini, Mme Nora & Mme Mouroy).*

(*The Times*, 30 December)

SIR GORE OUSELEY and some other gentlemen came to the house. After dinner we went to the Opera, which is a grand theatre like nothing I have seen before: it has seven magnificent tiers, all decorated in gold and azure, and hung with brocade curtains and paintings.[1]

Dancers and sweet-voiced singers appeared one after the other to entertain us, acting and dancing like Greeks and Russians and Turks. Their music and songs banished sorrow from the hearts of the audience. It is amazing that although 5000 people may gather in the theatre, they do not make a loud noise – when they enjoy a song they clap their hands together; if they think the singing bad, they say 'hiss'.

Sir Gore Ouseley remarked:'Truly, it is a splendid theatre. Sometimes the King and Queen and Prince also come to see a performance; they enter by a special door, which is always guarded by soldiers, and which you also had the honour to use.'

During the evening, a spectacle was produced in which an Italian named Tramezzani[2] played a king who is at war with another king of Greece. In English he is called Sidagero. When his castle is destroyed, he is thrown into prison with his two small children and condemned to death. This opera affected me deeply because of my exile.

After this there was a dance in which the dancers imitated the Emperor and the Empress of Russia and the Pasha of Turkey and

76

his wife and other Turks. A tiny woman from Italy danced and amazed us by remaining half an hour on the point of one foot. Her name is Angiolini.[3]

> . . . *[the Mirza] laughed heartily at the folly of bringing forward Peter the Great and his Empress as dancing to divert the throng. . . . Soon after, he jokingly said, 'When I get back to my own country, the King shall ask me, "What did the English do to divert you?" I will answer, "Sir, they brought before me your Majesty's enemies, the Emperor and Empress of Russia, and made them dance for my amusement."'*
>
> (from *Lord Radstock's Letter*, 10 January 1810)

When the curtain was lowered, the novelty of my appearance caused the English to talk about me among themselves.

---

[1] The King's Theatre (Royal Italian Opera House), in the Haymarket at the corner of Pall Mall, was London's most fashionable theatre for opera (sung in Italian) and ballet.

[2] Diomiro Tramezzani, the popular Italian tenor, appeared at the King's Theatre from 1809 to 1814.

[3] Mlle Angiolini performed at the King's Theatre each year from 1809 to 1814.

Sunday, 31 December

ECAUSE SUNDAY IS their holy day, the English go to church to worship in their own fashion. Then young and old, nobles and commoners alike, go out riding in carriages in clean and colourful clothes. Each carriage is attended by three grooms, two who ride at the back, and one at the front. The grooms of each carriage wear different coloured livery, for example, the driver of one lord might wear yellow, while the driver of another might wear green or some other colour. For pleasure and relaxation, they go to the parks, vast *maidans* or open spaces, which are the *Bagh-i Shah*, the King's Gardens, near the Royal Palace. In English, they are called Hyde Park and St James's Park.

In the park we saw some 100,000 men and women parading themselves on foot and on horseback. Elsewhere pretty girls and handsome youths were admiring the gardens: although it was winter, the verdure of the park rivalled the *Bagh-i Eram*, the Garden of Eden.

Everywhere there were groups chatting gaily together on the grass; but more remarkable were the wandering herds of beautifully spotted deer. I was told that the deer belong to the King. They are as free as London's citizens to roam in the pleasant parks, and they live and breed there; they are not afraid of people.

Indeed, it is a vast and delightful pleasure-ground – as exhilarating as a draught of wine. If a sorrowing soul traverse these heavenly fields, his head is crowned with flowers of joy, and looking on these saffron beds – luxurious as Kashmir's – he smiles despite himself. In the gardens and on the paths, beauteous women shine like the sun and rouse the envy of the stars; and the *houris* of paradise blush with shame to look upon the rose-cheeked beauties of the earth below. In absolute amazement, I said to Sir Gore Ouseley:

> *If there be paradise on earth*
> *It is this, oh! it is this!*[1]

78

He replied that it was winter now – in spring it is a thousand times better.

Then my sympathetic friend and I alighted from the carriage and walked around the edge of the park, which is enclosed with fencing, to the entrance of another garden.[2] Inside the garden are streams of running water and elegant avenues, lined with rows of stately trees which seem to touch the sky. Trees of fragrant oranges and lemons stand next to trees of other fruits; new green shoots emerging from their beds whisper to the green lawns.

After visiting the park and the garden, we got back into the carriage and returned home.

[1] The verse inscribed on the wall of the Hall of Private Audience in the Red Fort at Delhi.

[2] Kensington Gardens adjoin Hyde Park on the west.

JANUARY

1810

Monday, 1 January

EARLY THIS MORNING Sir Gore Ouseley came to the house. After exchanging compliments, he told me that it is a custom of the English that when ministers or councillors call on an ambassador, they leave a card the size of the palm of the hand at the ambassador's door. I was now obliged to return these calls.

To comply with this custom I wrote my name on a few cards, and set out with Sir Gore Ouseley to leave them at the homes of the ministers and other gentlemen who had called on me. A card is left so that the master of the house and his family will know that they have been honoured by a return visit from the Iranian Ambassador.

Wednesday, 3 January

AS THE ARMY OF DAY overcame the hosts of the night, the black soldiers retreated westward; but a black cloud so darkened the sky that the day was indistinguishable from night. As a result I was overcome with depression. I did not even have a book to occupy my mind, so I wrote a note to the Librarian of the Company asking him to send me a few history books.

When Sir Gore Ouseley arrived, he told me that today's newspaper[1] reported that I had attended a party at the home of the Librarian of the Company, together with himself and another friend. I said: '*Sobhanallah!* Good God! you know very well that I did not go out. This report in the newspaper is very strange indeed.'

The last time the newspaper made a mistake, we let it pass without correction.[2] But now Sir Gore Ouseley told Mr Morier to write a letter to the newspaper saying that the Ambassador of Iran had not been to that gentleman's house. He wrote to the publisher and in reply received a letter accusing him of falsehood.[3]

And so ended another day.

[1] Dr Wilkins' party was held on 10 January, one week after this entry in the journal. Abul Hassan was no doubt reminded of the news item when he came across the reference to the Librarian during a later revision, and inserted it here.

[2] This could refer to *The Times* article of 15 December which stated that the Persian Ambassador had sixty-three children. It is true that his monarch, Fath Ali Shah, could claim many more than this by his many wives; but Abul Hassan had only one wife and, at this time, only one son (who died before his return to Tehran).

[3] *The Morning Post*, the newspaper in question, did publish a correction on 13 January: 'The Persian Ambassador was not at Dr Wilkins' on Wednesday, as has been stated by mistake.'

Friday, 5 January

ACCOMPANIED BY Sir Gore Ouseley and Mr Morier, I drove in my carriage to the Bank,[1] which is near the India House in the City of London. The magnificent building was crowded with people, including some 400 soldiers on parade who are employees of the Bank.

Upon our arrival we were greeted with much ceremony by officials of the Bank. Then Sir Gore Ouseley and I were taken to visit several rooms in the building. In one of these we saw a group of clerks, who were seated busily writing with swift-moving pens. In this room I was asked to record the date of my visit.

A most extraordinary thing is the fact that they print thin pieces of paper each one of which is given a particular value from one *toman* to 1000 *tomans*. These printed papers are called 'notes', and they are just as valuable as gold. Some 200 clerks work from morning till night making these notes, which are printed with certain marks which make it extremely difficult to forge them. Just as it is impossible to create a likeness of the Incomparable Creator – so it is with these notes!

After making a complete tour of the building, we went to a room [the Great Parlour] where the directors' wives were already seated. We also sat down and ate some fruit. Each one had brought me a present of a gold coin. I felt I should refuse them, but Sir Gore Ouseley insisted.

I found the Bank – with its vast organization of clerks, soldiers and labourers – more impressive than the Court of a powerful Sultan.

[1] The Bank of England, Threadneedle Street in the City of London, was established by a company of Whig merchants and incorporated by William III in 1694.

Saturday, 6 January

THIS EVENING I was invited to the house of Lord Wellesley, the Minister for Foreign Affairs. I went with Sir Gore Ouseley. The Prime Minister, Mr Perceval, Lord Liverpool,[1] Mr Dundas, Lord Clive (who is now known as Lord Powis),[2] some gentlemen from the Company, and many lords were there. My friends made me very welcome.

Lord Wellesley said that he had heard so much from Malcolm about the healthy climate and fruits of Iran that he was inclined to appoint himself as Ambassador to Iran. I told him that he should send someone else as Ambassador and spare himself the affliction of being one!

The evening was spent in amusing and elegant conversation – and then I returned home with my friends.

[1] Robert Bankes Jenkinson (1770-1828), 2nd Earl of Liverpool; Secretary of State for War and the Colonies 1809-12; Prime Minister 1812-27.

[2] Edward Clive (1754-1839) was the son of Robert Clive (1725-74), 1st Baron Clive of Plassey, 'Clive of India'. In 1784 he married Henrietta Antonia Herbert, sister and heir of George Edward Herbert, last Earl of Powis of the Herbert family; in 1804 he became 1st Earl of Powis of the second creation. He was Governor of Madras 1798-1803.

Monday, 8 January

SIR GORE OUSELEY and I went by carriage five *farsakhs* out of London to his country house. When we went inside, he took my arm and led me to a magnificent library filled with all kinds of books. I remarked on the superb collection; and he told me he had acquired the books when he was in Lucknow. Sir Gore Ouseley told me he had built the house,[1] planted the crops and installed the herd of cattle. In spring and summer he invites his close and congenial friends here to enjoy themselves.

From the room where we sat we could see a fountain of clear and pure water; and Sir Gore Ouseley said he had planted the 30,000 trees of fir and pine himself. We went out to inspect the fountain, the envy of the Fountain of Life, and then we walked among the trees – cypress, fir, pine and juniper, citrus, apple and quince – and through the vineyards, planted with a variety of grapes.

Sir Gore Ouseley made no secret of the fact that he had bought the estate for 15,000 'guineas' (which are worth more than Iranian *tomans*).

The house is decorated with paintings on canvas, including portraits of Asaf od-Dowleh, that incomparable Vizir of Hindustan, and his estimable brother, Saadat Ali Khan,[2] and other officials universally famed for their handsome good looks and liberality. These paintings were acquired at great expense and hang beside the portraits of European nobles and men of distinction.

Sir Gore Ouseley went on to say that he has some 2000 books in English and 1500 volumes of Persian prose and poetry with fine calligraphy by famous Old Masters. Many of the books are illustrated with miniatures and gold illuminations by masters from India, Turkey and Iran. Then too there were examples of Indian calligraphy. Even I, who have travelled the world, looked at the library with wonder. When I asked about it, Sir Gore Ouseley told me that the books had been in the library of the Sultans of Lucknow, and that he had been able to acquire them for two *lakhs* of rupees during the time of troubles there. Perusing the collection is a delight for his friends, as it is for him.

We left the library and went next door to a storeroom where swords, shields, bows and arrows and daggers were displayed. I was surprised to learn that Sir Gore Ouseley is a skilled craftsman and needs no help to repair his collection of arms or the books in his library. He showed me some of his own carvings on ivory: the intricate designs reminded me of the work of Chinese or Indian masters. I was amazed that an Englishman should be so talented, and cried '*Marhaba!* Well done!'

As we left the house, we saw an extremely large dog guarding the entrance. When he recognized Sir Gore Ouseley he immediately lay his head at his master's feet and started to nuzzle him. I was amazed to learn that some masters take their dogs to market with them. They hang their purchases – chickens, fruit and so forth – around the dogs' necks and send them off home: the dogs obediently deliver the shopping to the mistress of the house! In this country dogs are bought and sold at very high prices.

We then got into the carriage and left for the city, enjoying the gardens we saw all along the way.

We reached home – and so ended another day.

[1] Ouseley bought Claramont (now Caldecote House), Goffs Lane, Cheshunt, Hertfordshire, in about 1807. The house was built in about 1781, so not by Ouseley.

[2] Saadat Ali Khan, Nawab Vizir of Oude 1798-1814, in whose service at Lucknow Gore Ouseley had held the appointment of Major-Commandant, had succeeded (after a brief interval) his brother, Asaf od-Doleh.

Tuesday, 9 January

L ORD TEIGNMOUTH ARRIVED. He is a good and dear friend and brought me the key to the square in front of his house,[1] so that whenever I wished I might take my ease there and so banish the grief and dust of my exile.

Many London houses are built around 'squares': these are large, open *maidans*, enclosed by iron railings as high as a man and set vertically a hand's breadth apart. The streets between the houses and the square are wide enough for three carriages to drive abreast; and streets for carriages, horse-riders and pedestrians lead out from each corner. Each square belongs to the owners of the houses surrounding it, and only they are allowed to go in. On each side there is an iron gate which the residents – men, women and children – use when they wish to spend some time walking and relaxing within. The squares are like pleasant gardens, planted with a variety of trees and beautiful, bright flowers. Most squares also have a pool of water and wide, straight paths to walk along. Three gardeners are kept busy in each square repairing the paths, planting trees and flowers and tending the shrubs. At night street lamps are lighted – like those outside each house. The doors and windows of all the houses look out on to the square. It is pleasant to walk there in all seasons: I always felt like singing and happily looked forward to walking in that pleasure-garden with Lord Teignmouth and his wife and children. The ladies of the square used to watch me from their windows.

---

[1] Lord Teignmouth lived at 4 Portman Square, not far from Mansfield Street.

PLATE 14

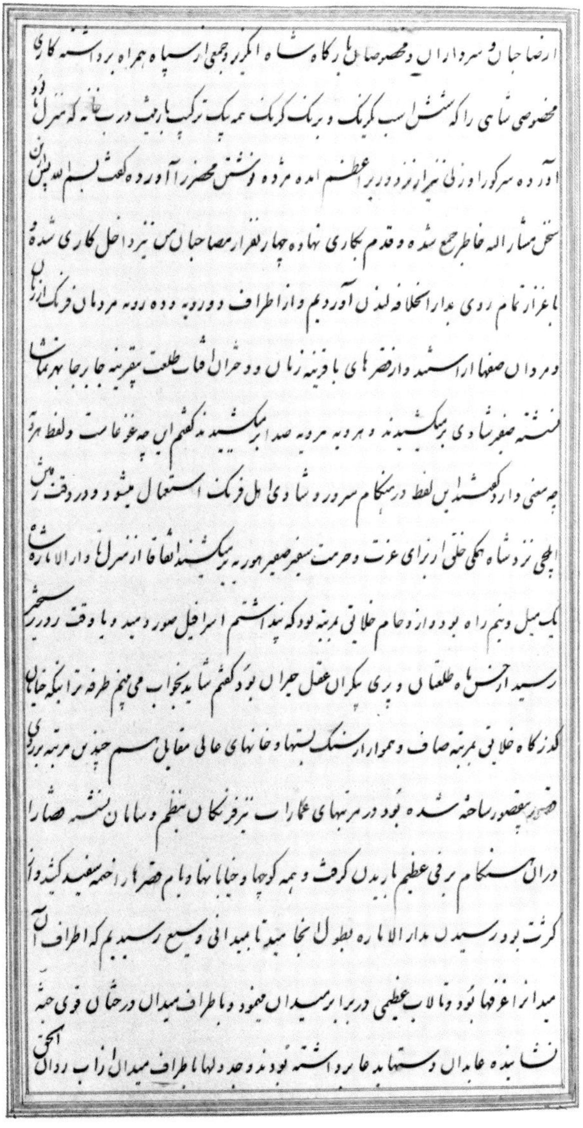

PLATE 15

Admiral William Waldegrave, 1st Baron Radstock, who was James Morier's uncle by marriage, became one of Abul Hassan's close companions in London. This engraving appeared in the Naval Chronicle, *vol* X *(1803).*

PLATE 16

James Morier (1819), the British diplomat and author of the Hajji Baba *books, who was Abul Hassan's interpreter in London. Portrait by Martin Cregan.*

PLATE 17

A drawing by James Morier of the fictional Persian
Ambassador in his two Hajji Baba *books.*

Wednesday, 10 January

THE SUN EMERGED from under a cloud as Colonel Desbrow[1] arrived to visit me on behalf of the Queen. He told me that the Queen regretted that, because of illness, she had been unable to come to London from Windsor to meet me as she wished. Besides, one of the King's daughters had also been taken ill.[2] But she was now recovering and was only slightly indisposed. So the Queen had arranged to come to town from Windsor on Wednesday next. She would send her coach for me, and Colonel Desbrow would accompany me to the audience.

Sir Gore Ouseley told me that Sir Harford Jones had not sent a translation of the illustrious letter of the *Mahd-i Olya*,[3] wife of the Omnipotent Shahanshah. He asked for the letter in order to translate it himself and said that he would act as my humble servant and interpreter on the day of the audience. I said that I had given Sir Harford Jones the letters entrusted to me by the Qibleh of the Universe and the Chamberlain of the *Mahd-i Olya*. He had kept them for a day and then returned them – I did not know why he had not translated the Queen's letter. In any case, I gave it to Sir Gore Ouseley.

---

[1] Colonel Edward Desbrow (or Disbrowe) of the 1st King's Own Stafford Militia was appointed Vice-Chamberlain to Queen Charlotte in 1801.

[2] Probably the Princess Amelia, youngest daughter of George III and Queen Charlotte, who died of consumption on 2 November 1810.

[3] *Mahd-i Olya* (Cradle of the Highest): a title of the Shah's principal wife.

Thursday, 11 January

Yesterday the Court of Directors of the East India Company gave an Entertainment to his Excellency Mirza Abdul [sic] Hassan, the Persian Envoy. The ball-room of the City of London Tavern was fitted up in a style of magnificence, truly oriental.

(*The Morning Post*, 12 January)

IN EVERY ROOM of the palace[1] there were so many hanging lanterns and crystal chandeliers of gold and silver that even the stars in the heavens were dazzled by the light. Everyone gazed upon them with wonder. And so many musicians were assembled there that Apollo laid down his lyre to listen.

Honourable ministers and princes, councillors and lords, Company directors, admirals of the fleet – so many that I cannot name them here – were all in their places in the vast hall prepared for the reception. Here, magnificent portraits of the King of England and the Shahanshah of Iran, the latter faithfully copied from Malcolm's painting, were suspended from arches in the ceiling. When I beheld the beauty of the Qibleh of the Universe I bowed, and others did the same. Indian musicians played popular tunes to which English dancers danced – it was a very merry scene.

After a while the Chairman of the East India Company invited his guests to the Banqueting Hall, where we all sat down at tables. I noticed gold and silver vessels inscribed with the name of the Shah, and dishes of crystal and porcelain also inscribed in gold. The table was set with every kind of delicacy.

After dinner the table was set for wine and all the guests, cut-crystal goblets in hand, became merry with the wine. In a loud voice, the Chairman called for silence and the attention of his guests. He filled his glass and lifted it to 'the Shahanshah of Iran' and 'the King and Queen of England': he recited a verse to the health of both Kings and drank his wine. Then he refilled his glass and said: 'To the

East India Company, the Directors, and all connected with it – may their pockets be forever lined with gold.'

Lord Wellesley, the Minister for Foreign Affairs, rose and spoke in English on my behalf: he expressed my satisfaction with the collaboration between the Governments of his Majesty the Shah of Iran and the King of England, and my hope that, *inshallah*, God willing, the Company would provide funds to enable the Iranian Army to repulse the Russians and regain Tiflis, thus strengthening the friendship between the two monarchs. After this speech, the guests applauded, thanked their host, and got into their carriages to go home.

Then Lord Wellesley said to me: 'Now you understand exactly what the Company's position is – there is no difference between it and that of the King of England.'

Then we left the assembly and went home.

<hr>

[1] The EIC gave its dinners at the London Tavern, Bishopsgate Street Within. Rebuilt by William Jupp and William Newton after a fire in 1765, it was renowned for the excellent meals provided in its dining-room which could accommodate 355 people.

Friday, 12 January

WHEN MY FRIENDS gathered at the house, Sir Gore Ouseley told me that tonight they planned to take me to a theatre called Covent Garden. Some time ago the theatre was destroyed by fire; it has been rebuilt with the help of a donation of 200,000 *tomans* from the King.[1]

And so we went there. On either side of the lofty stage there are galleries with painted ceilings. Although somewhat smaller than the Opera, the decoration is more elaborate. Musicians banished sorrow from our hearts with their songs. It seemed to me strange that the audience reacted to some of the tunes with such boisterous applause that it could be heard by the cherubim in heaven, but to others they appeared totally deaf.

The manager of the theatre, Mr Kemble,[2] acted the part of a King of Britain who divides his kingdom between two of his daughters, leaving the third without a share. In the end, however, the first two daughters show themselves ungrateful to their father, and the disinherited but dutiful daughter escapes from the bondage of her wicked sisters with the help of a general's son – a marquis – who is in love with her. When she succeeds to the throne, she accepts him as her husband.[3]

Next, several multi-coloured curtains were lowered, and from behind these curtains – in the manner of Iranian acrobats – appeared the fantastic figures of *divs* and *peris*, of birds and beasts. No one watching their antics could possibly have retained his composure. Grimaldi, a famous clown,[4] performed an act which I shall never forget: he would leap from a high window and just as easily leap back up again, returning each time as a different character and causing the noble audience to laugh uncontrollably.

Walking around the theatre, my companions and I saw beautiful ladies, beautifully dressed, casting flirtatious glances from their boxes. Then we left the theatre by the King's door and came home.

[1] The first theatre on the site of the present Royal Opera House, Covent Garden, burned to the ground in September 1808. The Duke of Northumberland contributed £10,000 towards the rebuilding, and the Prince of Wales gave £1000. But Abul Hassan must be misinformed about such a large donation from the King.

[2] John Philip Kemble (1757-1823) was the eldest son of the founder of the famous theatrical family.

[3] Abul Hassan was not confusing the plots of *King Lear* and *Cinderella* (which was playing at Drury Lane at the time). In his 1809 production, Kemble used much of the 'improved' version published in 1681 by the Poet Laureate Nahum Tate. Tate dropped the character of the King of France in order to introduce a love affair between Cordelia and Edgar (the Marquis) – their marriage brings the tragedy to a happy ending! The 'Tatefied' plot is given in Hazelton Spencer, *Shakespeare Improved*, Harvard University Press, Cambridge, Mass., 1927.

[4] Joseph Grimaldi (1778-1837), whose real name was Brooker, was the greatest of all English clowns.

Saturday, 13 January[1]

SIR GORE OUSELEY and Lord Liverpool, who is the Minister for War, came to see me. We talked of many things including the war with Russia and the kinds of artillery the Russians use.

That evening I was invited to Sir Gore Ouseley's house, so when the day ended I went there with my friends. The assembled guests greeted us with ceremony.

In addition to hired musicians, there was among the guests a lady called Miss Hume,[2] who played the violin very well. As Sir Gore Ouseley is accomplished in all the arts, and is second only to Hakim Farabi[3] in the art of music, he took the violin from Miss Hume and played a tune in the Indian manner which cleansed our minds and hearts of the dust of grief.

Later, Sir Gore Ouseley said that he was worried about his wife's poor health – there seemed to be no remedy. I told him that most Iranian doctors prescribe asses' milk for complaints of the chest, and that if fate decreed that he should go to Iran, he should take his wife with him to be treated with the milk cure.

Five or six hours passed and it was late, so we retired.

[1] This entry in the journal follows immediately after Thursday 11 January (5 Dhu al-Hijja), and is dated Thursday 6 Dhu al Hijja which must be incorrect. As there is no entry for Saturday 13 January, I have placed it here.

[2] Sophia Hume (died 1814) was the second daughter of Sir Abraham Hume, Bart, FRS, a well-known patron of the arts.

[3] Hakim Farabi: Abu Nasr al-Farabi (died 950) was the greatest philosopher of Islam before Avicenna.

Sunday, 14 January

A S THE FIRST glimmering of dawn emerged beneath the
indigo curtain and black night stole away to hide like an old
man, my *mehmandar* came in. Smiling, he told me that a
note addressed to me had just come from a newspaper office: it
referred to a report from Paris that the Governor of Isfahan had
been sent as an ambassador to discuss commercial relations with the
East India Company, and that the Shah of Iran knew nothing of my
own embassy. Although well aware that false rumours circulate in
newspapers, I was nonetheless disturbed. Recalling how the
Shahanshah had ordered General Gardane[1] to leave Iran, I felt sure
that this must be a plot devised by the French enemy to destroy the
friendship between the English and Iranian monarchs. But still –
Sobhanallah! Good God! I thought – this report was enough to dis-
quiet even me, who knew the true facts!

Sir Gore Ouseley said that the French had spread these rumours
out of enmity and that we should pay no attention to such nonsense.

> *The Marquis Wellesley gave a splendid dinner yesterday to the*
> *Foreign Ministers.*[2]
>
> *(The Morning Post, 15 January)*

I went with Sir Gore Ouseley to Lord Wellesley's house. A portrait of the English King hung in the entrance hall and paintings
decorated all the walls. Crystal chandeliers were lighted; but even
with the warmth from the wax candles and fur garments of sable and
squirrel, we all suffered from the cold.

Sir Gore Ouseley had been thoughtful enough to suggest that,
because the envoys of Spain and Portugal, of Sardinia and Sicily,
had also been invited this evening, I should wear my official Iranian
dress. This was good advice so, even though I was not feeling well, I
changed clothes and put on my robes of gold brocade trimmed with
sable.

When the other foreign envoys arrived, our host placed them on his left hand. Sir Gore Ouseley explained that the Minister wished to show greater honour and friendship to me by placing me on his right.

I told Sir Gore Ouseley that the task of the *farangi* ambassadors is made easier than mine because they are allied to the Minister by religion; besides, for them London is a refuge from Bonaparte. They are unable to return to their homelands because they are occupied by the French.

From there we returned home – and so ended another day.

---

[1] General Claude-Matthieu Gardane (1766-1817), a former aide-de camp to Napoleon, was sent to Tehran to secure Fath Ali Shah's ratification of the Franco-Persian Treaty of Finkenstein (4 May 1807), and to negotiate a commercial treaty: both were signed on 20 December 1807. Gardane left Tehran on 12 February 1809, just before Sir Harford Jones' arrival; the remaining members of his mission left on 29 March.

[2] Foreign Ministers: foreign envoys resident in London are meant.

PLATE 18

The Queen's Breakfast Room, Buckingham House.
Abul Hassan was much impressed by the lacquered
wall-panels decorated 'with divs *and* peris'.
Aquatint by G. Cattermole for Pyne's Royal
Residences, *1819.*

PLATE 19

*George IV as Prince of Wales (1803). Abul
Hassan was highly gratified by the Prince of Wales'
'extreme kindness and affability'. Portrait by Sir
William Beechey.*

Monday, 15 January

I WAS NOT FEELING well, so a doctor was sent for. He gave me some medicine, and because we were invited this evening to the house of Mr Perceval, the Prime Minister, I rested for a while after taking the medicine.

When evening came, I drove in the carriage with Sir Gore Ouseley and Lord Radstock to Mr Perceval's house. The house is like a Royal palace: the King ordered it to be built as a residence and office for successive Prime Ministers.[1]

When I entered the house, I was greeted by the Prime Minister's wife, Mrs Perceval, and her handsome sons and daughters. She is a lady of both physical and intellectual charms, not more than thirty years old.[2] She is called Mrs Perceval because it is the custom here for a woman to take her husband's name. This modest lady was exceedingly friendly and hospitable: she sat down next to me and showed such condescension and kindness that I found myself blushing and was quite cured of my fatigue. Never had I encountered an Englishwoman of such character and good humour! It was also the first time that Sir Gore Ouseley and Lord Radstock had met that sweet-spoken lady, and they too were greatly impressed by her civility. She might have had one hundred years' practice in the Ministry!

Mrs Perceval's older sister, Lady Arden,[3] a lady universally esteemed, also came to open the doors of affection and friendship to me and my companions.

After some time, Mrs Perceval rose from her chair, took my arm and said something to her guests which in English meant *bismallah*.[4] Everyone got up, and we proceeded to a spacious room with a domed ceiling, where we sat down to such a variety of dishes that we could not have consumed them all had we remained at table for a month. Since it is the custom for the host's wife to offer the first plate to each guest, she rose from her place and graciously presented me with a plate of sweetmeats. Similar plates were passed to the ministers, the lords, the officers and the gentlemen by handsome servants.

There were several varieties of fish, each cooked in a different way. Fish is so highly prized in London – each one costs two *tomans* – that salted fish is served with each course (even when the other dishes are salted as well).

Observing that such an assembly was strange to me, Mrs Perceval said: 'I see that you are surprised to find men and women eating together. But be fair! Is not our custom better than yours, which keeps a woman hidden behind the veil?'

I had to reply: 'Your custom is better indeed. A veiled woman, with downcast eyes, is like a caged bird: when she is released she lacks even the strength to fly around the rose-garden. I have travelled the world, but never have I encountered a woman such as you, possessed of such beauty and intelligence.'

> *Around the world my course I've set.*
> *many great beauties have I met,*
> *Who stole my heart – but never yet*
> *Was any one like you.*

On hearing these words, Mrs Perceval thanked me and made no effort to conceal her pleasure.

A few days previously Lady Buckinghamshire,[5] the widow of an important English nobleman, had invited me to an evening party on the same night as the invitation from the Prime Minister. I wanted to excuse myself from attending, but Mrs Perceval insisted that I go. So my friends and I left in the carriage for her house. We got lost on the way, but at last arrived.[6]

When we went in, some of the guests had still not arrived. Lady Buckinghamshire came forward immediately to open the doors of friendship. Although somewhat advanced in years, she was still a handsome woman. With a thousand courtesies she led me into a painted reception room where I noticed groups of sunny-faced girls and *houri*-like ladies chatting together, their beauty illuminated by the candle-light. Crystal lanterns and gold and silver chandeliers hung on all sides and the light from the wax candles was dazzling to the eye. But the guests were so engrossed in conversation, they did not seem to notice.

A young lady – a relative of the Buckinghamshires – who was adorned with pearls from head to foot, smiled at Sir Gore Ouseley and won a smile in return. 'What a rare beauty!' he exclaimed.

Only God the Creator could have made this!

We were talking about this pretty, smiling, pearl-bedecked girl, when another fairy creature entered the room with her mother and sister and banished all other thoughts from our minds. As this lovely jewel – she was Lady Emily Cecil, daughter of the Marquis of Salisbury[7] – made her entrance, my heart skipped a beat. I had learned a few words of English, so I spoke to the noble lady, and she smiled in return. I suggested that, if she would consent to give me lessons in English, I would teach her Persian. Flirtatiously, she asked in English why I wanted to learn the customs of her country.

At this moment, I noticed another young lady who had just arrived. Sir Gore Ouseley told me that she was the daughter of the brother of Lord Wellesley, the Minister for Foreign Affairs, and that her name was Miss Pole.[8] He said that the lady with her was her aunt, but that she looked so much like her sister, the young girl's mother, that most people could not tell them apart.

I told Sir Gore Ouseley that I should like a word with the young lady, because her brother had been to call on me.[9] With this introduction, we opened the door of conversation; but, as she had never met an Iranian, nor seen such a growth of beard, she retreated shyly. She inspired me to recite this quatrain:

Like a cypress you proudly stand, but when did a cypress walk?
Like a rosebud your ruby lips – but when did a rosebud talk?
*   Like a hyacinth's blooms are the ringlets of your sweet hair –*
But when were men's hearts enslaved by a hyacinth's stalk?

There were many lovely ladies and beautiful girls at the party, but I fancied none of them save this girl of noble birth whose beauty inflamed my heart with passion.

On the way home Sir Gore Ouseley tried to cheer me up – and so ended another day.[10]

[1] Downing Street was built by Sir George Downing in the 1680s, on land leased from the Crown. In 1733 George III bought back the lease of No. 10 and it was merged with a much larger house behind it (facing what is now Horse Guards Parade) to form a residence for his Chief Minister, Sir Robert Walpole.

[2] Spencer Perceval married in 1790 Jane Maryon Wilson, younger daughter of General Sir Thomas Spencer Wilson, Bart. Born in 1769, Mrs Perceval was almost forty years old.

[3] Mrs Perceval's older sister, Margaret Elizabeth Wilson (died 1851), married Spencer Perceval's brother, Charles George Perceval (1756-1840), who in 1784 inherited from his mother the title of Baron Arden.

[4] *Bismallah:* in the name of God (dinner is served).

[5] Albinia, Dowager Countess of Buckinghamshire (died 1816), married in 1757 George Hobart (1731-1804), 3rd Earl of Buckinghamshire.

[6] Hobart House, King's Road, World's End, Chelsea, no longer exists.

[7] Lady Emily Cecil (died 1858), second daughter of the 1st Marquis of Salisbury, married in 1812 George Nugent, Lord Devlin, later 7th Earl and 1st Marquis of Westmeath.

[8] The Marquis Wellesley's younger brother, William Wellesley-Pole, a Junior Lord at the Treasury in 1810, and his wife Katherine Forbes, had three daughters, the eldest of whom married in 1806. Abul Hassan's 'Miss Pole' was either Emily

Harriet, who married in 1814 Lord Fitzroy James Henry Somerset, youngest son of the 5th Duke of Beaufort, later Field Marshal the 1st Baron Raglan, or Priscilla Anne, who married in 1811 John Fane, Lord Burghersh, later the 11th Earl of Westmorland. Most probably she was Emily, who would have been known as 'Miss Pole' after her older sister's marriage, rather than Priscilla, who would have been known as 'Miss Priscilla Pole'. See also 6 July, note 2.

[9] Abul Hassan was probably thinking of Miss Pole's cousin, Henry Wellesley, who called on Abul Hassan with his father on 11 December.

[10] Abul Hassan makes no mention of meeting the Princess of Wales, as reported in *The Morning Post* on 17 January; presumably the thought of Miss Pole drove even such a prestigious encounter from his mind.

Tuesday, 16 January

THIS MORNING I FELT so ill with a high fever that I was quite unable to move.

Mrs Perceval, wife of the Prime Minister, kindly came in her carriage to enquire after my health. She left her card.

Then Sir Gore Ouseley arrived at my bedside. He expressed his concern and sent for the doctor.

He said that the Queen had come to London two days ago in order to meet me and that I should make every effort to attend her audience. I replied that I could not be blamed for my illness and that it was my greatest desire to attend if I possibly could.

Sir Gore Ouseley was distressed by my condition and begged the doctor to do his best for me. The doctor prescribed certain medicines for me to take at regular intervals day and night – and *alalham-dolillah*! praise God! I felt much better.

Wednesday, 17 January

SIR GORE OUSELEY came to the house and sent my Iranian servants to the Queen's House with my gifts. He kindly engaged me in conversation until they returned. Then the Queen's Master of the Ceremonies arrived with the Queen's carriage, drawn by six beautiful bay horses. The three of us mounted the carriage. The horses were so swift we reached the Queen's House in a short time.

When we went inside I saw the Queen's apartments were very similar to the King's, with the best rooms also on the upper floor. In one room, the walls were hung with pleasing portraits of the Kings of England and with paintings of *divs* and *peris* by Chinese masters.

I was astonished to see some paintings, close to the ceiling, of tall and muscular men carrying clocks on their backs – they actually seemed to be alive and moving.

Four or five of the Queen's ladies-in-waiting came in. They wore extraordinary dresses: from waist to toe they seemed to be standing in full-blown tents (the effect was awe-inspiring!), while from waist to shoulders the dresses were closely fitted. I was astounded! Sir Gore Ouseley explained that it was traditional for the Queen and Princesses to dress in this formal manner, and that the wives of ministers and lords and other distinguished guests were required to dress for an audience in the same way. It is called 'Court Dress'.[1]

Colonel Desbrow came in, paid his respects, and took me and Sir Gore Ouseley through an *iwan* to another room where the ceiling reached the constellations and the decorations overwhelmed the senses.

The Queen was standing on the Royal dais with four of her daughters and three of her sons.[2] I was looking at the ceiling and the decorations, but when my eye fell on that Royal lady, I took the *Mahd-i Olya*'s letter in my hand and advanced respectfully. The Queen also graciously came forward – she took the letter in both hands and touched it first to her forehead and then to her heart. She told me that the presents which had been delivered earlier had been opened and placed on a table, and she thanked me very kindly in English.

I begged leave to depart, but the Queen asked me about the pains and pleasures of the sea voyage. Her sons and daughters kindly asked about my ill health. The sparkle of their clothing and jewels lit up the room and their beauty transformed the place into a rose-garden.

From the Queen's House, we followed the established protocol and went to the house of the Prince of Wales and to the houses of the other Princes. I was shown great respect. Sir Gore Ouseley inscribed my name in the Visitors Book and then we returned home together in the carriage.

I was weeping uncontrollably for my love – melancholy songs and verses came unbidden to my mind – when the Italian Prince who had been on the ship with me[3] arrived at my house with a group of singers and musicians from the Opera to cheer me up. The doors of conversation were opened and the singing began. A sweet-voiced girl sang a song with this verse.

> *O dear God, how intense is the pain of the passion that I know.*
> *Let no person on earth be enslaved with the bondage that I know.*
> *If I am unworthy of having your love and your trust, then –*
> *In God's name set me free from the burden and torment that I know.*

On hearing these words I fell into a faint and took leave of my senses. My friends were greatly alarmed and crowded round me. One sympathetically rubbed my arms; another applied an ointment of almonds; the others began to pray. When I opened my eyes, I found the doctor at my side. He reassured me and told me that he would prepare a mixture of honey for my chest, but I could only reply:

> *For what ails me all treatment's vain.*
> *O Doctor, go, you cause me pain!*

The Opera singers formed a group and sang some agreeable – and some not so agreeable – songs. The slender dancer Angiolini performed a Spanish dance beautifully. While she was dancing I could see from her eyes that she was hopelessly in love with a handsome young man standing opposite me. I asked my friends who he was and they told me he was a Frenchman called Vestris.[4]

---

[1] Ladies' Court dress was unchanged throughout the reign of George III. Abul Hassan had become accustomed to the slim, high-waisted and often diaphanous 'Empire' style of 1810. No wonder he was surprised to see the hoop-skirt favoured in 1760, the year George III came to the throne.

[2] *The Morning Post,* 18 January, reported that the Queen was accompanied by the Dukes of Kent, Cambridge and Brunswick. Brunswick was in fact her nephew, son of the King's sister Princess Augusta, Duchess of Brunswick, and brother of the Princess of Wales.

[3] Abul Hassan makes no mention of an Italian prince in the shipboard entries of the journal.

[4] Armand Vestris (1787-1825), the French dancer and ballet-master, and Angiolini were dancing together at the King's Theatre.

Thursday, 18 January

SIR GORE OUSELEY came to enquire about my health. He told me that today is the anniversary of the Queen's Birthday and that, according to the English custom, the wives of ministers and lords are invited to the Queen's Drawing-room. Foreign ambassadors also attend and in the evening they are invited to dinner by the Minister for Foreign Affairs. They should also attend the Princess of Wales' evening reception. I replied that because of my illness I could not go; and I asked him to be kind enough to make my excuses to the Queen and to write notes to the Minister and to the wife of the Prince of Wales apologizing for my inability to attend either reception.[1]

[1] It is a pity that Abul Hassan did not feel well enough to attend the Queen's Drawing-room. The next day *The Morning Post* described the Queen's dress of green and gold velvet 'trimmed with an elegant embroidery agreeable to the costume of Persia; this was by far the most superb dress worn by the Queen on her own birth-day for many years past; we have heard that it was meant as complimentary to the Representative of the Persian Court.'

Friday, 19 January

THIS EVENING WE WERE invited to Lord Teignmouth's house. Among the guests were the Chairman of the Company and the Minister for the Company. I spoke to the Chairman about the Treaty of Friendship and my return to Iran.

He said: 'The knot of this problem must be tied by the skilful finger of the Minister, Lord Wellesley. He is your good friend and, very probably, he will soon make fast the thread with the help of the ministers and councillors and so set you free. But now, do not miss watching our host's daughters dancing!'

It happened that Lord Teignmouth's wife[1] knew the language of India: when she found that I did also, she was extremely hospitable to me.

Our host brought from his library a manuscript of the *Akhlagh-i Nasiri*,[2] copied by a fine calligraphist. He wished to make me a present of it, but I refused. So he hid it inside my carriage, and there I found it on the way home.

---

[1] Lord Teignmouth's wife was Charlotte, only daughter of James Cornish, a medical practitioner at Teignmouth, whom he married in 1786.

[2] *Akhlagh-i Nasiri:* a famous work on ethics by Nasir ud-Din of Tus (died 1274).

Sunday, 21 January

THE SERPENTINE RIVER. Was yesterday a scene of attrac-
tion. The banks on the north-side were lined with elegant equipages,
and those on the south with numerous groups of pedestrians. The day
was cheered by the rays of the sun having dispersed the fog. The air,
although keen, was invigorating. The ice was good, and the skaiters
were in numbers incalculable. . . .

(The Morning Post, 22 January)

I WENT IN THE CARRIAGE with Sir Gore Ouseley and some other friends to the park. The weather was so cold that the river[1] was frozen over and a large crowd of men and women was gathered there. Some of them had razor-sharp iron blades fixed to the soles of their boots and they moved like arrows across the ice. They say that ice-skating is a healthy winter exercise. If the ice should break and someone fall in, small boats are at hand to come to the rescue.

I conceived a fancy to slide on the ice in the English manner and we got out of the carriage. But there was such a crowd of milling people that I soon lost courage.

---

[1] The Serpentine.

Monday, 22 January

THIS MORNING MY sympathetic friend, Sir Gore Ouseley, came in and said that he had been approached by an Englishman who wanted to sell me two idols. Sir Gore Ouseley said that most people believe we Iranians are Zoroastrians from Fars and call us fire-worshippers. I told him they were wrong, but that in London I should be a sun-worshipper if the sun were not as invisible as the fabulous Phoenix.

Sir Gore Ouseley told me that at seven o'clock this evening we were invited to a ball at the house of Mrs Calvert's sister.[1] I asked what kind of party this was which lasted from seven o'clock until two, with only four hours left till dawn. He said that the rules of social etiquette in England are strict and must not be broken – whether you are invited to the homes of rich or poor, you must conform to these rules or lose in esteem. He promised to be my friendly guide in these matters.

I listened to Sir Gore Ouseley's advice and at the appointed hour we went to that kind lady's house. Lovely ladies came forward to greet me: they all wore dresses of silk and their radiant faces outshone the wax candles that lighted the painted rooms. Among those ladies, Mrs Calvert's daughter[2] shone like the sun.

She displayed so much kindness that she quite stole our hearts. Then she led us to a gallery of most unusual construction. I found her as beautiful as the women of Circassia.[3]

[1] The Hon. Frances Calvert (1767-1859) and the Hon. Diana Knox (1764-1839) were the daughters and co-heirs of Viscount Pery, a former Speaker of the Irish House of Commons. Frances married in 1789 Nicolson Calvert, who was Liberal MP for Hertford from 1802. Diana married in 1785 the Hon. Thomas Knox, son of

Viscount Northland; he succeeded his father in 1818 and was created 1st Earl of Ranfurly in 1831. The sisters were first cousins of the Earl of Limerick, Abul Hassan's neighbour in Mansfield Street. Mrs Calvert's journal was published by Mrs Warenne Blake in 1911 (see Bibliography).

[2] Isabella Calvert (1793-1862) was the third child and eldest surviving daughter of Frances and Nicolson Calvert.

[3] Women of the Circassian tribe in the western Caucasus were famed for their beauty and highly prized in Eastern harems. On his second embassy to London in 1819, Abul Hassan was accompanied by 'the fair Circassian', whom he had purchased in the Istanbul slave-market on the way to London. She was visited daily by the curious ladies of London until Abul Hassan tired of her and sent her home.

Tuesday, 23 January

TODAY A GENERAL CAME to the house on behalf of the Prince of Wales. He conveyed the Prince's compliments and said that since I had been to call on the Queen, I should now call on him. A Colonel – or some such distinguished person – also came to convey the compliments of the other Princes. He said that they had all been at their country houses, but were now returned to the city and desired the pleasure of my company.

It happened that there was a performance at the Opera this evening. I said that while I never tired of looking at the handsome singers, I was truly weary of the tale of *Sidagero* and of listening to the voice of that character who seemed constantly to be in tears. Sir Gore Ouseley said: 'Be of good cheer. This evening your companion is to be one of my favourite young ladies – she is the daughter of one of the Company directors and she speaks five languages.'

We had hardly set foot in the Opera House when the young lady came forward and flirtatiously began to recite some *ghazals* – romantic codes. I asked her what her name was, and she replied 'Miss Metcalfe.'[1] I complimented her on her Persian composition, but she protested that it was but a poor thing and her accomplishments few. I was enchanted with her conversation and her recitations of verse.

Content with the evening we returned home.

---

[1] Emily Metcalfe was the daughter of Sir Thomas Metcalfe, Bart (1745-1813), a director of the East India Company, who had served in India in a military capacity. In 1812 she married the 4th Viscount Ashbrook. In a letter to her father, Lord Minto, in India, Miss Elliott wrote: 'There is only one lady who can speak Persian to him, a Miss Metcalfe, who cracks Persian jokes to him, and laughs in Persian, just as if it was English. They say of course he is in love with her, but having two or three wives already, there is no room for her, the more's the pity.' Quoted in *Lord Minto of India* (see Bibliography), p. 137.

Wednesday, 24 January

THIS MORNING SIR GORE OUSELEY and I sat talking of this and that until shortly after noon when several footmen dressed in rich liveries arrived with the Prince of Wales' carriage. It was indeed a splendid carriage, drawn by six perfectly matched bays – I have never seen such handsome horses. Looking over the carriage I was delighted to ride in it. Sir Gore Ouseley and I mounted and the Prince of Wales' handsome footmen took their places together with my own servants. We set off.

When the citizens of London heard the news, they gathered in large numbers to see us pass. And when the ladies indoors heard the tumult, they came out on to their balconies to watch. We in turn were looking at them.

In a short time we arrived in a spacious courtyard enclosed by columns of mirror-like marble and flanked by pavilions which serve as guard-houses. We entered: it is a marvellous house, unsurpassed for beauty in London or indeed in all England.[1] It is more splendid even than the King's Palace, and has a garden to compare with the Garden of Eden. Huge mirrors and paintings were fixed to doors and walls.

Handsome servants in colourful liveries trimmed with gold braid and pretty bejewelled girls were in attendance. When they saw us, they bowed and curtseyed in the English manner. Red-liveried footmen respectfully conducted us to the upper floor, which is reserved for the Prince of Wales' exclusive use. Here we found the Prince and his brothers and a group of noblemen seated, their heartstrings being plucked by talented musicians playing English tunes.

As I joined the company, I dutifully paid my respects to the Prince who then opened the doors of affability and condescension to me and showed me such extreme kindness that my pen is incapable of describing it and my tongue is struck dumb trying to praise him. It is amazing that, although he is in his forty-eighth year, he looks

PLATE 20

*The gold dish, presented by Abul Hassan to the
East India Company during his second mission to
London in 1819, is a splendid example of Persian
enamel-work. The signature of the artist,
Mohammad Jaafar, the date 1233* AH *(1817/18*
AD*), and the Persian Lion and Sun appear in the
central medallion.*

PLATE 21

The Crimson Drawing-room, Carlton House.
Abul Hassan wrote that in Carlton House
'everything was perfection . . . gold and silver
plate, mirrors and paintings, huge chandeliers and
curtains of brocade.' Aquatint by C. Wild for
Payne's Royal Residences, *1819.*

no more than twenty. His face is marked with pride and dignity and in all my travels I have never encountered a more gracious prince. His brothers are all handsome and wise. Meeting the Princes, a verse sprang to my mind, but I was shy and whispered it only in my friend's ear:

Each native of your town in turn his fellows doth exceed
Perhaps it is the soil itself that rears so fine a breed.

Then the Prince spoke to me: 'The signs of homesickness are plainly to be seen in your countenance. It seems that the weather of London does not suit you.' I said that had I a thousand sorrows in my heart, they would be swept away by my consciousness of the great honour of being received by his Royal Highness. The Prince was pleased by my reply and sympathized with me. He said: 'I will do my utmost to effect your early departure and I urge you to tell your faithful companion, Sir Gore Ouseley, of any problems you may have, so that I – your affectionate friend – may be informed and come to your assistance. If ever you are feeling melancholy on a rainy day, come to my covered pavilion in the garden, relax and banish sorrow from your heart. Ride my own horses and visit the flower-strewn countryside round London.'

Then he asked me to choose a gift from among the many clocks to be found in the house – he suggested one that needs winding only once every six months. He said that he would send it to me.

Then I took my leave and returned home with Sir Gore Ouseley – and so ended another day.

[1] Carlton House, at the bottom of Lower Regent Street, facing on to Pall Mall, was given to the Prince of Wales when he came of age in 1783. When it was demolished in 1829 the columns were reused in the portico of the National Gallery in Trafalgar Square.

Thursday, 25 January

THE PERSIAN AMBASSADOR
BY THE TOWN CRIER
Tune – 'The Frog in an Opera Hat'

The Persian Ambassador's come to town;
    Heigho! says Boney:
And he is a person of rank and renown,
Says in Persia they'll knock all French politics down,
With their Parlez-vous, Voulez-vous, *gammon and spinach too;*
    Heigho! says Emperor Boney.

To see the Ambassador all the Folks ran;
    Heigho! says Boney:
He has sixty-three children, says Boney; well done*!*
What a dev'l of a fellow! while I haven't one*!*
With my Parlez-vous, Voulez-vous, *Josephine and others too;*
    Heigho! says the Emperor Boney.[1]

SIR GORE OUSELEY came to the house and we went riding in the Park on easy-paced horses. A great many people were leaping up and down on the ice like locusts. Sir Gore Ouseley pointed out a dignified-looking young man, saying that no one could move faster on the ice than he. But the moment the lion-hearted youth set foot on the ice, he slipped and was powerless to prevent his fall. The spectators laughed at his misfortune.

At this moment a messenger arrived from the Minister for Foreign Affairs with a note for Sir Gore Ouseley. It said that the Minister would call at my house this evening in order to complete my business. I was delighted to hear this good news and left the Park completely happy.

This evening we were invited to dinner at the home of Mr Dundas, the Minister for the Company.[2] Soon after we arrived I sat down and was joined by the Chairman of the Company with Lord Westmorland[3] and some other gentlemen.

114

Lord Westmorland is a councillor and the Keeper of the King's Seals. He remarked that it appears that there is some similarity between the Persian and Latin languages, and he asked me if I knew Latin. Then he asked for details about my religion. From his questions, I gathered he thought I was a fire-worshipper!

After dinner the Chairman of the Company and his Deputy rose from their places. Because of my appointment with the Minister, I took advantage of their move to rise myself. They left for the Houses of Parliament and I made my apologies to my kind and hospitable host and hostess (who have several sweet-spoken children) and left for home.

When we reached the entrance porch, I saw that more candles than usual had been lighted because of my appointment with the Minister. Sir Gore Ouseley and I waited for him until twelve o'clock; but he did not come nor did he send a messenger. I was in a desperate mood thinking of my ill fortune, but the army of sorrow overcame me and I slept until the sun rose in the east and auspicious Friday dawned.

[1] Part of the ten-verse satirical poem published in *The Statesman*, 25 January.

[2] The Dundases lived at 23 Hertford Street.

[3] John Fane (1759-1841), 10th Earl of Westmorland, was Lord Privy Seal 1798-1827. His second wife, Jane Saunders, was Mrs Dundas' sister.

Friday, 26 January

I WOKE UP EXTREMELY ANGRY and wrote a letter to the Minister which I prefaced with this verse:

A promise – either do not make it
Or, if it's made, then do not break it.

I continued: 'I must place on record that it is now two months since I came with my gifts, two months in which I have imposed on my friends in London, and still there is no sign that I shall be able to take my departure. . . .'

I ended the letter with *vasalaam*: 'What more can I say? May peace be upon you.'

Then I folded the letter and sent it off with my man Abbas, accompanied by his servant. He returned with the Minister's compliments and the message that he desired two or three hours to compose a reply.

In the afternoon Sir Gore Ouseley came to tell me that he had been summoned by the Minister, who had apologized so profusely for breaking our appointment that he had become quite embarrassed. The Minister explained that the questions and answers in Parliament had continued until dawn. To make up for last night he promised to devote himself to the resolution of my affairs and to meet me and Sir Gore Ouseley at his house soon to settle the matter.

I expressed the hope that my prayers would soon be answered.

And so ended another day.

Saturday, 27 January

I WENT IN THE CARRIAGE with Sir Gore Ouseley to the Minister's house – the sky was overcast with dark cloud and fog and many candles were lighted there.

When we entered, the wise Minister kindly showed me to the place of honour. He apologized profusely and asked me to tell Sir Gore Ouseley whatever I wished to say, so that he might translate it into English.

I read out in full the Treaty drawn up by Sir Harford Jones and the Iranian ministers[1] and I emphasized the mutual interests of both Governments. I reminded the Minister that the primary concern of his Majesty the Shah of Iran was the liberation of Tiflis from Russia's grasp – through the friendship of his Majesty the King of England and the assistance of the English Government. The Minister expressed the opinion that even if they helped drive the Russians out of Tiflis, the population would remain unsettled and ripe for Russian reoccupation.

But I told him that while there had previously been many traitors in the area, those loyal to the Qibleh of the Universe had seen to it that they were dealt with: some were blinded, some were put to the sword and some were buried alive. If we succeeded in liberating the city, the population would be relocated and replaced by brave and loyal citizens determined to defend it.

The Minister said that today we must both draft an agreement of mutual friendship between our two monarchs which could be signed and sealed by the accredited representatives. Then the business would be properly concluded.

Having agreed to this arrangement, I rose, took my leave together with Sir Gore Ouseley, and went home.

---

[1] The Preliminary Treaty concluded by Sir Harford Jones on 12 March 1809.

Sunday, 28 January

THIS MORNING, AFTER SAYING my prayers and invoking the assistance of the spirits of the Fourteen Innocent Ones,[1] I began to compose the auspicious treaty we had discussed yesterday. To explain its purpose and context, I wrote:

> *Keyumars was the first whose kingship won renown*
> *More great than any other king who ever wore a crown.*

Keyumars was the fortune-blessed son of Noah (may peace be upon him) who introduced monarchy and order into the world. Generations of that great Padeshah's descendants controlled the affairs of the world until the monarchy was grasped by the strong hand of Jamshid. Kings all over the world regard the shahs of Iran as the founders of monarchy and thus, in a sense, as their own ancestors. When waging war against their enemies they have always been able to rely on the shahs of Iran for unstinted support with men and money.

Witness the case of Humayun, Emperor of India,[2] who was forced to seek refuge in Iran when his country was in a state of insurrection: the Shah's army helped him to regain his throne from the traitor Shir Khan of Afghanistan.

A more recent example was the King of England's request to bring about the downfall of Zaman Shah's rule in Afghanistan, when Zaman was threatening India.

Therefore, in the best interests of the two great Governments – after due consultation and in accord with the strict instructions contained in the *farman* of the Solomon-wise Sultan of Iran – I do this day approve the Treaty of Friendship between the two exalted Kings and containing the following provisions: The Shah of Iran will do everything possible to defeat the enemies of the King of England, notably the French and the Afghans; and the King of England will likewise increase his assistance to Iran. He agrees to provide yearly to the Government of the eternal Shahanshah of Iran, Refuge of Sultans, 200,000 *tomans* in cash and 30,000 guns and other weapons of war, and he will endeavour to destroy utterly the Russian army and to liberate the city of Tiflis from the claws of the Russian crab.

I ended: What more can I say? May peace be upon you.

Then I sealed the document and gave it to Sir Gore Ouseley, who kindly translated it into English and took it to the wise Minister for his approval. After perusing it, the Minister praised it and said that we must write the treaty in just such sincere terms.

Late in the afternoon a distinguished company of friends gathered at the house, and we talked of many things. The subject of childbirth in England was raised and we discussed it at length. I could not help smiling when I learned that in England the midwives are not women, but men.

My friends asked about childbirth in Iran. I told them that in each district there are many midwives who are ready to assist when the need arises and who then become the child's nurse and the mother's help. They thought this was a good idea. One of the lords said that Englishwomen suffer exceedingly in childbirth because of their slim waists – and many of them die.

That evening Lord Radstock insisted on taking me to a church. When we were inside, I saw that many women had brought their new-born babies to be named. Each child's date of birth is written down and throughout his life a record is kept of his occupation and his abode.

I gathered that the religion of the other *farangis* differs from the faith of the English in much the same way as the Shias differ from the Sunnis[3] – that is to say, both groups follow Jesus Christ [as both the Shia and Sunni sects follow the Prophet Mohammad] and both are strict in their observance of the day set aside for prayer. They both have separate monasteries for men and women. But the other *farangis* eat less meat; and the customs of their Church require them

119

to have organ music and to hang pictures of Jesus and Mary all around the church.

After visiting the church we returned home – and so ended another day.

[1] The Fourteen Innocent Ones: the Prophet Mohammad, his daughter Fatimeh and the Twelve Imams. See note 3 below.

[2] The second Moghul Emperor, Humayun (reigned 1508-56), driven from India by an insurrection, took refuge in Persia, where Shah Tahmasp received him at Qazvin in 1544 and helped him with an army to regain his throne. The meeting is commemorated in a Safavid wall-painting in the Chehel Sotun (the Palace of Forty Pillars) at Isfahan.

[3] The Sunnis and the Shias are the two main sects within Islam. The former accept a line of caliphs descending from Mohammad through a process of election which eliminated his descendants with the exception of his son-in-law Ali. The vast majority of Iranians are Shias, who recognize the Twelve Imams, or spiritual leaders, who were all blood descendants of Ali and the Prophet's daughter Fatimeh.

Monday, 29 January

I WENT WITH SIR GORE OUSELEY and Mr Morier to the house of Sir William Beechey, the portrait painter who lives near the church and my house.[1] Sir Gore Ouseley told me that the East India Company had asked him to arrange for a likeness of me to be made – and for this reason he troubled me to accompany him to the artist's studio.

The artist took us into his studio: the walls were hung with paintings of animals and birds and fairy creatures, and with canvases of all sizes portraying men of distinction. The house was decorated with mirrors and furniture of ebony: truly, it was a charming and cheerful home. Sir William Beechey received us with great courtesy and hospitality. He introduced his thirteen children, pretty as shining stars, and each one modestly greeted me in the English fashion.

Then Sir Gore Ouseley told him that the Company desired a portrait of the Iranian Ambassador.[2] Sir William Beechey asked me to be good enough to come to his studio for two hours each day, in the early morning. He said he would be delighted to have the opportunity of conversing with me while he painted. The rooms pleased me so much that I readily agreed.

[1] Sir William Beechey, RA (1753-1839) lived at 13 Harley Street, one street west of Abul Hassan's Mansfield Street.

[2] The East India Company paid 250 guineas for the full-length portrait of Abul Hassan in August 1810. It was exhibited at the Royal Academy (see the entry for 27 April) and was subsequently hung in the Finance Committee Room of East India House. It now hangs in the Foreign and Commonwealth Office in Whitehall.

121

Tuesday, 30 January

ABOUT NOON I WENT with Sir Gore Ouseley and a General to a workshop where they make cobblers' tools and articles such as scissors, razors and knife blades.

Sir Gore Ouseley spoke with the master-craftsman and ordered some things for me which might prove useful in Iran.

From there we went to Lord Radstock's house and with him to an enamel-works. The place was hung all round with countless mirrors, dazzling to the eye.

When we were seated, the master-enameller brought a few things he had made for the nobility for us to see – among them a lady's *étui* or patch-box decorated on the lid with a likeness of the Prince of Wales, which quite took my breath away.

I told my friends that the Shahanshah of Iran was very interested in enamel-work[1] and painting, and that if the master-enameller would agree to journey with me to Iran, the Shah would place him in charge of an enamel-works – among the many other art workshops which he has commanded to be established.

[1] The earliest surviving Persian enamels date from the Zand dynasty (1750-94), but there is no evidence that the art was not practised earlier. The most brilliant enamels, characterized by translucent ruby reds, royal blues and emerald greens on a gold ground, were produced in the reign of Fath Ali Shah (1798-1834). A particularly splendid example is the flat-rimmed gold dish, with a central enamelled medallion of the Lion and Sun, which Abul Hassan presented to the directors of the East India Company on 18 June 1819, during his second Embassy to London.

Wednesday, 31 January

AFTER I HAD PERFORMED my morning prayers, Sir David Dundas[1] came to call on me. He is the Commander-in-Chief of the English King's armed forces, a just and modest man. His conversation with me is one that I shall recall with particular pleasure and excitement.

We exchanged compliments and began to talk. He said: 'A few days ago a review was held in honour of the Queen's Birthday. I was sorry to learn that you had not been informed and very much regretted that you were not present. In future when I review the troops I shall invite you myself and we shall go together.'

He told me that he was the author of an instruction manual for the infantry and the cavalry. He said he would send a copy for his Royal Highness the *Valiahd*, the Crown Prince of Iran, as he had heard that he took a lively interest in these matters.

I commented that although the great Prince is himself most skilled in the arts of war, to send the book to him would help to cement the friendship between our two countries.

---

[1] Sir David Dundas KCB (1735-1820) had retired from the army as a full General in 1805. He was recalled and appointed Commander-in-Chief in March 1809 when the Duke of York was forced to resign after his mistress, Mary Anne Clarke, had been found guilty of selling army commissions. Dundas served until May 1811, by which time the scandal had died down and the Duke of York resumed command.

FEBRUARY

1810

Thursday, 1 February

SIR GORE OUSELEY called on this unhappy exile to say that the Minister had promised to conclude my business within four or five days and to obtain permission for my departure.

These words perturbed me and I perceived that the best course of action was to write to the Minister myself. Sir Gore Ouseley agreed; and I wrote a note to the effect that, as the wise and distinguished Minister well knew, much time had passed since the arrival of the letter from his Majesty the Shahanshah of Iran to the exalted King of England. I had given much trouble to my friends and companions and in particular to the peerless Minister and his colleagues and to Sir Gore Ouseley and his family. I could be patient no longer, for I stood in fear and trembling before the awesome Majesty of the Sultan of Iran.

> *Do not procrastinate and so prolong my persecution –*
> *Release me from my misery and fix my execution.*

When I finished writing the letter, I gave it to Sir Gore Ouseley and we went out together in the carriage. During the drive I gave him some oral instructions. When we neared the Foreign Office Sir Gore Ouseley got out, and I returned home.

Mr Morier then arrived to enquire about my health. He expressed his concern, saying: 'You have not yet completed your course of treatment; you are not yet cured of your indisposition. Remain at least a few more days so that your health and strength may be fully restored and you will be able to withstand the hardships of travel. Then you may hasten to depart.'

'English customs are indeed pleasing to my heart,' I replied, 'but truly I must depart. What can be your motive in keeping me here? There is no time to waste, for it is clear that Bonaparte's greed knows no bounds; he covets the entire world.'

We were conversing thus when Sir Gore Ouseley returned from the Minister's house. He was clearly upset. He said that the Minister had been hurt by the contents of my note – it was impossible to hurry the King. Sir Gore Ouseley had tried to be firm on my behalf, but this only irritated the Minister more. Feeling ill at ease, he returned home.

Friday, 2 February

I have received a letter from the Envoy this morning, hoping that he would be allowed to go away in a Carriage with conveyances for his Servants and baggage, but that if it was not considered proper to comply with his wishes on this subject, he must proceed on foot – I shall wait upon him immediately and use every possible means to divest him from his imprudent determination.

(Letter from Sir Gore Ouseley to the Marquis Wellesley, 2 February)[1]

SIR GORE OUSELEY came through the door in a happy, joyful mood. After compliments he said: 'Your mission has been accomplished, thank God! The Prime Minister has written to all the members of the Council: they are to meet today for the precise purpose of drawing up the terms of the Treaty of Friendship between our two great countries. Your work will be at an end.'

Sir Gore Ouseley continued: 'Now banish sorrow from your heart and prepare to attend a banquet at the home of my friend Sir Sidney Smith,[2] who has spread the cloth of hospitality and invited you to dine with a number of lords and gentlemen. Friendship aside, he is a clever and brave man. Once when Bonaparte mounted an attack against fortifications in Egypt,[3] Smith's victory cost the French 5000 lives. He would prove an influential friend, so it is important that you attend his party.'

'So be it,' I said. And, with Sir Gore Ouseley and Mr Morier, we drove in the carriage to our rendez-vous.

It happened that our host had recently married. His wife is extremely beautiful and she greeted her guests with perfect hospitality. *Houri*-like girls and beautiful ladies eclipsed the brilliance of the candles with their own radiance.

Mrs Perceval, wife of the Prime Minister, was seated among the guests. She opened the gates of kindness and condescension to me and my companions; but after some time she politely excused herself and went home.

PLATE 22

*Sir Harford Jones Brydges, Bart (1829). Portrait
by Sir Thomas Lawrence.*

PLATE 23

This drawing by James Morier of The Prime
Vizir, A Little Old Man *for his book,* Hajji
Baba of Ispahan, *is undoubtedly a portrait from
life of Persia's Prime Minister, Mirza Shafi, with
whom Abul Hassan corresponded while in London.*

I then tried to converse with a lovely lady to whom I was introduced by Sir Gore Ouseley. I tried a few words of English, but she only blushed and hid her face; I received no response at all. Sir Gore Ouseley explained that she was deaf and that – because my illness had weakened my voice – she was unable to hear me. Sir Gore Ouseley and I went to say good-night to Miss Pole. We got into our carriage and that charming, star-kissed girl waved us off.

[1] BL Add.37285, ff.221-2.

[2] Admiral Sir (William) Sidney Smith (1764-1840) married in 1809 Caroline, widow of the diplomatist Sir George Berriman Rumbold. They lived in Cleveland Row.

[3] This probably refers not to Egypt but to Smith's most notable success, the defence of Acre in Syria (1799).

Saturday, 3 February

THE SUN EMERGED through the azure curtain of heaven; but it was soon enveloped in a veil of cloud and raindrops fell. After praying to the Great Creator, I fearfully reflected on the power of his Majesty the Shahanshah, from whom all justice flows, and I waited for news from the Prime Minister.

Sir Gore Ouseley, my support in sorrow, arrived. After explaining at length why I had received no news from the Foreign Office, he said: 'Tonight his Royal Highness the Prince of Wales has invited the Prime Minister and his ministers, the nobility, Company officials and army officers to an entertainment in your honour. They must dress in a manner worthy of such an occasion; and you too must change your clothes so that we may set off together.'

When evening came we drove together in the carriage to the house of that peerless Prince. We proceeded through rows of handsome footmen, richly attired, and saw a myriad beautifully coiffed ladies standing beneath the gold and silver and crystal chandeliers. Thousands of wax candles lighted the rooms and alcoves which I have previously described with the pen of praise.

The guests were seated on golden chairs at a banquet-table spread with a profusion of tasty dishes. The Prince graciously placed me on his right hand and showed me great condescension. He said: 'The weather of London in winter is hardly agreeable, especially to one like yourself, who is accustomed to the fair climate of Shiraz.'

As Sheikh Saadi[1] wrote:

> *A fairer place than Shiraz I did never see*
> *God's blessing is upon it – may it ever be!*

'Still,' continued the Prince, 'every place has its particular attractions. God the Creator has given us the flowers of spring and the fruits of summer – as well as pomegranate-breasted beauties! Since

He has brought you to this land, banish sorrow from your heart and enjoy it!'

Then the conversation turned to affairs of the heart. The Prince asked: 'Thin women or fat – which do you prefer?'

'I like a woman as plump and as tall as a cypress tree,' I answered. 'Thin women do not attract me at all.'

The Prince was greatly pleased by my poetic allusion and congratulated me; it seems our tastes are similar. He wanted to know if I had found a woman in England, but I had to reply that, though I wished it were otherwise, none desired me because of my beard.

The Prince replied: 'If indeed they flee from your hairy face, you may at least be thankful to be spared their hairy intellects!' We could not help laughing at his joke!

Then the Prince decided he wanted to go to the Opera. He stood up and all the guests rose, mounted into golden carriages and left for the Opera.

<hr />

[1] Sheikh Saadi of Shiraz (?1184-1291) is one of the most popular Persian poets. He is best known for his *Gulistan* (Rose-garden), a collection of ethical anecdotes and maxims of worldly wisdom composed in prose and poetry; and his *ghazals*, or odes, are considered to rival those of Hafez.

Sunday, 4 February

IN THE EVENING THE Turkish Ambassador joined our agreeable company. I thought he looked upset and I asked him the reason. He said that his French translator, a friend and companion, had today passed from this world. Having spent seven years in his company, he was deeply affected by his death.

I asked the Ambassador why his embassy had been of such long duration and why his mission had not yet been accomplished. He told me that the King's ministers refused to receive him: they appeared to have blotted his name from the pages of their memory. I felt very sympathetic, thinking of my own similar circumstances, and I prayed to God Almighty for my release.

Monday, 5 February

TODAY IS THE FIRST DAY of *Moharram* and I wept thinking of Iran and of the *tazieh* representing the young *sayids'* journey to Paradise.[1]

[1] *Moharram* is the first month of the Islamic religious (lunar) calendar, the years of which are dated from the *hijra*, Mohammad's migration from Mecca to Medina in 622 AD; 5 February 1810 was the first day of 1225 AH. Shia Moslems regard the whole of *Moharram* as a period of mourning for the Imam Hussein, grandson of the Prophet Mohammad, who died in battle at Kerbala in Iraq. Episodes from the lives of Hussein and his brother Hassan are enacted in passion plays called *tazieh*. A *sayid* is a descendant of the Prophet.

Tuesday, 6 February

L ORD HARCOURT,[1] Master of the Queen's Horse, called with Lord Radstock. They found me in low spirits, but their kind words cheered me up.

I went with their Excellencies to a glass and mirror manufactory, where we observed stones and other ingredients combined and melted in furnaces to produce clear, jewel-like glass. I enquired about the glass and mirror industry and asked if there were any other, superior, manufacturers of mirrors. The man replied honestly: 'English artisans are highly skilled and unrivalled throughout Europe. But the French produce a better-quality mirror because of the different materials they use.' The fairness of the master's reply pleased me and I ordered two *qalians* from him. They made two sets for me by hand.

From there we went to a crystal-cutting factory. We looked around and were told the prices of the various patterns. English cut-crystal is superior to that of other countries because the English have a greater appreciation of the art.

Finally we visited a gunsmith renowned for the manufacture of shotguns and pistols. The perfection of his workmanship is universally recognized – he has no peer in all of Europe.

The artisans of London excel in every craft with the exception of brocade-weaving. But European brocades are rarely used here because their import is prohibited by Royal decree. English leather and metal-work are also of high quality. But prices are high in London. For example: a knife costs four 'guineas', a pair of leather boots three 'guineas', and a pair of shoes one 'guinea'. (A 'guinea' is the equivalent of one Iranian *toman*, sometimes more.) Even the drinking water is sold and brings a revenue of 90,000 *tomans* a year.

This evening, after dinner, Sadri Effendi, the Turkish Ambassador, wanted to go to the Opera, so we went there in the carriage with

Sir Gore Ouseley. The audience, of all classes, were already in their places.

The ballet concerned a war between Russia and Turkey, during which the Turkish commander offered to sell his country to the Russians for money.[2] The dancers wore Russian and Turkish costumes.

During the whole of his stay in London, the Ambassador had never been to the theatre. He expressed great surprise and said: 'I have you to thank for this – without you I should never have visited the Opera House.'

'The nights are long in every country,' I replied, 'but especially in London. From now on, I shall take you to the Opera every night, and you will see strange and wonderful things.'

When the evening came to an end, we all returned to our homes.

[1] William Harcourt (1742/3-1830), 3rd Earl Harcourt.

[2] The ballet, *Pietro il Grande*, was about Peter the Great's campaign against the Turks on the River Purth in 1711.

Wednesday, 7 February

M Y TRUE AND DEVOTED friend Lord Radstock told Sir Gore
Ouseley that someone had complained to him that the
Persian Ambassador had slandered English womanhood.
Sir Gore Ouseley answered Lord Radstock: 'This man's accusation
is nonsense. The Persian Ambassador's character is honourable and
blameless and we have heard him utter nothing but praise for the
ladies of London. As it happens, however, he is but little acquainted
with Englishwomen; how, then, could he be acquainted with either
their virtues or their vices?'

When Sir Gore Ouseley reported this conversation to me, I said:
'*Sobhanallah*! Good God! How could anyone be so ungrateful as to
eat salt from the table of friendship and then break the salt-cellar! As
God is my witness I wish the women of Iran could be more like the
women of England. Iranian women are chaste because they are
forced to be – they are shut away from men; but Englishwomen are
chaste by choice. They are free and independent and responsible
only to their husbands, whom they look upon as the only men in the
world. They do not hide themselves away, but appear veil-less in
society; and they honour their husbands' guests as their own friends.'

Then I said to my faithful and sympathetic friend Sir Gore
Ouseley: 'From now on I shall remain at home alone. I shall attend
no more assemblies and I shall shun society lest I hurt my friends.'

Sir Gore Ouseley replied: 'Rest assured that the people of London
are shrewd enough and wise enough to distinguish between truth
and falsehood. It is true, you know, that the sea was never contami-
nated by one dog's mouth!' And so saying, he left for home.

I spent the evening reading Persian poetry and thinking of my
country and my fellow countrymen.

Thursday, 8 February

THE DAY DAWNED AND I rose and prayed to the One God. Then I left the house intending to go by carriage to the home of my dear *mehmandar*, my sympathetic friend Sir Gore Ouseley. I wanted to apologize for what I had said yesterday in my state of agitation. But I found that the carriage was missing. When the coachman returned I rebuked him, not realizing that Mr Morier had taken the carriage on a necessary errand.

Hearing that I was angry, Mr Morier told Sir Gore Ouseley that it was clear I was not pleased to have him living in my house! Sir Gore Ouseley reassured him: 'You are imagining things: the Ambassador was only annoyed with the coachman. You must know how dear you are to his heart.'

When all of this was repeated to me, I summoned Mr Morier and said: 'I am amazed! How little you seem to know me. I thought our journey together on land and sea had been a sufficient test of our friendship.' Mr Morier agreed and apologized for what he had said to Sir Gore Ouseley.

> *The Persian Ambassador appeared much astonished at the elegant suite of rooms, at St. James's Palace, and at a numerous assemblage of beautiful Englishwomen, elegantly dressed, attending as spectators. His Excellency expressed his acknowledgements, by his actions, at the attention shewn him by the attendants about the Palace, especially those who conducted him to his carriage.*
>
> (*The Morning Chronicle*, 9 February)

Today the Queen came to the city from her country palace, and all the ministers and high-ranking officials, together with their wives and daughters, went to call on her. Those who have the honour of being received by the Queen, and who have business with the King, hope to reach the King's ear through her. An invitation from her Majesty also arrived for me, requesting my attendance at the Palace.[1]

Sir Gore Ouseley and I drove there in the carriage. The street was blocked with such a multitude of carriages, large and small, that none could move forward, even though the road was closed to ordinary traffic. Everyone was impatient, but it is the rule that one should not overtake someone of higher rank: everyone knows his own place and respects the rank of others. The world would do well to emulate such politeness.

At last we arrived and entered the house by the door reserved for princes. Handsome footmen conducted us to the Fairy Queen's Audience Chamber – they call it a 'Drawing-room'. A house may have many rooms decorated with taste, but the best room is called the drawing-room. The Queen's Drawing-room is also known as the Throne Room.

The guests were lined up on all sides and we tried in vain to make our way through the crowd. Then the Queen entered from another room, followed by ladies-in-waiting, beautiful as the Pleiades, three of the Princesses[2] and a young page, the son of a lord, who carried her long train so that it would not drag on the floor. There must have been 1000 guests. The ladies wore the 'hoop' skirts I have already described. Some wore Phoenix-like feathers in their hair; others wore jewels. The Queen mounted the dais and the loud acclaim of the crowd might have turned even Afrasiyab's[3] heart to water from fear and trembling!

I found the ladies' dresses unattractive and I said so to my good friend. 'These strange costumes truly depress me – their everyday gowns are much more flattering to waists and bosoms than these tightly boned bodices!' As for English men's clothes, they are immodest and unflattering to the figure, especially their trousers which look just like under-drawers – could they be designed to appeal to the ladies? The ladies admire small feet – I have seen men wearing shoes so tight that their feet bulge over the sides! Both men and women consider small feet to be elegant and a sign of high birth.

The Queen stood on the Royal dais while the ladies brought their daughters forward to be presented individually by the Deputy Master of the Ceremonies. Their names and titles were announced and the Queen spoke to each one.

At last the presentations were over and a young colonel made a passage for us through the crowd and brought us into the Queen's presence. A handsome lady offered me her place. When the Queen saw me and Sir Gore Ouseley she spoke to us with extreme condescension, elegance and wit. She addressed Sir Gore Ouseley: 'I have heard that the Iranian Ambassador is so enamoured of a certain young lady that the affairs of Iran are far from his thoughts!'

Sir Gore Ouseley replied with a smile: 'It is as your Majesty says.'

Then the Queen asked if I had met the Prince of Wales. I told her that I had and that we had discussed the protocol of being presented to his Royal mother. The Queen said she hoped to be of some help to me in accomplishing my mission and then graciously gave us leave to withdraw.

We left the dais and busied ourselves admiring the lovely ladies of London. I learned that young ladies are not presented to the Queen before they reach the age of seventeen, and that, until they have had that honour, they do not go out in society or attend dinner parties and receptions. No member of a family touched by scandal is received at Court.

<hr />

[1] St James's Palace.

[2] *The Morning Post,* 9 February, reported the presence of the Princesses Augusta, Elizabeth and Sophia.

[3] Afrasiyab: a king of Turan, legendary foe of Iran, who was killed by Key Khosrow after a long pursuit.

Friday, 9 February

WHEN THE SUN APPEARED in the azure sky to bathe the land with light, Sir Gore Ouseley arrived. After the usual exchange of compliments, he said: 'The ministers and councillors have met to deliberate the details of your release and departure for Iran. The Prime Minister will fix a time agreeable to the King when your business may be satisfactorily concluded.'

I said to Sir Gore Ouseley:

> *Naught in the world will go aright*
> *If you're not there to set it right,*

and I thanked him for his many kindnesses on my behalf.

Sir Gore Ouseley continued: 'I spoke at length of your anxiety to return to Iran and the Prime Minister said he would make every effort to that end – on condition that I accept the post of Ambassador to Iran. I told the Prime Minister that I must have a few days to consider his proposal and that he also must be completely satisfied of my worthiness to undertake this important mission.'[1]

I was delighted to hear this news and said: 'I thank God for my good fortune to have you as my guide. And I congratulate the wise Minister on making an appointment calculated to strengthen the Government and the monarchy!'

In the evening we were invited to dine at Lord Radstock's house and my friends and I drove there in the carriage.

After dinner cup-bearers served us with the wine of hospitality. Mrs Perceval and Lady Arden and their pretty daughters were the stars of the assembly. Mrs Perceval's second daughter, Miss Fanny,[2] who is lovely to look at and amiable of disposition, sought my company and paid me particular attention, treating me as a sister would her brother.

Lord Keith's daughter, Miss Mercer,[3] was also among the guests. Among her accomplishments, she is a portrait painter, as skilful as Mani,[4] and like the French masters, she paints with a hair brush. It was most extraordinary that after a single glance she was able to sketch my likeness. I begged her to send me the picture so that I might have a souvenir of her talent.

[1] Ouseley himself had written to Wellesley on 7 February asking for the post (BL Add.37285, f.223).

[2] Frances (Fanny) Perceval, born 1792.

[3] Margaret Mercer Elphinstone (1788-1867), daughter of Admiral George Keith Elphinstone (1745/6-1823), 1st Baron (later 1st Viscount) Keith, was known as 'Mercer'.

[4] Mani (Manes c. 216-76 AD), the founder of Manichaeanism. He was executed by Shapur I for idolatory; but according to the *Shahnameh* (The Book of Kings, Iran's national epic written by Ferdowsi, 1020-5), he was a renowned artist who came to Shapur's court from China.

Saturday, 10 February

IN THE EVENING I went to the theatre with Sir Gore Ouse-ley. The audience were annoyed by the irritating voice of one of the women on stage and they made those noises which the English call 'hiss' and which indicate displeasure. But the actress had one admirer at least – across from us two arrogant gentle-men began to fight with their fists. One of them put his hand in his pocket and drew out a card; and the other, according to the custom, produced a card of his own.

I was amazed by this behaviour and I asked Sir Gore Ouseley to explain. He told me that since it was not possible to continue fighting in the theatre, they exchanged cards in order to settle their dispute with pistols at an agreed time and place. Any man who feels he has been insulted may call out the other – be he prince or peasant – for satisfaction. The opponents take their positions twenty paces apart and two men of their own choosing prepare the pistols. They may fire twice and may not turn aside for fear of being labelled a coward and banished from society. If one of them is killed, the other is not blamed; but if both survive, they must make peace and cease their enmity – otherwise they are considered ungentlemanly and are received nowhere.

It happened that Mr Canning, the former Minister for Foreign Affairs, for whom I had brought letters from the ministers in Iran, engaged in just such a pistol fight with Lord Castlereagh, the former Minister for War. Mr Canning was hit by a bullet, but was not seriously hurt; and afterwards, God be praised, they embraced and became as brothers.[1]

---

[1] Robert Stewart (1769-1822), Viscount Castlereagh (later 2nd Marquis of London-derry), Minister for War in the Portland Administration, accused the Minister for Foreign Affairs, George Canning (1770-1827), of intriguing to remove him from office. The duel took place on Putney Heath on 21 September 1809.

Sunday, 11 February

THIS EVENING WE WERE invited to the house of Lord Harrowby.[1] Two lords – one of them was Lord Dartmouth – came up to invite me to their parties. They were very insistent. When I told Sir Gore Ouseley of the invitations, he reminded me that we were engaged on those evenings, and he exclaimed: 'Good God, Londoners are so hospitable to foreigners and entertain them so lavishly, there is no end to it!' So he decided to prepare a scroll with dates to be filled in by my hosts. If anyone asked me for an evening, I was to ask him to seek permission from Sir Gore Ouseley.

After dinner we discussed my departure from London, and I said: 'You are all very kind to wish me to remain in London, but you place me in a difficult position. I fear the displeasure of the Shahanshah of Iran and my anxiety increases exceedingly the longer I am prevented from returning to the Shah's radiant presence.'[2]

[1] 39 Grosvenor Square.

[2] There are no journal entries for 12-20 February, except for a note clearly relating to 14 February. A similar gap occurs in the Hoare and British Library manuscripts. Yet this was the period when Abul Hassan's diplomatic mission finally achieved a break-through, as is evidenced by other documents.

On 16 February Lord Wellesley sent a detailed written reply to the points raised by Abul Hassan (IO L/PS/3/3, Appendix 19). On the subsidy issue, he wrote that details had to be settled with the East India Company, to whom the matter had been referred.

This led Abul Hassan to write to Mr Dundas on 18 February. Dundas wrote back immediately to say that he had spoken to the Directors of the Company and hoped to be able to give an early and satisfactory reply. On 22 February (when Mr Grant told Abul Hassan that all was settled) the Directors' agreement was conveyed to Dundas. (IO L/PS/3/3, f.226).

Wednesday, 14 February

TODAY IS THE DAY which the English call 'Valentine's Day': it is the custom on this day for lovers to send letters and love-poems to their sweethearts, but they do not sign their names. Elegant dandies also send each other caricature drawings as jokes.

While I was at home a letter was delivered to me containing some verses and several drawings. I passed it to Mr Morier and asked him what it was. He told me they were verses which the Minister had commissioned for me from a poet of taste and elegance and he assured me that they contained no element of satire.

Wednesday, 21 February

SIR GORE OUSELEY came to the house to say that Mrs Perceval's mother[1] had come to town from the country and that she had sent an invitation for me to call on her. So we rode out to visit that good lady. She is indeed a worthy woman and proud to claim forty children and grandchildren. After making me feel very much at home, she asked me to write something for her in Persian. Lady Arden also came to see her, with two of her daughters.

While we were exchanging farewell compliments, Mrs Perceval's mother invited us to spend a night at her country house.

From there we went to the Office of the Minister for Foreign Affairs, which was on our way home. A packet of letters had arrived from Iran and we learned that the Padeshah, Asylum of the Universe, had honoured the capital Tehran with the return of his retinue from Azerbaijan.

As if by the hand of Mercury, I was honoured with letters from the *valiahd*, the Crown Prince, and from officials of the Court – jewel-like words, written more than two months previously. At the sight of them my eyes grew bright.

There were several despatches bearing the seal of the First Vizir, Mirza Mohammad Shafi, to the Nobles of the English Government. They dealt with my departure from London and with several other matters concerning the strengthening of friendship between our two countries: they pointed out that the *ilchi* of the French Emperor had been ordered to leave the country because of Iran's friendship with England; it was now up to England to demonstrate that friendship by providing assistance.

After perusing the letters, Sir Gore Ouseley exclaimed: 'Thank God! I was correct in what I first told the ministers and councillors: both his Royal Highness the Crown Prince and your honourable Minister have addressed you as *ilchi*. Sir Harford Jones first

PLATE 24

*The Marquis Wellesley who was Foreign Secretary
at the time of Abul Hassan's mission to London.
Portrait by R. Home.*

PLATE 25

Spencer Perceval as Prime Minister, a posthumous portrait by G. F. Joseph from a death mask by Joseph Nollekens. Spencer Perceval was assassinated in the House of Commons on 11 May 1812.

reported your title as *chargé d'affaires*; but from the moment I saw the word *vakil* – written in the Shah of Iran's letter to the King of England – I maintained that your position was higher than that of envoy. The members of the Council accepted my word: they acknowledged your high rank and your right to be addressed as Excellency. Thank goodness I can hold up my head, for I was not mistaken.'

I replied: 'Sir Harford Jones is an "envoy", is he not? Jaafar Ali Khan, Sir Harford Jones' translator in Iran, said that Sir Harford Jones is treated like the Shah's fourth Minister and that the Shah addresses him as brother. Do you now tell me that an "envoy" is not an ambassador of the first rank?'[2]

Sir Gore Ouseley explained: 'There are three ranks of diplomatic representative: (1) *chargé d'affaires*, which is the lowest; (2) envoy; and (3) ambassador, like Mr Adair[3] in Constantinople.'

Sir Gore Ouseley took the letters from Iran saying he would read them to the Minister for Foreign Affairs at a convenient moment. Then he left to call on that Minister and also on the Minister for the Company in order to obtain answers to the questions I had previously submitted. He said he would return in the evening.

---

[1] Lady (Jane Maryon) Wilson, widow of Sir Thomas Spencer Wilson (1726-98), 6th Baronet. She died in 1818.

[2] Sir Harford Jones' title was Envoy Extraordinary and Minister Plenipotentiary. The British Government recognized Abul Hassan as the same; but, as Jones had been accorded in Persia honours 'superior to those due to his rank' (in Wellesley's words), Abul Hassan was in turn granted extra privileges. Wellesley had recommended (and the King had agreed to) a public audience, though in the event a private audience (with extra ceremony) was agreed, because it could be arranged sooner (BL Add.37285, f.200).

[3] Later Sir Robert Adair (1768-1855).

Thursday, 22 February

THE SERPENTINE RIVER. Yesterday the river exhibited one uniform sheet of transparent ice. The skaiters, however, were not numerous. . . . His Excellency the Persian Ambassador sat in his carriage, for some time, a delighted spectator of, to him, a nouvelle scene. . . .

(*The Morning Post*, 23 February)

I DROVE TO A FRIEND'S HOUSE. Mr Grant, the chairman of the Company, who was also there, told me that all of my requests had been accepted by Mr Dundas, the Minister for the Company, and forwarded to Lord Wellesley. He said they were considering the appointment of an ambassador – a learned man – to Iran.

I said that the ambassador must be a linguist as well as an eloquent and clever speaker; and he should be committed to the interests of both countries because there were no adequate interpreters in Iran. We talked at length on this subject until the day came to an end.

Friday, 23 February

THIS MORNING I WENT out riding; but I returned quickly because I was expecting Mr Dundas to call. However, he came before my return and, not finding me at home, he left a note to say that he had talked to the Minister about each of my requests, one by one.

Then Sir Gore Ouseley arrived. Finding me downcast, he asked the reason. I told him it was because of the Council's continued procrastination in replying to my letters. He said: 'I have received splendid news which means that your affairs will soon be resolved. Do not be despondent. I have been told that I am appointed Ambassador to the Shah of Iran and that we are to travel there together.'

He showed me the letter he had received from the Minister for Foreign Affairs: it said that in view of Sir Gore Ouseley's merit and accomplishments, the Council could not have failed to approve his appointment; and it instructed Sir Gore Ouseley to accompany me on the difficult journey to Iran where we would work together to secure the ratification of the treaty, to create a firm foundation of friendship between our two exalted monarchs, and to bring about the downfall of their enemies. On hearing these glad tidings, I said:

> *What my heart sought is now revealed*
> *Behind this veil it lay concealed.*

If it has pleased God to raise us to these important tasks, in spite of the efforts of our enemies, then my happiness – and that of my dear friend Sir Gore Ouseley – is complete. We passed the day in perfect contentment.

Saturday, 24 February

AFTER THE SUN ROSE I wrote a letter to the wise Minister congratulating him on naming Sir Gore Ouseley as Ambassador to Iran – never has such a brilliant appointment been made! His wisdom and intelligence can only result, *inshallah*, God willing, in increased friendship and good relations between our two great countries. I also expressed my own gratitude for his help and friendship. I sealed the letter and despatched it.

Tonight my companions and I drove to the Opera House in the carriage. When we arrived, Sir Gore Ouseley was already there talking to Miss Pole's sister – she is so beautiful that the beauties of paradise are obliged to pay her compliments. Her name is Mrs Bagot[1] and her husband is one of the most handsome and generous young men in England. They were standing in a group of lovely ladies waiting to go in, and they kindly asked us to join them. Mrs Perceval's sister was also there.

Among the cast was [Tramezzani] who had made me weep on the first night I went to the Opera. But tonight I did not enjoy the performance at all, and I wished that mysterious hands would appear to squeeze the breath from his throat. Our friends were bored too and we all went home.

---

[1] Mary Charlotte Anne (died 1845), eldest daughter of William Wellesley-Pole, married in 1806 the diplomatist (later Sir) Charles Bagot, second son of the 1st Baron Bagot.

Sunday, 25 February

ON SUNDAY, WHICH IS their holy day, the world-illuminating sun appeared to brighten the city of London with its blazing countenance! I gave thanks to see the sun's face after such an age, and I praised God the Creator!

By invitation we drove to the house of Lady Arden, a devout woman who is a true and compassionate friend. It happened that her worthy sister Mrs Perceval honoured us with her presence – her affectionate nature always gladdens my heart. The children all crowded round me and paid me such kind attentions that I was able to forget for a moment the long separation from my own loved ones.

One of the little girls, who has completed only ten years of life's journey, bitterly deplored my departure for Iran and vowed to accompany me. She gripped my hand tightly, as if I were a brother about to set off on a long journey. I consoled her by saying that the date of my departure was not yet fixed and that she should not distress herself.

I diverted them by writing each of their names in a notebook in English letters.

From there we returned home and I spent the evening with my friends.

Monday, 26 February

IN THE EVENING WE WERE invited to a children's dance at Lord Darnley's house.[1] The ladies gathered around banquet tables covered with all sorts of delicacies – it could have been paradise.

The Prince of Wales kindly agreed to open the candle-lit ball. A little girl of ten years, who sang a song and danced, stole the Prince's heart. He made a great fuss of her and all the guests admired his interest in even the youngest of his subjects and his obvious delight in children.

Later, the Prince said to me: 'These entertainments are hardly worthy of an ambassador from Iran; still, we hope they may help to lessen the pain of your exile.'

I told the Prince that his condescension and concern for me were thus:

> *To treat a beggar with a kindly grace*
> *The standing of a king did ne're disgrace.*

Never has a prince possessed such a kind heart.

I spent the evening happily.

---

[1] John Bligh (1767-1831), 4th Earl of Darnley, married in 1791 Elizabeth Brownlow of Lurgan. The Darnleys, who lived at 46 Berkeley Square, had two surviving sons, aged fifteen and twelve.

Tuesday, 27 February

WHEN THE SUN ROSE, I awoke with a severe pain in my chest – I thought I would die! But walking for a time in Lord Teignmouth's square, I gained some measure of relief.

THE DUKE OF YORK'S DINNER TO THE PERSIAN AMBASSADOR.
The Duke of York gave a grand entertainment yesterday to the Persian Ambassador. Among the company present were the following distinguished personnages: – The Prince of Wales, Dukes of Clarence, Kent, Cumberland, Sussex and Cambridge, Marquis of Hertford and Earl of Yarmouth.

(*The Morning Post*, 28 February)

This evening we were invited to the house of the second Royal Prince, the Duke of York,[1] and we went there in the carriage. The Prince of Wales and his other brothers were there, and ministers and prominent personages of this happy land were assembled, like moths attracted to a candle.

Our host's wife, who is the daughter of the King of Denmark [*sic*], sat between me and the Prince of Wales. Lord Wellesley's sister[2] sat on my left. No other ladies were present.

The Prince of Wales was so amusing that I and the other guests could not contain our mirth. I laughed so much that my sides hurt and this verse came unbidden to my mind:

I'm out of control, for the Prince is so droll,
Come quick, catch my head – from my neck it may roll.

The Prince of Wales directed so many jokes and winks at Lord Wellesley that even that serious-minded Minister could not help laughing. And he exchanged such rare anecdotes with his brothers that they too became quite insensible with laughter.

One of his stories was about the huge size of the penis of one of his Royal brothers – a fact which he had discovered one night while riding with him in a carriage. His brother had felt the need to

151

relieve himself: when he did so out of the carriage window, the water flowed as from a fountain and the driver urged the horses forward to escape what he thought was a rainstorm! 'That is how I found out,' said the Prince, 'and I am letting you into his secret too!'

All of the guests told jokes, and some were even directed at me. It was a very amusing evening.

Since there was a performance this evening, we went on to the Opera.[3] The star was Tramezzani. He sang with emotion and seemed very pleased with himself. He bragged and swaggered about the stage, and acted as if he were giving lessons in love to the young people in the audience.

When the spectacle was over, we all returned home.

[1] Prince Frederick, Duke of York and Albany (1763-1827), formerly Commander-in-Chief of the army (see entry for 31 January), was the second and favourite son of George III. His wife was Princess Frederica, eldest daughter of Frederick William II of Prussia. While the Duke devoted himself to a succession of mistresses, she was content to remain at their country house at Oatlands, near Weybridge. She rarely appeared in London, but must have done so on this occasion. In London, the Duke of York lived (from 1807) in York House, Stable Yard, St James's Palace, the site now occupied by Lancaster House.

[2] Richard Wellesley had one sister, Anne, who was Lady-in-Waiting to the Duchess of York. In 1799 she married, as her second husband, Charles Culling Smith, who in 1810 was one of Wellesley's Under-Secretaries of State for Foreign Affairs.

[3] *Romeo e Giulietta* by Guglielmi.

MARCH

1810

Thursday, 1 March

THIS EVENING WE WERE invited to an entertainment, a 'party', at the house of the Marquis of Salisbury,[1] and I went there with Sir Gore Ouseley. All the luminaries of London were gathered together in a brilliant assembly, which included the Prince of Wales. He shone in witty conversation with the ladies.

Even the dowagers are flirtatious. They rouge their cheeks and love to converse with the young men. Among them was a certain high-born lady who was very kind and flattering to me. I noticed there were white hairs on her face – Sir Gore Ouseley told me she had grown a beard out of admiration for my own!

At supper, I sat next to the Prince and the conversation was so pleasant that the hours seemed to pass in a flash. It was dawn before we all got into our carriages and went home.

I will now set down the rules governing entertaining in London. Invitations are issued on cards which give the day, the month, the hour of arriving and the hour of leaving. For example:

A 'dinner' lasts for four hours, from six o'clock until ten o'clock.

A 'ball' is a large gathering attended by the nobility. It begins late in the evening, at ten o'clock, and lasts until five o'clock in the morning – seven hours are spent dancing! Balls are held in large rooms which have been cleared of carpets. Three or four musicians play instruments which resemble the *kamancheh*. When the music begins, each gentleman asks a lady if she wishes to dance; if she says no, he asks another.

Another kind of entertainment is called 'music', which may also mean singing. This also lasts for four hours, from ten o'clock until two o'clock in the morning. Guests are invited to hear a distinguished musician; and when he appears they become silent out of respect. The host makes a speech of welcome and appears to have to persuade him to perform, even though it is well known that he will receive a fee.

An 'assembly' is a form of entertainment which I have told my faithful friend Sir Gore Ouseley I think could well be done away with – and he agrees! This lasts for six hours, from ten o'clock until four o'clock in the morning and resembles nothing so much as the crowd at a ladies' *hammam* or the great gathering of souls at the Last Judgement.[2]

There is one other type of entertainment, which the English call 'breakfast': this means the morning meal. Guests present themselves at their host's table, partake of some food, and return home.

Night and day, it seems, the English think only of pleasure.

---

[1] James Cecil (1748-1823), 7th Earl and 1st Marquis of Salisbury, Lord Chamberlain 1783-1804, married in 1773 Mary Amelia, daughter of the 1st Marquis of Downshire, who died in a fire at Hatfield House in 1835. The Salisburys' London house was at 20 Arlington Street.

[2] In his second book of travels, p. 404, James Morier wrote: 'When it is known that a Persian *mejlis* or assembly is composed of people seated in a formal row on the ground, with their backs against the wall, some idea may be had of the Persian Ambassador's surprise upon entering an English rout. The perfect ease of his manners and unembarrassed conduct on such occasions, will be as surprising to us, as the great crowd of men and women hotly pressed together for no one apparent purpose, was to him.'

Friday, 2 March

MR MORIER ARRIVED. 'Ah, my dear friend,' I said, 'it is ages since I have seen you – does my company begin to bore you?'

For many a day the gate's been closed
That stands across affection's road.

He replied: 'But you knew I had to go out of London! From the day of our arrival I have acceded to your wish that I remain in this house with you. But some of my other friends have been anxious to see me and I have been obliged to deprive myself of the pleasure of your company for a few days.'

I also complained that my good friend Lord Radstock had not called on me for several days – this saddened me. But Mr Morier told me that he too was very busy.

Sunday, 4 March

As day dawned in the east, I realized that it was the Londoner's holy day and that most of them would be in the country – so I sat disconsolate in my lonely corner.

After a while a messenger came to deliver a pen-and-ink portrait of me from Miss Mercer. He said that Miss Mercer sent her compliments and her apologies – had she seen me more than once the portrait might have been better.

For years your portrait has been sketched by the pen of fate.
It's taken quite a lifetime, for your stature is so great!

I examined the drawing closely and found no defect save its small size. '*Sobhanallah!* Good God!' I exclaimed, 'the Eternal Artist has endowed the women of this city with all the talents and spared them all the defects.'

In the evening I was invited to the house of Mr Arbuthnot, Joint Secretary to the Treasury, and I went there in the carriage.[1] I arrived to find a truly sumptuous banquet lighted by a thousand candles. Soon after my arrival the Minister for Foreign Affairs and Mr Wellesley-Pole came in with the latter's son-in-law Mr Bagot. He is a handsome youth, tall as a cypress:

The cypress tree sank to the ground and the moon hid in disgrace
So tall and fine a figure was his, and such a radiant face.

We sat down and Mr Bagot said, with a smile, that he had heard my heart was breaking with love for Miss Pole. That sweet-tongued youth assured me that gentlemen do not repeat each other's secrets and begged me to tell him all about it. 'In truth,' I replied, 'she is far distanced from me, and I, forlorn, from her; but surely I can dream that:

When day is breaking, when day is done
Like honey and sugar we blend as one.

157

My friends applauded and cried, 'Bravo!'

After dinner the conversation turned to good horses and agreeable women. Mr Bagot kindly offered to send one of his horses for me to ride. He also offered to arrange a private party for me one evening with a girl whose beauty would rouse the envy of Venus: I could judge for myself if she were not more charming and affectionate than my own loved one!

The evening passed pleasantly and we all returned home.

[1] Charles Arbuthnot lived at 11 Downing Street. It was acquired by the Crown in 1805 and is still used by the Chancellor of the Exchequer.

Monday, 5 March

THE SUN APPEARED IN THE TURQUOISE SKY —

Risen from the hidden fire the great magician came
And, like a waking dragon, breathed his shining ray of flame.
Then from the vaulted mouth of heaven the sun at last uncurled
Its rapier tongue, and licked to life the still unconscious world.

I sat in a corner of the terrace excited by the prospect of the promised horse. But I waited in vain, reflecting on the promises of drunkards. There are two things you cannot rely on: youthful beauty which never lasts and a drunkard's generosity which profits no one.

In this deceitful world don't seek to find
Fidelity in horse, or sword, or womankind.

I went out to a nursery garden where I inspected a myriad bright flowers and orange and lemon trees. I ordered some potted plants and gave the gardener a gold coin to deliver them to the house.

When I returned home I found Sir Gore Ouseley and I praised God – his two days' absence had seemed like two years! He told me he had just been informed that the King would soon summon him to appoint him Ambassador to the capital of the exalted Padeshah of Iran. And this verse came unbidden to my mind:

Now I've heard this, to death I'd be resigned
For this good news has brought such peace of mind.

I was as delighted by this news as if he had made me a present of the world! Then I thought of Mr Morier and insisted that he too accompany us. Sir Gore Ouseley kindly agreed. Although he has already promised to take his brother,[1] who is eager to visit Iran, he said that he would arrange with Lord Wellesley today that Mr Morier be appointed Second Gentleman.

We were in the middle of this conversation when we received

159

news of the death of a lady very close to Mrs Perceval. I was distressed by the news and said we must go to escort the funeral procession. But my dear friend explained that in England, in the case of heart failure, it is the custom to delay burial. Apparently some years ago a man who had been declared dead rose living from his coffin: he had only suffered a heart attack. After this, King and Council had ordered that dead bodies be left in their beds and buried only when they begin to stink![2]

[1] Sir William Ouseley (1767-1842), a notable Persian scholar, served as his brother's Private Secretary in Tehran and published an account of the embassy: *Travels in Various Countries of the East, more particularly Persia*, 3 vols, Rodwell & Martin, London, 1819, 1821, 1823. He brought home a large collection of Persian manuscripts, many of which are in the Bodleian Library, Oxford.

[2] Here I have omitted a three-page discussion of ancient Greek and Roman burial rites.

A 'Drawing-room' in the Council Chamber of St James's Palace. Abul Hassan much preferred the slim, high-waisted dresses of contemporary fashion to the 'tent-like' hoop skirts worn by the ladies at Court. Aquatint by Pugin and Rowlandson for Ackermann's Microcosm of London, *1808-10.*

PLATE 27

*A miniature from the manuscript which the Shah
presented to Sir Gore Ouseley in July 1812.*

Wednesday, 7 March

WHEN THE EARLY MORNING SKY turned to turquoise, my faithful friend Sir Gore Ouseley came in. He sat down on a gilt chair, and he might have quoted this old saying:

> *Good news I bring; my reward I claim,*
> *From the plains of Khotan a musk-deer came.*

He brought the reply, which he had drafted for the Minister, in answer to my letters and he asked if I had any comments.

He also told me that the Ministers in Council had arranged for him to have a farewell audience of the King on Wednesday next, and that we might leave by ship in about six weeks' time when the weather would be favourable and when, undoubtedly, the replies to all my requests would be prepared.

I was so happy and exhilarated by this news that I rode out into the country to practise throwing the javelin.

Thursday, 8 March

I RECEIVED A NOTE FROM my friend Sir Gore Ouseley telling me that he will be honoured with an audience of the King of England on his appointment as Ambassador to Iran, and that the King will grant my request for Mr Morier to fill the post of Second Gentleman. These two pieces of good news overwhelmed me with joy.

In this happy mood, I went to the house of Sir William Beechey, the portrait painter. He was holding a canvas to rouse the envy of Mani and Shapur. It was a marvellous portrait and I told him it was the best one he had painted since I had first made his acquaintance.

Sir William Beechey told me that, by command of the King, an exhibition is held yearly to judge progress or decline in the arts. Each artist takes his best canvas to the place appointed for the exhibition and they are hung for people of all classes to see. An entrance fee is charged, which yields about 4000 *tomans*, and the money is used to support artists who have lost their eyesight or poor young art students during the coming year. I congratulated him and said what an excellent custom this was: Blessed is he who gives from the heart.

Sir William Beechey told me that his own reward would be my coming to the studio so that he could paint my portrait for the exhibition. He hoped that the public would be so pleased with an Iranian figure that they would increase their donations – and at the same time increase his reputation.

I remarked that he had already painted my likeness, but he said that he had delivered that portrait to the East India Company. So I stayed for a while and that skilful artist made a rapid sketch.[1]

I returned home to greet the wife of Sir Harford Jones, who had kindly and politely come to thank me for securing his Majesty the King of England's permission for her husband to include heraldic emblems of his Majesty the Shahanshah of Iran in his own coat of arms and to emblazon them on his carriage.[2] Her speech pleased me greatly.

[1] This sketch must have been for the half-length portrait exhibited at the Royal Academy in 1811 and which was last recorded at Rainy's auction in 1839. The EIC full-length portrait appeared at the 1810 exhibition. See the entry for 27 April.

[2] Harford Jones refused the Persian Order of the Sun because it had been bestowed on the French Envoy, General Gardane, in 1807. In its stead the Shah issued a *farman* authorizing him to incorporate the Royal arms of Persia into his own coat of arms. Sir Denis Wright points out that this was a unique distinction: see *The English Amongst the Persians*, Heinemann, London, 1977, p. 38.

Saturday, 10 March

A FAITHFUL COURIER ARRIVED: like the hoopoe sent by Solomon to the Queen of Sheba, he had crossed mountains and deserts and seas to bring welcome news from Mirza Mohammad Shafi, the *Motamad od-Doleh*, and the *Amin od-Doleh*.

I removed the seals from the letter and learned that my own letters had reached Iran and that my Government was aware of my situation here. By the highest authority I am commanded to complete the Treaty of Friendship with the utmost speed and to return to Iran with the money and arms stipulated in the Treaty. I am to make this clear to the English Government and to brook no delay. In addition, they desire that an ambassador of the highest stature be appointed to represent this Christian state both in times of peace and in times of war with Russia: the presence of a skilled diplomatist should secure the just return to Iran of Tiflis and the surrounding area.

Of course, the English ministers and councillors have already consulted and complied with the requests of the First Vizir of Iran: the agreement has already been drafted as described in the pages of this journal; the embassy has already been entrusted to Sir Gore Ouseley, a skilful and prudent counsellor who is fluent in Persian and Arabic, and eloquent in Turkish, Greek and English; and scribes of elegant calligraphy attached to the King's Office in London have already been assigned to write out his Letters of Credence.

The arrival of news from Iran filled me with such great happiness that I wanted to celebrate with my sympathetic English friends. I gathered them all together and we mounted horses to ride out into the country for a game of polo.

In that same meadow some lovely ladies were riding: the curved daggers of their eyebrows could have drawn blood from the hearts of the bravest men! I thought to myself how wonderful it would be if the men – and indeed the ladies – of the Iranian Court could be in that meadow to learn how to ride and gallop. I was completely captivated watching the ladies ride, and I struggled to suppress my desires.

In the evening we were all invited to dine at Lord Dartmouth's house.[1] After dinner musicians played reed-like instruments to cleanse our hearts of sorrow and one of the musicians sang a melancholy English song.

Later, Lady Arden rose and remarked that a beautiful Italian woman named Catalani,[2] who has not appeared in London for three years, was singing at the Opera this evening. She suggested that we all go and we agreed.

When we arrived we found so many people drawn there by her fame that it took much searching to find seats. Her performance was superb and her talent was highly praised by those who attended the Opera regularly. I asked about her, wondering why, after all this time, I had not heard her sing until this evening. Had she been ill? One of the lords explained to me that during the six-month Opera season Madame Catalani appears only two or three times because such is her reputation that she commands a fee of 5000 *tomans*.

The lord asked me if I were surprised by this sum and I admitted to being astonished: a high-ranking general is said to receive a salary of 1000 *tomans* a year, yet a female entertainer is paid 5000 *tomans* for three nights' work!

It was very late when I returned home to rest.

[1] George Legge (1755-1810), 3rd Earl of Dartmouth, lived at 12 Berkeley Square.

[2] Angelica Catalani (1789-1849), the famous Italian soprano, sang in London with huge success from 1806.

Monday, 12 March

The Princess of Wales gave a most sumptuous dinner to the Persian Ambassador, and his suite, on Monday last, at Kensington Palace. A grand Concert succeeded in the evening, at which Madame Catalani, Naldi, &c. assisted. The whole entertainment was so fascinatingly festive as to arrest the visitors till between four and five the next morning.

(*The Morning Herald*, 17 March)

WE RODE TO THE HOUSE of the Princess of Wales,[1] which is by the King's Gardens. The rooms are beautifully decorated and hung with large mirrors, but the ceilings are so low that the guests were afraid of hitting their heads while they are dancing.

The Italian singer, Madame Catalani, banished sorrow from our hearts with her beautiful voice. Miss Pole and her pretty sister were ornaments of the assembly. They danced with such enthusiasm that all the nobles and their wives applauded and cried, 'Bravo!'

Today was the Princess of Wales' anniversary.[2] It seems that the Prince and Princess of Wales feel no affection for each other – they live apart. This house belongs to the Princess and that is why the celebration was held there.

[1] The Prince of Wales married in 1795 his first cousin Princess Caroline (1768-1821), daughter of George III's sister Augusta and the Duke Karl II of Brunswick-Wolfenbüttel. The marriage was a disaster from the beginning and the couple lived apart.

[2] The Princess of Wales' birthday was 17 May. Abul Hassan must have misunderstood the occasion for the party, which *The Morning Herald* reported was in his honour.

Wednesday, 14 March

THIS MORNING SIR GORE OUSELEY and Mr Morier came to the house to tell me that today Sir Gore Ouseley was to have the honour of kissing the King of England's hand before leaving to take up his appointment as Ambassador to Iran. They left and I awaited their return.

Several hours later they came in and Sir Gore Ouseley said: 'I wish you had been with us at the levée – you would have enjoyed his Majesty's pleasantries!'

When I asked about the Royal humour, he said: 'After enquiring about your health, the King asked if you had learned to dance in the English manner and if you had learned to cope with the coquetry of Englishwomen. He told me not to allow you to dance if it embarrasses you!'

I replied that if ever it occurred to an Englishwoman to ask me to dance, I should certainly not refuse!

Then I asked about the state of our affairs and Sir Gore Ouseley said that although his ambassadorship had been approved, certain details will take a few more days.

Thursday, 15 March

WE MOUNTED HURRICANE-FAST HORSES and rode out into the country. It happened that we met the noble Prince, the Duke of Cumberland, who is also fond of the countryside. The Prince remarked that I had lately abandoned the society of my friends, and he kindly asked the reason why.

I told him that for a while I had not been very well. Then I had been busy with correspondence and the conclusion of my mission, the writing of the Treaty of Friendship between our two countries. I had therefore been deprived of the honour of meeting the noble Prince. I was out riding in the country to relieve my anxiety and highly delighted by the honour of encountering his Royal Highness.

The Prince was pleased by my speech and said that in the spring he would take me hunting every day.

'If you have any affection for me,' I replied, 'help me to achieve my greatest wish: to return to Iran and kiss the foot of the Throne of the Shahanshah, Refuge of Iran.'

> *Not a night goes by that in grief is not spent,*
> *The stars are my sighs, the sky is my lament.*

The Prince said: 'Thank God, the Treaty will strengthen the friendship between our two exalted monarchs and enable them to triumph over their enemies. Your embassy is nearing its completion, so do not despair. I shall do my best for you.'

In the evening I went to a party crowded with people, including the Prince of Wales, the third Prince, the Duke of Clarence, and ministers and lords whose wives adorned the assembly with their beauty.[1] The din of their drinking reached the shining heavens!

This was the first time I had taken my Iranian servants with me. They were ignorant of English customs and they all exclaimed: 'What a unique place this is! Princes and ministers and high-ranking dignitaries mix happily with sunny-faced women, singing and dancing to banish care! Would that our own country could adopt the customs of the English nobility!'

Miss Wellesley, daughter of the Minister for Foreign Affairs, arrived with her sister and their distinguished mother[2] to decorate the assembly with their presence. They were very kind and friendly to me.

Truly, it would be impossible to choose the most beautiful among English beauties, but if one could name that unique pearl, then this verse of Khajeh Hhafez (may God's blessing be upon him) would apply:

> *The crown of womankind alone you wear,*
> *To you all beauties must their tribute bear.*

I recited the verse and my dear friend, Sir Gore Ouseley, translated it for the lovely ladies. They all applauded with enthusiasm!

Then all the young ladies – fairy-figured, rose-cheeked, jasmine-scented – joined hands with the handsome and graceful, cypress-tall young men, and they began to dance in friendly fashion: it might have been the Garden of Eden. They had all been drinking wine, but none of them was over-amorous or tipsy!

The Prince of Wales had the kindness to ask, with a smile, if the fortune-blessed girl who had been frightened by my huge beard had finally been tamed; and I replied:

> *If that strong-willed maid were a wild gazelle,*
> *I'd have tamed her now, I have tried so well,*
> *But she never a moment slackens her pace*
> *To allow my heart to relax a spell.*

The Prince was pleased with my verse. He said he was coming to my party tomorrow evening and that he would try to banish anxiety from my heart. At once, I replied with this verse of Saadi:

> *So royal a falcon I greet you.*
> *Come into my nest I entreat you.*
> *It is but a humble dark dwelling,*
> *You'll light it the moment I seat you.*

That Ornament of the Kingdom said, 'Bravo!' and then rose from his place. All the guests left for home and also said goodbye to our host.

At home I gave instructions to the servants about my reception tomorrow in honour of the Prince of Wales. I told them that they could borrow anything they needed from the house of my dear friend Sir Gore Ouseley, and that they must take the greatest care in preparing the food lest the tender digestion of the exalted Prince should suffer.

And so ended another day

[1] The only large party reported in the newspapers was the Duchess of Newcastle's, but there was no mention of Abul Hassan or the Prince of Wales.

[2] The Marquis Wellesley married the French actress Hyacinthe Gabrielle Roland in 1794, after the birth of their five children, who were illegitimate. By early 1810 the Wellesleys were seeking a legal separation; *The Morning Post*, 21 February, reported that the Marchioness and her family had moved to a house in Grosvenor Square at the corner of South Audley Street. Their two daughters were Anne, Lady Abdy, and Hyacinthe.

Friday, 16 March

THIS EVENING I ENTERTAINED an assembly of guests including beautiful, jasmine-scented, heart-ravishing ladies. There was an uproar when the Prince of Wales arrived,

171

preceded by footmen in gold-trimmed livery bearing jewel-studded torches. With great joy I rushed forward to greet the noble Prince: 'Your Royal Highness' auspicious presence illuminates a humble foreigner's abode – a thousand times welcome!'[1]

The Prince thanked me and said: 'Now that the highest degree of amity and concord has been established between our two Governments and heartfelt affection exists between our two high-minded monarchs, it is time to shut the doors on ceremony and protocol – let us eat, drink and be merry!' The Prince asked me what news I had from my heart-ravishing sweetheart! Then he sat down on a gilded chair and ordered the musicians to strike up the music for dancing. During the evening the illustrious Prince was so amusing and clever with words that the guests could not contain their laughter.

At the end of the evening, when the Prince rose to leave, I accompanied him – a shadow beside the brilliant sun. He thanked me and left for home.

'*Sobhanallah!* Good God!' I said to Sir Gore Ouseley. 'How extraordinary it is that so powerful a Prince acts with such condescension to ordinary people!' My dear friend explained that it was because of this that the people of England and her colonies revere the monarchy and are willing to sacrifice themselves in time of war.

England is a country full of wonders: her Government of ministers, general and admirals, her architecture and inventions amaze even the wisest of men. It seems that God who created the Universe chooses special people on whom to shower special blessings.

---

[1] *The Morning Herald,* 17 March, reported that all the Royal Dukes were present 'to pay their compliments to the Illustrious Stranger'.

Monday, 19 March

I ROSE AND SAID MY PRAYERS. I was sitting with my head bowed in the collar of reflection when a note arrived from Sir Gore Ouseley saying that he had news from Calcutta which he would tell me when we met. Mr Morier was with me and I told him it appeared that Malcolm may have gone on an embassy to Iran.[1]

In the evening, at Lord Keith's house,[2] Sir Gore Ouseley told me that Lord Minto had written to say that a representative of the East India Company at Bushire had gone to the capital of the Sultan of Sultans and that Malcolm would soon follow.

I was surprised and said: 'How could the Company send an envoy to Iran who, two years before, had been refused an audience by the Shah and forced to return to India; who said that he would have been arrested if he had not fled from Iran? How could the Iranians trust a man who threatened an invasion of their country – a plan supported by Lord Minto? How could the Company, instead of honouring Sir Harford Jones, wish to dismiss him – the man who has succeeded in evicting the French and gaining the respect of the Iranians? This is an insult to the King of England, whose representative he is! The Company knows that I am in England as the devoted servant of my country and yet they do not wait to see the outcome of my mission: once again they send Malcolm to Iran!'

[1] Malcolm's three missions to Persia are outlined in the Introduction, pp. 15-18.

[2] The Keiths lived at 45 Harley Street, one block from Abul Hassan.

Tuesday, 20 March

THIS MORNING I TOOK the letters I had written to officials of the Government of his Majesty the Shahanshah of Iran to Lord Wellesley's office and gave them to the young Englishman who is leaving for Istanbul. In my letters I explained that Sir Harford Jones would be expected to vacate his house and leave for England before the arrival of Sir Gore Ouseley.

This evening I went to the Opera with my friends. Because there was a new programme, the theatre was fuller than usual and many of the beautiful ladies had trouble finding seats.

From there we went on to a musical evening at the house of a lady. Mrs Perceval was there. A middle-aged lady said to Sir Gore Ouseley: 'I hear that what's-his-name speaks English!' 'Yes,' said Sir Gore Ouseley, 'would you like to talk to him?' She said yes, and I asked her in English how many children she had. The lady laughed and said she was not married – yet!

It was a very pleasant evening.

Thursday, 22 March

The dialogue between the Persian Ambassador and an illustrious lady, as given in some of the papers, is pretty well for the close of a Persian Tale, *but will make a sorry figure among* matters of fact.

(*The Morning Post*, March 22)

THE KING'S DEPUTY MASTER of the Ceremonies called on me. He conveyed the King's good wishes and expressed his concern because I seemed to be hiding myself away. He also brought friendly greetings from Lord Wellesley.[1]

While we were talking, Sir Gore Ouseley arrived in happy mood: 'Today, Thursday, I met with the Prime Minister and it was arranged that next Wednesday we have an audience of the King to complete our business.'

---

[1] On 21 March Abul Hassan failed to attend the King's Levée at which all the other foreign envoys were present, claiming that he was unwell.

Friday, 23 March

Mirza Abul Hassan was one day waited upon by a deputation from the Society for Promoting Christian Knowledge, composed of three Reverend Gentlemen, who in their robes presented him with a Bible and prayer-book superbly bound, and addressed him a speech written on parchment. As they spoke the address he was requested to stand up, which he willingly did; but when they had departed, his servants were all unanimous that he had been made an Isauvi, *that is, a Christian.*

[*(Morier II*, Appendix, p. 404)

AFTER RISING AND SAYING my morning prayers, I intended to go out into the country, but Mr Morier came in with some 'padres' – that is to say, priests of the church – who had come to call on me.

Their leader, who was dressed in black, held a long piece of leather, like the deer-skins they tan in India, which was inscribed with passages from the Gospels. He opened it and read a passage.

My Iranian servants became extremely agitated, believing the priest had converted me to Christianity! But I explained that he was simply reciting a few prayers.

He promised that before I left for Iran he would send me a few Bibles for the edification of the Iranian people. Then the priests said good-bye and left.

PLATE 28

Persian Musicians: the first plays the violin-like
kamancheh; *the second sings, fanning his mouth
with a piece of paper to aid his ululations; the third
plays the tambourine; and the last beats two small
drums. Engraved from a drawing by James
Morier for his second book of* Travels.

PLATE 29

*Sir Harford Jones Brydges' Coat of Arms, showing
the Qajar crown, the Persian Lion and Sun, and
the motto 'By Royal Favour' in Persian.*

Saturday, 24 March

SIR GORE OUSELEY CAME. After the usual compliments I showed him the books the priests had brought for me the day before. I told him about the prayers they had recited and, with a smile, I said: 'I told the priests I was no longer content just to be an ambassador. I had become weary of Islam and wished to study other religions and to find a guide along the path of truth. The priests were delighted: they recited the prayers of their faith for me and promised to explain fully the Books of the Gospel!' We laughed together and Sir Gore Ouseley said how happy they would be to make converts from all religions!

As we were invited to the house of Mr [?Dent][1] we rode there together. When we arrived, our host took us first into his library, where he keeps a wonderful collection of Persian and Arabic books and European paintings. I looked at each book carefully.

Then we went to the dining-room where we found a distinguished assembly of nobles gathered around the beautifully decorated table. Lovely ladies illuminated the party with their radiance. The Duke of York honoured the assembly with his presence.

Also present was Mr Sheridan,[2] a distinguished Member of Parliament, who is possessed of all the talents and is famous for his wit. He had heard of my meeting with the priests and, with some humour, suggested that I should have exchanged a copy of the Qoran for the Bible they had given me. It happened that at that moment I was holding a rather large knife in my hand, so I replied: 'Not having a Qoran immediately to hand, perhaps I should send them this!' Everyone laughed.

---

[1] Possibly John Dent, Tory MP for Lancaster, who lived at 10 Hertford Street. He had served in the Bengal Army.

[2] Richard Brinsley Sheridan (1751-1816), theatre manager and dramatist.

Sunday, 25 March

SIR GORE OUSELEY came to the house. 'Spring is here!' he said. 'Although ten days still remain until the first of Rabi ul-Awal,[1] there are already signs of spring in the fields and meadows. Today I am going to take you to the country, to the home of the widow of a German prince.'[2]

So we drove through the pleasant countryside for four miles until we came to a heavenly house overlooking the Thames.[3] The good lady welcomed us with so much kindness and affection that I still blush to think of it. She led us to an upper storey:

> *To heaven it says, as it towers so high,*
> *'You are the earth; it is I am the sky!'*

The house is magnificently designed; there is even a charming small theatre. The lovely garden is planted with junipers and cypress trees. The tops of the firs seem to touch the firmament.

We entered a room overlooking the river which they call the 'gallery', where a rare collection of Chinese porcelain is arranged on glass shelves. Another room houses every kind of musical instrument: I was told that our hostess can play them all and that she is without peer in her knowledge of music. She also has a splendid library. In her youth she was incomparable in beauty, grace and charm; and even now, in old age, her face bears the traces of youthful beauty.

The evening passed delightfully, eating and drinking, in that exhilarating place.

---

[1] In 1810 the first day of Rabi ul-Awal corresponded with 5 April.

[2] The Margravine of Anspach: Elizabeth Berkeley (1750-1828), daughter of the 4th Earl of Berkeley. She married first William Craven (1738-91), 6th Baron Craven, by whom she had three sons and three daughters. They separated in 1783 and she travelled on the continent, finally making her home in Anspach. On the death of Lord Craven she married Christian Frederick Charles Alexander, Margrave of Brandenburgh, Anspach and Beyreuth (1736-1806). In 1792 the Margrave ceded his principality to Prussia and they came to live in England. The Margravine was a musician and dramatist whose plays were performed publicly as well as in her private theatre at Brandenburgh House. Her memoirs, first published in 1826, have been edited by A. M. Broadley and Lewis Melville in *The Beautiful Lady Craven*, 2 vols, John Lane, London, 1914.

[3] In 1792 the Anspachs purchased the mid-seventeenth-century mansion on the river at Hammersmith which they named Brandenburgh House.

179

Monday, 26 March

IN THE MORNING we got into the carriage and that kind lady gave us some provisions for the journey. As a souvenir, she gave us an excellent cheese for which the region is famous, and which is said to strengthen the five senses.

Sir Gore Ouseley told me that we were to call on the wife of the Prime Minister before going on to the house of the fifth Royal Prince, the Duke of Cumberland,[1] where we were invited in the evening.

When we arrived at the house of that modest lady, she opened the doors of kindness and affection to us. She paid us so much attention that I was quite overwhelmed.

I asked her to intercede with her husband on my behalf and she readily agreed; but she insisted that the Prime Minister was so well disposed towards me that I had no need of her recommendation.

> THE DUKE OF CUMBERLAND'S DINNER TO THE PERSIAN AMBAS-
> SADOR. *Tuesday* [sic], *his Royal Highness entertained his Excellency
> Mirza Abul Hassan and a distinguished circle of friends, &c. at his
> superb apartments in the Palace of St. James's. . . .*
>
> (*The Morning Post*, 28 March)[2]

Then my dear friend and I went on to the house of the Duke of Cumberland, where we found the Prince of Wales in conversation with the Minister for Foreign Affairs. When we joined the brilliant assembly, the wise Minister greeted me jovially: 'How well you look, God be praised! You must give me the name of the doctor who cured you, so that I may consult him about my own aches and pains!'

I answered that dear Englishman by saying that I knew of no better doctor than chastity, and I quoted a long passage from Jami's *Joseph and Zuleika* which relates that when Joseph (may peace be upon him) was sold as a slave in Egypt, he remained so pure and chaste that God took him under His protection and rewarded his virtue by raising him to the Vizir's throne. The story also appears in the pages of the glorious Qoran. Sir Gore Ouseley gave an elegant translation of the verses which won the praise of the distinguished Duke and the peerless Minister.

I went on to explain why it was necessary to avoid the company of women: 'God the Creator fashioned women and endowed them with great charms in order to test his servants: to observe which ones would choose the path of virtue and which ones the path of perdition. So I have resolved to avoid the coquetry and alluring glances of London's ladies and not to fall victim to their curling locks and dimpled chins. So God has redeemed me and I am free to enjoy conversing with my dear friends, the illustrious Duke, the distinguished ministers, officials and gentlemen, and their lovely ladies.'

Then the Prince ordered the cup-bearers to bring more wine and the musicians to entertain his guests with their songs. The English beauties took cups overflowing with wine and were soon tipsy. Each took the arm of a partner and captured the hearts of those watching with the twists and turns of their dancing.

The room became so overheated that I felt quite breathless and feared my soul might fly from the cage of my body! The Prince of Wales remarked to Lord Eldon, the Lord Chancellor,[3] and the Minister for Foreign Affairs that it was so hot one could hardly speak!

The Prince of Wales put his hand in his pocket and brought out an ivory comb which he gave me as a present. Then he very kindly showed me to another room where I rested with my companions and recovered my breath.

We went on to a party at the house of the Marquis of Salisbury where beautiful ladies with glowing faces to delight their husbands were dancing, free from the cares of the world.

But I saw one bewildered old lady – who might have sailed in the Ark with Noah – who was trembling like a willow-tree. I feared she would be trampled on in the crowd.

When the party ended the guests left for home.
And so ended another day.

[1] Prince Ernest Augustus (1771-1851), Duke of Cumberland and, on the death of William IV, King of Hanover.

[2] *The Times* of 29 March reported that the Duke of Cumberland's party for Abul Hassan took place on the Monday. As Abul Hassan went on to the Salisburys' assembly, this is probably correct.

[3] John Scott (1751-1838), 1st Earl of Eldon, Lord Chancellor from 1801 (with a fourteen-month interval) until 1827.

Tuesday, 27 March

I HAD FINISHED SAYING MY MORNING prayers when Sir Gore Ouseley came in with a broadly built lord and a colonel. After the usual friendly compliments, Sir Gore Ouseley took my arm and we went to a sculptor's studio where I saw works of art even more marvellous than the rock carvings at Bisitun.[1] Just as the painter paints a man's likeness on canvas, this master carves a man's likeness in marble. First he makes a clay model; then he copies it in stone.

He showed us an image of the Minister for Foreign Affairs which was so good it seemed that the stone was alive and the Minister himself was with us. I was told that when a man dies his relations often console themselves by ordering his image carved on a stone tablet. Rather in the same way, a group of Lord Wellesley's friends in India, where he was Governor-General, have sent this sculptor 10,000 *tomans* to carve his portrait in stone.[2]

Sir Gore Ouseley then explained that the reason for taking me to visit the sculptor was that he wanted a bust of me to take with him to Iran. I am to return in a week's time so that the master can begin the work.[3]

On our way out we went through a vast gallery containing statues of men and women like those of ancient Rome.

---

[1] The famous rock carving at Bisitun, near Kermanshah in north-west Iran, celebrates the triumph of the Achaemenian King Darius (reigned 521-485 BC) over nine of his enemies.

[2] John Bacon junior (1777-1859) exhibited a statue of Marquis Wellesley, destined for Calcutta, at the Royal Academy in 1808. In the same year he also exhibited a bust of Wellesley. In 1809 he exhibited a 'group for Bombay – Marquis Wellesley'.

[3] Bacon made two busts of Abul Hassan, one of which was exhibited at the Royal Academy in 1811. See Graves, *ibid*. Both busts have disappeared.

Wednesday, 28 March

The Persian Ambassador attended the Levée yesterday, to pay his respects to his Majesty in consequence of his Excellency being indisposed last week when all the other Foreign Ministers attended his Majesty's Levée.

(*The Times*, 29 March)

I WOKE FROM SLEEP hoping to have confirmation of my audience with the King. A note arrived for Sir Gore Ouseley from the Minister for Foreign Affairs saying that although his Majesty had expected to see me last Wednesday, he would nevertheless be pleased to receive me today. Accordingly, we set out together for the King's Palace.

On the occasion of my first audience I did not take sufficient notice of the Court ceremonial. So today I watched with special care. Footmen lined the route from the entrance to the Throne Room, which is on the upper floor. There, the great ministers and councillors, in formal Court dress, formed a semi-circle, like heavenly stars – about fifty in all.

The King entered from a small private room adjoining and spoke with great condescension to each one in turn. Because his eyesight is so poor, a Court official stands behind him to announce each person's name.

When it came to my turn, his Majesty said: 'Alas, in England the sun is veiled, but of moonlight we have plenty at this time of year!' I dared to say that I preferred the sunshine of Iran to the moonlight of London! And as I had by now learned a few words of English from my dear friend Sir Gore Ouseley, I went on to apologize for my inability to attend last week's levée – illness had deprived me of that pleasure.

The King was surprised that I spoke in English, and in return he asked me if I had seen anything remarkable in his city. 'At this very moment,' I replied, 'in your Majesty's presence, I am looking at the most extraordinary thing yet! Only two nights ago, at the house of the Duke of Cumberland, I met Lord Eldon. He looked just like all the other gentlemen; but today – he has covered his head with the fleece of a sheep!' The King smiled and said I must record his question and my answer in my journal. I promised to do so.

Then the Minister for Foreign Affairs came up to ask how I was; and the King spoke to Sir Gore Ouseley at length about Persian books.

When the levée was at an end, all those who had had the honour of being presented knelt on one knee and kissed the King's hand. We were then given permission to leave the King's presence and we returned home.

Thursday, 29 March

I WAS INVITED TO THE HOUSE of Mr Hope,[1] which is not far from my own. Mr Hope is a Dutch merchant who has lived in London for some time. His house is magnificent, with a forecourt like a palace. Inside, there was a large assembly of English ladies and gentlemen, but the house is so vast it seemed almost empty! The paintings and porcelains – which are displayed on shelves – are said to be worth 100,000 *tomans*.

Mrs Hope is an Irish beauty – her mouth and teeth are particularly striking. Her husband, on the contrary, is incredibly ugly[2] – if you were to see him in a dream, you would never wake again! They say that she was married to him for his money – that her father was a 'padre' who forced her into a union she was not eager to accept.

Among the guests was a handsome Armenian youth, dressed in Turkish clothes, who was surrounded by gentlemen and their ladies. A high-ranking nobleman, whom I had met in Bath on my way to London, grasped him by the arm, and the ladies were very attentive. They danced with him constantly. I was pleased that they showed such hospitality to a stranger, but I thought to myself: '*Sobhanallah!* Good God! These distinguished ladies and gentlemen show as much attention and courtesy to an Armenian nobody as if he were one of their own brothers returned from a long journey; whereas he should be standing at attention by their chairs, to serve their commands!'

I said to Sir Gore Ouseley: 'This display of condescension to an Armenian is excessive and – in my opinion – wrong!' He agreed; and when we returned home, he promised that in future he would not allow the Armenian to be admitted to any party I attended. I replied: 'The English know that I wish only the best for our two Governments. They invite me to their homes because they know me as a trustworthy ambassador; but consorting with an Armenian can only bring them dishonour.' Sir Gore Ouseley apologized.

[1] Thomas Hope (1770?-1831), antiquarian, collector and author of several books on interior decoration, came from a wealthy family of English merchants who settled in Holland in the seventeenth century. He returned to England in about 1796 after the French occupation of Holland. In 1806 he married Louisa Beresford, daughter of William de la Poer Beresford, Archbishop of Tuam in Ireland. They lived in Duchess Street.

[2] Following a dispute over the price of a picture, a French artist named Dubost painted a caricature of Mr and Mrs Hope called *Beauty and the Beast*, which he exhibited publicly in 1810.

Friday, 30 March

The Persian Ambassador attracts the particular attention of the Hyde
Park Belles *as an* Equestrian *of a singular order, for he rides in
silken pantaloons of such wide dimensions, that, being inflated by the
wind, make his Excellency appear like flying to a* Turkish Haram,
than riding for the pure air in Rotten Row.

(*The Morning Herald,* 29 March)

I WAS FEELING BILIOUS and unwell, so Sir Gore Ouseley and
Mr Morier went by themselves to keep an engagement and
I went riding in the King's Garden. There, I happened to
meet Lady Arden and her second daughter, Helena. I dismounted
and relaxed with my friends – we talked about that Armenian.

And so passed another day.

Saturday, 31 March

SIR GORE OUSELEY'S distinguished brother, Sir William Ouseley, who will accompany him to Iran, has arrived in London. He is extremely intelligent and knows six languages. Although he has had no formal lessons in Persian, he has translated several Persian books into English and is an expert on calligraphy, the construction of prose and poetry, and the history of the shahs of Iran. He is now occupied with a translation of the *Iskandar-nameh*.[1]

In the evening we were invited to the house of Lord Mountnorris[2], father of Lord Valentia. The Duke of Sussex was also invited, but did not attend. There was dancing and, after dinner, general conversation and music. Smiling, our host's wife said to Sir Gore Ouseley: 'I hear the Ambassador has a pleasing voice – perhaps he will sing for us!' I realized they were teasing me, so I said that my chest was bothering me and my voice was affected – otherwise I should not refuse.

The evening came to an end and everyone went home.

[1] *Iskandar-nameh:* The Book of Alexander the Great, the fifth of the poems in the *Khamseh* (Quintet) of Nizami.

[2] Arthur Annesley (1744-1816), 1st Earl of Mountnorris, married second in 1783 Sarah, daughter of Sir Henry Cavendish. He was succeeded by his son, the Viscount Valentia. The Mountnorrises lived at 2 Stratford Place.

APRIL

1810

Sunday, 1 April

SIR GORE OUSELEY and his family have gone to spend three days in the country to make plans for the embassy to Iran. I went with Mr Hamilton[1] and Sir William and Lady Ouseley[2] to the house of Lord Elgin,[3] who was formerly Ambassador to Istanbul. We went there to see the marbles he brought back from Greece: they are carved with men and women, birds and beasts. Lord Elgin spent 25,000 *tomans* shipping the ancient marbles to England so that they might be studied by English masters. Mr Hamilton asked me what I thought of the sculptures and what value I would place on them. I said I would not give five *tomans* for the lot of them!

When we left, after seeing the collection, it was raining heavily and we hurried home.

[1] As Private Secretary to Lord Elgin at Constantinople, William Richard Hamilton (1777-1859) had superintended the removal of the Grecian marbles to England. In 1809 he was appointed an Under-Secretary of State at the Foreign Office.

[2] Sir William Ouseley married in 1796 Julia, daughter of Lieutenant-Colonel John Irving. She did not accompany him to Persia.

[3] Thomas Bruce (1766-1841), 7th Earl of Elgin, was appointed Ambassador to Constantinople in 1799.

PLATE 30

Lamplighter and Apprentice, an engraving for
Pyne's Costumes of Great Britain, *1805.*

PLATE 31

Lord Radstock's house appears on the left in this
engraving of All Souls Church, Langham Place.

Monday, 2 April

*THE DUCHESS DOWAGER OF NEWCASTLE'S BALL On Monday
evening, at her Grace's residence in Charles-street, Berkeley-square,
far excelled every similar entertainment yet produced this season. . . .
The Persian Ambassador wore, for the first time, his state costume,
almost wholly composed or real gold; he wore many jewels. . . .*

(*The Morning Post*, 4 April)

MR MORIER AND I went first to the house of the artist who makes portraits out of clay and stone. As Sir Gore Ouseley wished, I sat for him an hour and he fashioned a perfect likeness of me.

From there we went to visit two painters: the first was a famous artist, appointed by the Royal Family, who has created many large canvases for the Royal Palace; and the second was the artist who painted Sir Harford Jones being received in audience by the Padeshah of Iran.[1] Truly, both are masters of their art.

---

[1] This is almost certainly the painting by Robert Smirke (1752-1845) in the collection of John Lucas-Scudamore, Esq.

Tuesday, 3 April

SIR GORE OUSELEY had arranged for a tutor to give me English lessons; and in return I was teaching him Persian from my own books. But I found that writing English is so different and so much more difficult than speaking it – it would take the lifetime of a Noah – that I made my excuses and dismissed him.

Wednesday, 4 April

SIR GORE OUSELEY returned from his country house. Happily, he told me that the fresh country air, which is far better than London's, has cured his charming wife of her illness.

In the evening I went to an assembly at Lady Stafford's.[1] The house is a splendid one, fit for a King. It is hung with Old Masters: they say that just one of them is worth 10,000 *tomans*.

Mr Morier is in love with Miss Hume, and he was deep in conversation with her.

---

[1] George Granville Leveson-Gower (1758-1833), 2nd Marquis of Stafford (later 1st Duke of Sutherland), married in 1785 Elizabeth, daughter of the 18th Earl of Sutherland, who was Countess of Sutherland in her own right. They lived in what had been Cleveland House, in Cleveland Row off St James's Street.

Thursday, 5 April

Last night Mrs Thomas Hope had a splendid rout at her mansion in Duchess Street.

(The Morning Herald, 6 April)

WITH MY COMPANIONS I went to Mr Hope's house. I have already described his excellent paintings and his beautiful wife. Unfortunately, this evening she was ill in bed.

> *No fever thy delicate frame should endure*
> *I would sacrifice Hope, for the hope of thy cure.*

I thought: 'What a pity your illness is not his; what a pity that you cannot give your fever to Mr Hope in return for your marriage settlement; what a pity that such a delicate creature should burn with fever, while his hideous self should be free from pain!'

Sir William Abdy,[1] whose wife is the daughter of the Minister for Foreign Affairs, greeted me. He too is so ugly that he might be Mr Hope's brother, and I could not help thinking of two Iranian proverbs: 'A sweet melon is devoured by the hyena'; and 'Wherever a fairy is, there is a demon by her side.'

I could not enjoy the splendid assembly, so I went home.

---

[1] Sir William Abdy (1779-1868), 7th and last Baronet, married in 1806 Anne Wellesley, daughter of the Marquis Wellesley.

Friday, 6 April

AFTER SAYING MY PRAYERS, I went riding in the open fields of London and spent some time relaxing. When I returned home, Mr Morier's brother, Mr John Morier, kindly came to call on me. He told me the good news of his appointment to America.[1] I was delighted by this news because he is an intelligent and clever young man who speaks several languages: his Turkish is fluent and his Persian melodious. Truly, all the Morier brothers are equally gifted. The youngest is a lieutenant on a ship, an expert in his field.[2] Their mother is a charming, gracious lady who also has three beautiful, star-blessed daughters. She takes great pains with their education and also teaches them dancing.

In the evening my good friends and I went to the house of the Margravine of Anspach.

On our way there we saw that lamps were lighted at the door of every house and cottage and that the roads were blocked by a multitude of carriages. I asked the reason for the tumult and I was told that a man called Sir Francis Burdett,[3] who is a member of Parliament for London, had spoken against the Government and the King and caused an uproar in Parliament. He was therefore sentenced to two to three months in prison; if the Council agrees, he will be released after the prorogation of Parliament. This evening his supporters were trying to prevent his arrest: they called for every house to light up and they threw stones at the windows of all those who refused.

We went on our way with great difficulty. When we neared Burdett's house,[4] our carriage was stopped and we were ordered to remove our hats; but when our driver told them I was the Iranian Ambassador, they respectfully doffed their hats to *me* and allowed us to pass.

When my friends and I reached our hostess's house we found among the nobles the fat Duke and his Duchess who are always so

196

kind to me at parties. He has some connection with the Americas.

Two Portuguese girls were dancing beautifully for the guests when Lord Keith and Miss Mercer came in – totally dishevelled and covered with mud. I asked what had happened and they said that they had refused to remove their hats to the mob – as a result, stones had been thrown at them. For the same reason, many people had turned back and I did not enjoy the evening very much because so many of my friends were absent.

The guests began to dance and asked me to join them, but I said I did not wish to dance, especially on such a depressing evening. So I left and got into the carriage with my friends. On our way home we passed Lord Wellesley's house and I saw that his windows had been broken in the rioting.

[1] John Morier had just been promoted to be Secretary of Legation at Washington.

[2] William Morier (1790-1864) served in the Mediterranean and Lisbon in 1807-10. He rose to the rank of vice-admiral.

[3] Sir Francis Burdett (1770-1844), 5th Baronet, MP for Westminster; radical Whig and parliamentary reformer; one of the most popular politicians of the day. The Burdett 'affair' arose from a letter he published in *The Political Register*, 24 March 1810, accusing the House of Commons of abuse of privilege by excluding strangers, including the press, from debates on the disastrous Walcheren expedition. As the result of a motion arguing that the letter was 'libellous and scandalous, reflecting on the just rights and privileges of the House', he was arrested and taken to the Tower on 9 April. He was released in late June after Parliament had recessed.

[4] Burdett lived at 80 Piccadilly, near the corner of Bolton Street.

Saturday, 7 April

Scarcely an hotel at the west end of town escaped a species of domicili-
ary visit from the mob on Friday and last night. . . . we understand
the windows of Marquis Wellesley's house, those of Lord Dart-
mouth's, the Duke of Montrose's, Sir Robert Peel's and Mr Wellesley
Pole's, were entirely demolished on Friday, and most of the houses
entirely covered with mud.

(The News, 8 April)

IN THE MORNING IT WAS reported that most of the ministers' and councillors' houses were stoned and damaged last
night, including those of the Prime Minister and Lord
Westmorland, who is one of the councillors. The King's Army was
called out to quell the rioting and soldiers of the cavalry and infantry
are posted around the city.

I left the house to go riding as usual. I met some English friends
and acquaintances who tried to discourage me from going out today.
But I paid no attention to their warnings and went into the Park.

I met Mrs Perceval, wife of the Prime Minister, riding in a
handsome carriage. She, too, advised me against being out of doors
and warned me that today's rioting was worse than last night's. She
asked me not to stay out lest, God forbid, I should meet with
violence or disrespect. I did not heed her advice and when I encountered the soldiers they all took off their hats to me as a sign of respect.
When I asked why the rioting had not yet been suppressed, they said
that the councillors were still deliberating and that without a warrant
from the Council they could not remove the criminal from his house
to the King's prison.

I was utterly amazed! If such a situation had lasted for several days
in one of Iran's cities, 2000 or more people would have been executed by now. I was even more perplexed by the length of time the
Council was taking to order the criminal's arrest.

I am recording these facts to demonstrate the freedom and bene-volence enjoyed by the citizens of London. Because the Government is concerned that no innocent person should be molested, no one is arrested until his crime has been proven.

After making my enquiries into this affair, I returned home. And so passed another day.

Monday, 9 April

IN THE MORNING I HEARD that Sir Francis Burdett has been arrested and taken to the Tower. Ten to fifteen of his sup-porters have been killed. His term of imprisonment is three months, after which he will be able to resume his seat in Parlia-ment. In the Tower he is not kept in chains and he may even receive visits from his friends.

Calm was restored to the city and in the evening I went to a party at the house of Lady Saltoun,[1] a young and kind neighbour of mine. It was late when I returned home.

[1] Margery, Lady Saltoun (died 1851), was the widow of Alexander Fraser, 15th Lord Saltoun of Abernethy, who had died in 1793 at the age of thirty-five. She was herself a Fraser, daughter of Simon Fraser of Ness Castle.

Tuesday, 10 April

SIR GORE OUSELEY came to see me with Mr Grant, the Chairman of the Company, and the Deputy Chairman, Mr Astell. Mr Astell informed me that he is to be raised to the position of Chairman of the Court of Directors.[1] I thought Mr Astell looked very young for the post.[2]

I congratulated Mr Grant on his skilled handling of Iranian affairs. He told me that the guns destined for Iran have been collected together and are ready for shipping.

We discussed the riots and the fact that the glaziers are doing a flourishing business because of all the broken windows.

In the evening my faithful friend and I went to the Opera.[3] The theatre was much more crowded than usual and our special box was changed.

After watching the performance we returned home.

[1] At the yearly election of officers of the Court of Directors of the East India Company, the Deputy Chairman always succeeded the Chairman.

[2] William Astell was thirty-six; Charles Grant sixty-four.

[3] *Atalida,* with Catalani and Tramezzani.

Wednesday, 11 April

IN THE EVENING I WENT with my faithful friend Sir Gore Ouseley to a concert in a very large house with high ceilings, where a raised platform had been erected.[1] The nobility took part: about 300 of them had gathered to listen to music and English songs. Each lord pays a subscription of some 500 *tomans*; in addition to his wife, he may invite one guest.

A special box was designated for the King. There was also a special entrance for the King and Queen and the Royal Princesses; I entered the house by this special door.

Four of the Royal Dukes were present. The Duke of Cambridge introduced me to the King's sister,[2] who is about eighty years old. After the formalities, he said to her: 'The Persian Ambassador may share his state secrets with some of the ladies, but he's not likely to share them with an old lady like you!' Sir Gore Ouseley and I laughed at this, but she was clearly embarrassed. At this moment Mrs Perceval and Lady Arden joined us and we had some pleasant conversation.

We went on to the house of Lord Limerick:[3] I always call him my 'fellow countryman' because his house is so close to mine and because he is always so friendly towards me.

Miss Pole, the niece of my good friend the Minister for Foreign Affairs, was there. I was especially glad to see her because I had not had recent news of the Minister. I thoroughly enjoyed myself talking to that charming girl and her mother.

[1] The Hanover Square Rooms.

[2] George III's sister, mother of the Princess of Wales, was Princess Augusta (1737-1813). She returned to England in 1807, after the death of her husband Prince Karl, Duke of Brunswick-Wolfenbüttel.

[3] Edmond Henry Pery (1758-1844), 1st Earl of Limerick.

Friday, 13 April

SIR GORE OUSELEY came to the house early in the morning. He kindly helped me to compose a letter to the Prime Minister, asking him to instruct the Minister for Foreign Affairs to arrange for a ship to take us back to Iran. He said that we might be able to leave in one month's time.

Now that early spring has come the sun sometimes shows its face; but sometimes it hides behind the clouds. Every day I take pleasure in going to the open fields of London and meeting the charming lords and lovely ladies who go there too. The trees wear their New Year's robes of honour[1] and fresh breezes blow: it is a paradise.

But at home, in the evenings, I realize that one year has passed since my farewell audience with the Shahanshah of Iran and I weep heartfelt tears of blood. I console myself with verse:

> *O Qibleh of my heart where shall I seek thee?*
> *Within my heart and with my heart I seek thee.*

---

[1] On New Year's Day in Iran, 21 March, it was the custom for the Shah to present new *khalats* – robes of honour – to his courtiers.

Monday, 16 April

SIR DAVID DUNDAS, Commander-in-Chief of the Army, sent two of his officers to my house to invite me to a review of the armed forces in the Park. I accepted the invitation and Sir Gore Ouseley and I mounted our horses and accompanied them to the parade ground.

When we arrived we saw all the soldiers lined up in rows in front of a reviewing stand. The Commander-in-Chief was very kind and complimentary to me and told me he very much wanted me to see this review of the English army.

The youngest Royal Prince, the Duke of Cambridge, marched on with a troop of his brave soldiers.[1] They doffed their caps to the Commander-in-Chief and moved to one side. He was followed by some 100 lords, generals and colonels who led their men past the Commander-in-Chief, removed their caps according to the English custom, and took their places. Then they demonstrated various methods of attack and combat. I was told there are about 3000 cavalry troops; each of the Royal Princes has 500 under his command.

I was viewing the parade with some astonishment and Sir Gore Ouseley asked me the reason. When I said I was amazed to see the Duke of Cambridge removing his hat, he told me that in this country even a prince must salute his Commander-in-Chief.

In England the people are free and no man is forced to serve in the army; every soldier is a volunteer. But it is true that recruiting officers sometimes get young men of eighteen or twenty years so drunk with wine that they readily consent to join the King's service. They are then given red tunics and hats decorated with feathers and marched through the streets to the sound of fife and drum in order to encourage others to join. No soldier may leave the army – he may serve for fifty years or more – even if he was drunk when he agreed to join.

I am told that the nobility willingly send their sons to sea to learn the arts of war. I was amazed to learn that a prince may serve as a 'midshipman', which is several ranks lower than a captain.

After watching the march-past, Sir Gore Ouseley and I walked in the Park, enjoying the trees and the flowers.

From there we went to a vast three-storey building set in a large wooded park on the river at Chelsea. It is called the Royal Hospital[2] and it houses retired soldiers over fifty years of age who spend the rest of their lives in peace and comfort. They are provided with clothing and food by the English Government: 500 men sit down together for meals. Most of the men I saw there had suffered wounds in battle and had had an arm or a leg amputated.

In addition to these soldiers, 12,000 pensioners live at home with their families: they each receive twelve *tomans* a year from the Government. Near the Hospital is another large stone building built eight years ago by the second Royal Prince, the Duke of York, for children whose fathers were killed in the wars.[3]

I do not know if the King is a religious man, but God must be pleased with him for building this house and caring for orphans. And his soldiers must be all the more loyal and willing to risk their lives in battle if they can look forward to a comfortable old age in the Chelsea Hospital.

After touring these buildings we had lunch at General Hulse's[4] house. His house and that of the Commander-in-Chief[5] adjoin the Hospital.

[1] The Duke of Cambridge, a general in the army, was Colonel of the 2nd, or Coldstream, Regiment of Foot Guards.

[2] The Royal Hospital, Chelsea, completed in 1691, was founded by Charles II as an asylum for some 500 old or disabled soldiers.

[3] The Duke of York's Headquarters, King's Road, Chelsea, was begun in 1801 as the Duke of York's School or the Royal Military Asylum for the children of soldiers' widows.

[4] General Sir Samuel Hulse (1747-1837), 3rd Baronet, became Lieutenant-Governor of Chelsea Hospital in 1806 and Governor in 1820.

[5] The Commander-in-Chief, Sir David Dundas, was also Governor of Chelsea Hospital.

Wednesday, 18 April

I WENT TO THE KING'S GARDEN and on my return Sir Gore Ouseley told me that a newspaper had reported that the Iranian Ambassador had taken two Iranian women, dressed in men's clothes, to the military review in the Park.[1] I said to Sir Gore Ouseley: 'What nonsense! There is not a word of truth to it!' Sir Gore Ouseley replied that such false rumours were not uncommon.

In the evening we went to a party where Miss Elphinstone, Lord Keith's beautiful daughter, was extremely courteous and conversed with me in friendly fashion.

It was late when we returned home.

---

[1] *The Morning Post,* 17 April reported: 'The Persian Ambassador was on horseback, with his attendants, and two Ladies dressed in Persian costume. They attracted much notice.'

Good Friday, 20 April

WHEN THE SUN ROSE from the horizon, I mounted my horse and rode to the open fields.

Today was an important holy day for the English, the anniversary of the day Jesus (may peace be upon Him) was crucified on a gallows with four nails. But there were so many people out in the country that it looked more like the day of the Last Judgement.

Saturday, 21 April

IN THE MORNING I got into the carriage with my good friend Sir Gore Ouseley, Mr Morier, Mr John Morier, and the eldest son of the Prime Minister, Mr Perceval. Several of my Iranian servants accompanied us in another carriage.

During the six-mile journey to Greenwich I mentioned to Sir Gore Ouseley that I thought parties should be held in the early hours of the morning before dawn – when it was impossible to sleep anyway because of the noise made by the night watchmen calling out the hours!

We entered a magnificent four-storey building set in a square and surrounded by green parkland traversed by two streams. Nearby were a large church built of marble and another, older building which contained many paintings by masters of that art.[1]

Some 500 sons of naval pensioners were lined up in the principal building. The 2500 old sailors are housed in the adjoining buildings with all their needs provided.

The Governor of the Hospital is Lord Hood,[2] who is eighty-eight years old. He has a house in the grounds. The Governor has a staff of officers and servants to administer the Hospital. Our guide was a very fine man called Sir John Colpoys.[3] He took us to visit the kitchens: the cooking utensils and the food – meat and bread – were very clean. I heard my Iranian servants talking among themselves: one of them, who is particularly lazy, said he would like to live here with the old people – they lead such tranquil lives, he thought it unlikely they would ever die!

Then we went to look at the paintings of historic battles on land and sea and the portraits of past kings of England.

Accompanied by Sir John Colpoys, we left Greenwich in a Royal barge and travelled three miles down the River Thames. In many places on the river straight canals have been dug to cut across meanders and thus shorten the journey. A charge is made to boats for the

PLATE 32

272

*Abul Hassan in riding-dress, by John Kay for his
Original Portraits and Caricature Etchings, 1819.*

PLATE 33

*Claramont, Sir Gore Ouseley's country house at
Cheshunt, Hertfordshire, an engraving made about
1840.*

use of these canals.

The East India Company has constructed its own docks for ship-building and for the unloading of merchandise brought from India by ship.[4] When we arrived, some 10,000 people had already gathered to watch the launching of the new ship.

One of the Royal Princes, the Duke of Clarence, who serves in the Royal Navy, was there to launch the ship. He was accompanied by one of his pretty daughters and he introduced me to her.[5]

The Prince struck the bow of the ship with a bottle of wine and she slipped smoothly into the river. There were many guests on board and a young child shouted: 'We are off! Goodbye!'

[1] Christopher Wren's splendid Naval Hospital, now the Royal Naval College, dates from the end of the seventeenth century.

[2] Admiral Samuel Hood (1724-1816), 1st Viscount Hood, held the post of Governor of the Royal Hospital at Greenwich from 1796 until his death.

[3] Admiral Sir John Colpoys KB (1742?-1821) was Treasurer of the Royal Hospital at Greenwich from 1805 until he succeeded Lord Hood as Governor in 1816.

[4] The East India Docks at Blackwall, on the north bank of the Thames, were opened in 1806.

[5] Prince William Henry, Duke of Clarence (1765-1837), who succeeded to the throne as William IV in 1830, was in 1810 an admiral of the Red.

Monday, 23 April

SIR GORE OUSELEY came to the house early to tell me that in the evening we were invited to a banquet by the Lord Mayor of the City of London which would be attended by many people. He explained that each year the merchants and craftsmen of the City meet to choose a Lord Mayor from among themselves. He is conducted to a church where he solemnly swears that he will govern the people with truth and justice during the coming year. He becomes, in fact, King of the City for a year. He receives a salary of 10,000 *tomans*.

At the end of his year in office, the Lord Mayor invites people of all classes to a banquet in his house, where the tools of trade and the products of all the craft-guilds, even weapons of war, are displayed.

I had heard the title 'Lord Mayor' before and I had assumed that he was like other lords, like the ones whose houses I visit. But it is not a condition for selection that the Lord Mayor be of noble birth: he might be a cobbler or a blacksmith, and he will return to his trade at the end of his year in office.

In the evening Sir Gore Ouseley and I travelled together the several miles to the Lord Mayor's house.[1] The street was so blocked with carriages that we had to wait one hour before alighting. Then several footmen, carrying staffs of gold, made a path for us and conducted us into the house.

The Lord Mayor was standing to greet his guests with great cordiality; but his daughter, who is called the Lady Mayoress, remained seated and (unlike the Queen!) did not bow to anyone. She was, indeed, dressed like a queen and wore diamonds in her hair. It angered me that this girl should be so discourteous to me. I am not, after all, a subject of England! How can it be that the exalted Queen of England stands talking graciously to her subjects while this haughty girl took no notice of anybody? I told Sir Gore Ouseley I wanted to go home: the Lord Mayor is nothing but a brandy-seller –

not even a wine-seller! (In England, a brandy-seller, like a seller of *araq* in Iran, is of lower class than a wine-seller.) The Lord Mayor is called Mr Smith[2] and that girl who took on the airs of a queen is called Miss Smith. Sir Gore Ouseley said I must try to ignore her – she is rude even to princes! He was so insistent that I agreed to stay.

The Lord Mayor was strangely dressed: extraordinary gold chains hung from his neck and, in spite of the heat, he wore a black velvet cloak (like that of a priest) covered with gold lace. He held out his arm to me as if to say: 'See how splendidly and expensively I am dressed; see how far I have come from my little brandy shop!'

Then we went into the dining-room. It was a truly magnificent room: high stone columns were hung with multi-coloured lanterns, ablaze with wax candles. Two sides of the room were lined with tables covered with a profusion of dishes.

Sir Gore Ouseley asked the Lord Mayor where the Iranian Ambassador should sit. The Lord Mayor replied that he did not know where *he* was to sit: the Master of the Ceremonies would seat us, and I would be placed next to him and some of his councillors – representatives of the trades like cobblers and blacksmiths.

At dinner, the Lord Mayor told me that he had invited 500 people to dinner and 4500 to dance afterwards. But none of the Royal Princes or ministers were present, and very few lords. The Lord Mayor did not seem to know what he should eat; he kept asking the footman standing behind him which dishes to choose.

Eventually, the Lady Mayoress was so gracious as to look in my direction and raise her glass to me.

After dinner – according to custom – one of the Lord Mayor's councillors took out a long scroll and called for silence. As usual, the first toast was drunk to the health of the Shah of Iran; then the glasses were raised to the other guests. Sir Gore Ouseley told me that I must now propose a toast to the health of the Lord Mayor. I had not yet risen from my seat when the Master of the Ceremonies loudly called for silence and announced that the Shah of Iran would propose the toast to the Lord Mayor! The guests laughed uproariously at his mistake. Then we drank to the health of 365 merchants who were members of the various guilds, the number corresponding to the number of days in the Lord Mayor's reign.

We rose from the table and went to another room. I sat down and my companions began to dance. The room was long but narrow and the 5000-6000 men and women there could hardly breathe or move.

Miss Mercer and her cousin Miss Elphinstone had come to the ball with Lord Keith. They were standing with me in a corner when there was a disturbance: two ladies had swooned to the floor. A crowd gathered round them, fanning them and trying to give them air.

There was such a mob it was difficult to move. We tried to leave, but Sir Gore Ouseley said it was impossible. Then I completely lost patience and told him that unless he managed to find a way out I would surely expire! As soon as I had said this I fainted; and it was not until one hour later that I came to my senses – in the Lady Mayoress's bedroom!

When I was sufficiently recovered my friends managed with great difficulty to get me outside and into the Lord Mayor's coach (which is even more splendid than the King's).

I am truly amazed that the dignitaries of this land torture themselves by attending receptions where they must mix and converse with tradespeople. That night I did not get a moment's rest. I kept thinking of the office of Lord Mayor and how useless it is. I can only hope it will be abolished.

---

[1] The Mansion House was built in 1739-53 to provide an official residence for the Lord Mayor of the City of London.

[2] Thomas Smith (died 1823) was a leatherseller and Master of the Leathersellers Company 1812-13. Abul Hassan was mistaken about his trade. See A. B. Beaven, *The Aldermen of the City of London*, London, 1908.

Tuesday, 24 April

AFTER LAST NIGHT I was not feeling very well and I stayed in bed late. Lord Keith and some other kind friends who were concerned about me came to ask how I was.

Sir Gore Ouseley decided that I needed a change and insisted that I should spend a few days in the country. So we got into the carriage with Mr Morier and went fifteen miles to the house of one of Sir Gore Ouseley's neighbours in the country. We spent the day there and our host and his family were extremely kind and considerate. Their kindness and the fresh country air – which is so much better than London's – quite cured me of the shock I suffered at the Lord Mayor's banquet.

In the afternoon we drove in the countryside. We returned to the house to find that our host had invited some agreeable friends to dinner in our honour.

It was late when I retired to my comfortable bed.

Wednesday, 25 April

I WOKE UP AND, AFTER praying to God, I walked along the garden paths admiring the flowers and trees planted by the stream. In the garden there is a fountain like those we have in Iran, with a water-jet in the centre. The fish swimming in it are red and white, gold and violet; I was told they are descended from fish originally brought from China.

Then we went to see our host's hunting dogs; they were held on leads by the grooms responsible for feeding them. Each dog has a large box in which to sleep. I was told that these dogs are used to retrieve birds, pheasants in particular. People who do not own their own dogs may hire them from kennels for a certain fee.

There are many varieties of hunting dog, large and small. Those used for birds have an excellent sense of smell which they use to track down the prey for their masters to shoot. Hounds are used to chase foxes and greyhounds to chase hares.

Hunting dogs are very clever and intelligent. But they are faithful to only one master, as Mr Morier related in this story about a vicar who borrowed a dog from one of his friends. When they reached the hunting ground, the dog, as usual, put up some birds from the fields. But the vicar missed them all. The poor dog flushed some more from another field, but the vicar only managed to hit some tail feathers. When, a third time, the vicar failed to bring down even one bird, the dog turned to look at him, pissed on his trousers, and bounded back to his own master's house.

The English praise the faithfulness of dogs and they told me two stories to illustrate this. The first concerned two Frenchmen who set out on a journey together. One was accompanied by his faithful dog. He had a few *dinars* in gold and for these his wicked companion murdered him and buried him deep in a forest. The dog managed to return to the city, to the house of one of his master's friends. The friend was puzzled to see the dog, exhausted and without his master.

Friend and dog went out together; by chance, the dog recognized the murderer in the market-place and leaped upon him. Some people thought the dog had gone mad and should be put down. But the dog made digging movements and ran off towards the wood. His master's friend's suspicions were now thoroughly aroused and he followed the dog to the place in the wood where the dog started to dig again – and the victim's body was discovered. The murderer was brought before the Court of Justice and sentenced to fight the dog to the death in the arena. He was killed in a bloody battle. This story is recorded in many French books.

In Europe a murderer's freedom cannot be bought by money, even if the victim's heirs consent; if murder is proved, the law requires a life for a life.

The second story was about a dog who saved the life of a duke. The dog seemed to know that a servant planned to murder his master and howled so continually that the Duke finally allowed him to stay overnight in his bedroom. When the servant entered the room with a razor, intending to cut his master's throat, the dog leaped upon him and was injured in the struggle. The Duke, realizing that the dog had saved his life, dressed the dog's wounds himself and afterwards kept him constantly at his side. Many such tales are recorded and recounted.

There are no deer in England except in the King's parks. They are ugly, with mouths like a cow's. I could not find out when and from where these deer were introduced into the Royal parks. They are tame; they roam and feed freely and they are not afraid of people.

Many wild animals – lions, leopards, wolves and bears – have been brought to England from America and Africa. They are kept in cages for the people to see.

We were invited that day to Sir Abraham Hume's house,[1] eight miles away, and I went there with Sir Gore Ouseley and Mr Morier. The house is very large, set in a flower-filled garden where we found our host's daughter, Miss Hume, walking with Lord

Brownlow.[2]

Because Sir Abraham Hume is commander of the local Volunteers, 300 mounted artillerymen were assembled outside the house in our honour.[3] A tent had been erected on flat ground, and many local people had gathered to watch the soldiers practise their drills.

I suspected that Miss Hume and Lord Brownlow were in love. Lord Brownlow had been staying the previous night and after he took his leave, I spoke to Miss Hume, advising her, when she married, to choose a handsome husband. But she replied that it did not matter to her if he were handsome or not as long as he was intelligent.

I asked Sir Gore Ouseley if Lord Brownlow were married and he told me that he did not yet have that good fortune. I predicted that Miss Hume and Lord Brownlow would surely become engaged.

In the evening we dined and listened to music. Then we returned to our host's house to spend the night; Sir Gore Ouseley's wife had remained there.

And so passed another day.

[1] Wormleybury, near Cheshunt, Hertfordshire.

[2] Sofia Hume married on 24 July 1810 John Cust (1779-1853), 2nd Baron (later 1st Earl) Brownlow.

[3] Sir Abraham Hume was Major Commandant of the Southern Troop of Hertford Cavalry, made up of eight troops of cavalry and one of horse artillery. Three hundred 'mounted artillerymen' probably represents the entire regiment.

PLATE 34

Madame Catalani (1807). The huge fees she
commanded impressed Abul Hassan much more
than her voice! Stipple engraving by S. Freeman.

PLATE 35

The Egyptian Hall of the Mansion House. At the Lord Mayor's banquet held on St George's Day 1810, Abul Hassan was overcome by the heat and woke up in the Lady Mayoress' bedroom! Aquatint by Pugin and Rowlandson for Ackermann's Microcosm of London, *1808-10.*

PLATE 36

His Excellency the Persian Ambassador (1819).
An etching made by Richard Dighton during Abul
Hassan's second mission to London.

PLATE 37

Fath Ali Shah receiving Sir Harford Jones in audience in 1809. James Morier, Secretary to Sir Harford Jones, stands behind the seated Envoy; the central figure, with his back turned, is probably Abul Hassan. It seems likely that the artist, Robert Smirke, worked from a drawing made by James Morier at the time of the Audience.

Thursday, 26 April

M Y FRIENDS AND I walked in the flower-garden. Then we took leave of our host, got into the carriage, and travelled the fifteen miles to the city.

In the evening we went to Lady Saltoun's house where we were invited to a dance for young people about fifteen years of age.[1] I talked to most of the ladies there including the Duchess of Manchester, who was very kind and gracious. She is one of the most important ladies in London.

[1] Lady Saltoun had three sons and two daughters under twenty-five. The eldest, an officer in the Guards, had succeeded his father in 1793 as 16th Lord Saltoun.

Friday, 27 April

E ARLY IN THE MORNING Sir Gore Ouseley and I went to Somerset House, a large and magnificent mansion built of stone, like a small castle, overlooking the river. In one part of the building about 1000 naval officers and clerks administer the affairs of the Royal Navy.

In another part of the building famous artists show their paintings to the general public, who pay two shillings to look at what they call an 'exhibition'. The money collected is given to poor painters and their children. By showing their paintings here, artists may gain in reputation and attract sitters to have their portraits painted. The work is well paid.

My portrait by Sir William Beechey was among those in the exhibition.

Monday, 30 April

Last Monday night the Marquis and Marchioness of Hertford gave a grand concert to the Persian Ambassador and a numerous party of the Nobility and Gentry at their noble mansion in Manchester-square.
(*The Morning Chronicle*, 2 May)

IN THE MORNING Sir Gore Ouseley, Mr Morier and I were invited to the house of the Duchess of Devonshire at Chiswick, near London. But first we went to Richmond, where there is a Royal Palace.[1] In this season of early spring, the fields are green and the flowers are blooming – never in all my travels have I seen such a pleasing view.

I got out of the carriage and I begged Sir Gore Ouseley to let me stay here for a few days, to relax and banish sorrow, to look upon the tulips and the hyacinths, and to escape for a moment the gloom of London (where even if the sun does emerge from behind its veil of cloud, it is often obscured by high walls). But Sir Gore Ouseley replied that it would not be possible to find a suitable house for me here.

We went on to the Duchess of Devonshire's. Her house[2] stands in the middle of a delightful garden, planted with pine trees and surrounded by a stream, like the Garden of Eden. It is beautifully laid out with flower-beds and walk-ways.

I was greeted by the Duke of Devonshire.[3] He is a friend of Mr Adair, the English Ambassador at Istanbul, who had given me a letter of introduction to him. The Duke took my arm and we walked through the gardens with some guests; among them was Lord Aberdeen. We were followed by musicians: he called them a 'band'.

Then we went into the house. It is a unique mansion, decorated with statues of marble and paintings by European masters. Conversation among the guests was lively. A meal was served which, although it was almost afternoon, they called 'breakfast'.

We returned to town through beautiful green hills and valleys.

In the evening we were invited to Lady Hertford's[4] splendid house in Manchester Square.[5] The Prince of Wales was among the ladies and gentlemen dancing. He was exceedingly kind to me and appeared to be in a very cheerful mood.

[1] The Royal Palace at Richmond was largely destroyed in the 1650s. George II had a house in 'the Old Deer Park', but George III moved from there to Kew in 1772. Kew was a country retreat where the Royal Family used to go to escape from the formality of the Court at Windsor.

[2] Chiswick House.

[3] William Cavendish (1748-1811), 5th Duke of Devonshire, married second in October 1809 Lady Elizabeth Hervey, daughter of the 4th Earl of Bristol, and widow of John Thomas Foster MP.

[4] Francis Seymour-Conway (1743-1822), 2nd Marquis of Hertford, was a Lord of the Treasury 1774-80; Ambassador to Berlin and Vienna 1793-4; Master of the Horse 1804-6; Lord Chamberlain 1812-21. He married second in 1776 Isabella Anne Ingram-Shepherd, eldest daughter of the 9th Viscount Irvine. By 1810 she had replaced Mrs Fitzherbert in the affections of the Prince of Wales.

[5] Hertford House, 20 Manchester Square, was built in 1776 as the Duke of Manchester's own house. The lease was acquired by the 2nd Marquis of Hertford in 1797; by 1807 he had added two first-floor rooms on each wing and a conservatory outside the central Venetian window. In 1872-5 it was completely altered by Sir Richard Wallace, the illegitimate son and heir of the 4th Marquis; it is now the museum housing the Wallace Collection.

MAY

1810

Tuesday, 1 May

The children and I walked to-day in Kensington Gardens, where we met the Persian Ambassador who walked a little way with us. We saw him throw the javelin several times at one of his attendants on horse-back, who had to show his dexterity by avoiding the blow, which to say the truth seemed rather a service of danger.

(*Mrs Calvert's Journal,* 1 May 1810)

I RODE WITH LADY ARDEN, Mrs Perceval and Sir Gore Ouseley to a building they call the 'Panorama', where they exhibit paintings by master artists of the famous cities of Rum, Farang, Iran, Turkestan and India[1].

One panorama I saw was of a city in Egypt with citadels, mosques and monasteries, mountains and the River Nile; camel caravans approached the city. The painting was so detailed that an Egyptian would have been able to pick out his own house. An even more striking panorama was of the battle on the island of Walcheren[2], a Dutch possession before it was occupied by the French. It showed the city in flames, the smoke of the cannon and the bodies of the dead.

Artists who have travelled to many countries paint pictures of the various cities they have seen and hang them in this house to increase their reputation. Each visitor pays two 'shillings' to enter.

After seeing these wonderful paintings we left for home.

[1] Baker opened his famous Panorama in 1793 on a site in Leicester Place that runs north from the south-east corner of Leicester Square.

[2] The Walcheren expedition: a disastrous attempt, in the summer of 1809, to take Antwerp and reopen navigation on the Scheldt. The British troops got no further than the island of Walcheren. A parliamentary inquest into the failure was the principal preoccupation of the Government at this period.

Wednesday, 2 May

I DROVE INTO THE COUNTRY with Sir Gore Ouseley. After travelling about three miles we came to a magnificent house set in a large garden. Our young host, Lord Mansfield,[1] graceful as a cypress, gracious and soft-spoken, greeted us with much ceremony. He conducted us to his splendid house[2] through woods of juniper, box and spruce, as pleasing as the gardens of Kashmir or the flowering Garden of Eden.

Our host's wife was hospitable and charming and her children are noted for their beauty. We joined the assembly and there were the usual compliments on all sides. Among the guests was a young lord, very handsome, but so poor that no girl would have him for a husband. After lunch there was dancing: the English beauties and handsome youths gladdened our hearts.

When the dance ended the children took me on a tour of the gardens and we walked along the garden paths. Then we were served with a kind of fruit which resembles the mulberry – it had been grown in the hot-house. I asked to see the tree which produced this fruit and they showed me a bush like the lentil. In English this fruit is called 'strawberry'. Then we returned home.

[1] David William Murray (1777-1840), 3rd Earl of Mansfield, married in 1797 Frederica, daughter of Dr William Markham, Archbishop of York.

[2] Kenwood House, Hampstead.

Friday, 4 May

IN THE MORNING SIR GORE OUSELEY announced that we would visit the church known as St Paul's[1] and several other interesting buildings, including a fortress which houses a fine collection of armour. So I rose and prepared to set out for the church.

I was completely overwhelmed by this splendid building and its masterly paintings and sculpture. Its magnificent dome would dwarf the Tagh-i Khosrow! The windows circling the dome are leaded with small mirror-bright panes which reflect the sun's rays and dazzle the eye. Looking at this dome one can understand why the circle is considered the most perfect of forms.

Immediately below the dome clever engineers have built a gallery which is reached by a spiral staircase and where one can walk with ease. The acoustics are extraordinary. I was standing with Sir Gore Ouseley and his brother, Sir William Ouseley, when a small door in the gallery was slammed shut: the sound echoed through the dome like cannon-fire. Then Sir William Ouseley went to the far side of the gallery; with his face to the wall, he whispered in English: 'You speak English very well.' I heard the words perfectly!

With much trepidation (on my part), we climbed wooden ladders to another gallery higher in the dome. There we had a splendid view of London and the surrounding countryside for ten miles: the great houses and humble dwellings, the horse-drawn carriages, all looked like children's toys. We looked briefly at the marvellous paintings inside the dome, but it was so cold we were forced to come down.

We went to visit the Royal fortress in the City which they call the Tower of London. It is built of stone and is surrounded on three sides by a broad moat filled with water; on the fourth side is the River Thames. The Tower is in the middle of the fortress.

We went first to a chamber where they keep old weapons captured from the enemy: iron shields, spears and arrows. Any Londoner

PLATE 38

*The Shah of Persia's name and one of his many
titles enclosed in c-scroll cartouches in the
Wedgwood Crest Book for 1810. Above, 'The
Sultan son of the Sultan'; below, 'Fath Ali Shah
Qajar'. An East India Company Minute of 27
June 1810 records the payment of about £1300 for
'two Table Services of Wedgewood's [sic] Ware for
his Persian Majesty.'*

PLATE 39

PLATE 40

*Plate 39: A View of the Tower of London and the
Mint (1821), drawn and engraved by Robert Havell.*

*Plate 40: Astley's Royal Amphitheatre. Aquatint by
Pugin and Rowlandson for Ackermann's*
Microcosm of London, *1808-10.*

who wishes to may come to see these exhibits. In this room we also saw a figure of a Queen dressed in armour sitting on a horse holding the reins. This Queen had herself ruled as King.[2] It happens that in most of the countries of Europe women have ruled at times; if a king dies without a direct male heir, even if he has brothers, his daughter will succeed to the throne.

Then we went to another large and splendid room where we saw the figures of seventeen Kings in full armour on horseback. These figures, representing the ancestors of the present King, were arranged in order and each was dressed in armour of the period in which he reigned. Their boots and helmets were also of iron and their horses were covered with iron plates. Almost nothing could be seen of horse or rider. Most of them wore beards, for in times past most Europeans were bearded.

In this same fortress there is another building where they keep all sorts of wild animals:[3] black and white lions, leopards, wolves, foxes and monkeys. A keeper is assigned to each one. The black and white lions were brought from India and the New World: I have never seen their like before. There are also sweet-singing birds from all over the world. I was told that when they die, their insides are removed and their bodies are stuffed so that the shape is retained and not a feather is lost. They are then kept in show-cases.

[1] Christopher Wren's baroque masterpiece, the fifth St Paul's Cathedral on the site, was built to replace the church destroyed in the Great Fire of London in 1666. It was completed in 1710.

[2] Queen Elizabeth I.

[3] A Royal Menagerie was maintained at the Tower from 1235 when the Holy Roman Emperor presented Henry III with three leopards (an allusion to the leopards on the Plantagenet coat of arms) until 1834 when the animals were removed to the Regent's Park Zoo. The Menagerie was in the Lion Tower, where the ticket office is now.

Saturday, 5 May

IN THE MORNING I went with Mr Morier to Mrs Perceval's house. Her daughters were having a dancing lesson. Miss Fanny, the second daughter, performed a variety of dances very well.

The Prime Minister came in and was extremely friendly.

From there we went to the house of Mr Astell, the new Chairman of the East India Company, where we were invited to dinner. It is a splendid house, four or five miles from London, set in a pleasant garden planted with all kinds of flowers and herbs – a truly delightful, peaceful place.[1] Our host's wife[2] was very kind and gracious. She has several handsome children.

Several of the Company directors and Mr Dundas were also there. After dinner the ladies joined the party. Seldom have I spent a more pleasant evening, especially as the weather was so fine.

[1] Astell's principal country house was Everton House, Bedfordshire; he must have had another, week-end house, 'four or five miles' from London.

[2] Charles Astell married in 1800 Sarah, daughter of John Harvey of Ickwellbury, Bedfordshire. She died in 1841.

Sunday, 6 May

IN THE MORNING I went to the house of the Margravine, about whom I have written previously. Sir Gore Ouseley's brother, Sir William Ouseley, went with me. It had been decided that I should spend a few days there so that I might forget my troubles in those pleasant surroundings and in the company of that charming lady.

Among the guests assembled for dinner were Sir William's wife and her young and handsome brother. Our hostess had taken great care over the preparation of the meal – there were several different kinds of fruit drinks.

Each guest was given a separate bedroom. Mine was decorated in the Turkish style – the Margravine has visited Istanbul and become familiar with Turkish customs. My bed was therefore placed on a raised platform, but it was so narrow that every time I moved a little I rolled out on to the floor; I spent a very sleepless night!

Tuesday, 8 May

UNTIL MIDDAY THE MARGRAVINE and I sat talking in a pavilion on the riverside near the house – it looks like a Roman temple. She lamented the fact that her eldest son is mixing with people of inferior rank. 'My son is a lord,' she explained, 'and should therefore have chosen the daughter of a lord; but he has married a common woman and broken my heart.'[1] She wept.

Then we said goodbye and returned to the city.

When we got home Sir Gore Ouseley came in and told us that a large ship with sixty-four guns is being made ready for our journey and that, God willing, we might sail for Iran in two weeks' time. This news pleased me greatly and the day ended happily.

---

[1] The Margravine's eldest son by her first husband was William Craven (1770-1825), who succeeded his father as 7th Baron Craven in 1791 and was created 1st Earl of Craven in 1801. He married in December 1807 the celebrated actress Louisa Brunton. Her father was an actor and theatre manager; but he had been a soap dealer in Norwich and then a grocer in Drury Lane.

Friday, 11 May

FIRST THING THIS MORNING I heard my Iranian servants whispering among themselves: they had learned we were to return to Iran by way of India. They were frightened of the sea voyage and wanted to go via Istanbul. Mr Morier did too, but Sir Gore Ouseley said it would be impossible for his Secretary to travel by a different route.

Saturday, 12 May

WE WERE INVITED TO A large party at the house of Mr Dundas, the Minister for the Company. Among the guests was Lord Westmorland, one of the King's councillors and the Keeper of the King's Seals. He is very fond of riding and spoke to me with pride about one of his mares.

My friends asked me about the size of the Shahanshah of Iran's army. I said 120,000 men. Mr Dundas asked Mr Morier if this were correct, and Mr Morier replied: 'Perfectly true – all but three-quarters!' I was furious and protested angrily that no one had ever, until today, accused me of lying, and certainly not in the middle of a distinguished assembly!

Later I asked Mrs Dundas how she would like living in India if Mr Dundas were appointed Governor-General. She said she was anxious about the hot weather.

Lady Westmorland, who is Mrs Dundas' sister, was also there. It is clear that she was a great beauty in her youth. She has just returned from a tour of Istanbul and Spain.

And so ended another day.

Sunday, 13 May

SIR GORE OUSELEY came to the house and we drove in the carriage to the Park.

In the evening Sir Gore Ouseley and some other gentlemen, including Captain Heathcote,[1] Captain of the ship which is to take us to Iran, were invited to dinner at my house. When all were seated, Captain Heathcote told us that all the necessary provisions were now on board the ship – the rest was in the hands of Providence. I found him a very sympathetic person.

We went on to the Portuguese Ambassador's reception in honour of the anniversary of the King of Portugal [sic].[2] A great many people were there, including the Prince of Wales and the Duke of Cumberland.

The sounds of music came from all sides and the Italian singer, Madame Catalani, sang beautifully. I was told that she had once sung for the Prince Regent of Portugal (who ruled in the place of his mother the Queen) in Lisbon, before he left for the New World. The Prince presented Madame Catalani with a diamond ring valued at 10,000 *tomans*. If this is true, she was generously rewarded indeed!

And so ended another day.

[1] Captain (later Admiral Sir) Henry Heathcote (1777-1851), was the fourth son of Sir William Heathcote, 4th Baronet. Henry Heathcote was promoted captain at the remarkably early age of twenty-one.

[2] Prince John of Portugal ruled as Regent for his mad mother Maria I from 1792 to 1816 and as King from 1816 to 1826. When Napoleon invaded the Iberian Peninsula, he went into exile in Brazil (1807-21). Abul Hassan and Sir Gore Ouseley were guests of the Prince Regent during their fortnight's stay in Rio de Janeiro (11-26 September 1810) *en route* to Iran. See *Morier II*, pp. 3-8.

Monday, 14 May

MY FRIENDS TOLD ME ABOUT a theatre on the outskirts of London called 'Astley's Amphitheatre',[1] which opens in the spring, and where one can watch horses dancing. I went there with Sir Gore Ouseley. The theatre is somewhat smaller than the others I have seen and described in this journal.

I will describe the performance of one of the nimble riders who stood on a horse's back, without holding the reins, while the horse continued to run around the circular arena. Sometimes he jumped down to the ground and back up again; sometimes he stood on one foot, or lay down, or stood on his head with his legs in the air; sometimes he would vault himself from one side of the horse to the other; or, grasping the horse's body with his legs, he would hang underneath with his hands trailing on the ground. Then a second horse was brought in to run alongside the first. The rider jumped back and forth from one horse to the other, dancing and clapping his hands. A third horse was added and he continued dancing. Most amazing of all was his feat of jumping from one side to the other over all three horses!

The owner of the theatre was a friendly man; he explained to me how the horses are trained to perform these tricks. My Iranian servants were amazed and astonished by what they had seen.

As we left the theatre, I told Sir Gore Ouseley I thought the horses performed so well that it should be called the 'Horse Opera'.

---

[1] Philip Astley was a retired cavalryman who presented equestrian displays and melodramas under canvas from 1769.

Tuesday, 15 May

I have found a very handsome Carriage ready made which would answer with a little painting and blazoning exactly for the Persian King. . . .

(Letter from Sir Gore Ouseley to the Marquis Wellesley, 5 May)[1]

I WENT WITH SIR GORE OUSELEY to the workshop where they are making the carriage ordered for the Qibleh of the Universe.

We also went to visit some other shops: Sir Gore Ouseley, on behalf of the Government, asked me to order anything I wished. As he was so insistent, I ordered a few things and we returned home.

[1]BL ADD.37285, f.229.

Wednesday, 16 May

I WENT RIDING IN the Park. For no apparent reason, Sir Gore Ouseley's mare, which I ride every day, fell while we were galloping; but I did not fall heavily and was not injured at all. Even so, because it is their custom to show kindness to foreigners, all the riders in the Park rushed to see if I had been hurt and to offer help. They dismounted and expressed much anxiety about me. A lady and gentleman who were driving along the path in their carriage got down and came to ask if I was all right. Everyone was very glad that I was unhurt. What a contrast to Iranians who feel no compassion or concern for one another's welfare – in such a case they would simply say, 'What a shame – he's not hurt!' and go on their way. I was touched by the sympathy shown by these English people to a perfect stranger.

In the evening I went to party at the Margravine's house. There was a performance in her theatre which featured an actress and her two daughters: one of them was twelve years old and the other ten.[1] They were also accomplished actresses, singers and dancers. An audience of friends was gathered to watch.

---

[1] Julia Augusta and Jane Cramer were the two daughters of the violinist William Cramer (1745-99) and his second wife, the singer Maria Madden. The girls must have been older than twelve and ten: Jane made her much applauded debut on the public stage in Collins's *Ode on the Passions* at the Haymarket Theatre, 22 June 1810.

Thursday, 17 May

I DROVE IN MY CARRIAGE to Cavendish Square, where there was a crowd of some 3000 people. It was cold and raining heavily. Nonetheless, ten lords and distinguished gentlemen had taken the place of their drivers in splendid and shining four-horse carriages and were preparing to race each other along a road which had been closed to other traffic.[1] I was amazed that these gentlemen should choose to dress in the livery of carriage-drivers and apparently enjoy driving in the pouring rain! My friends assured me that in this season it is the custom for these gentlemen to parade in drivers' livery and demonstrate how well they can drive their own carriages. Still, I felt sorry for them in the rain.

I thought about this sport and concluded that these young men are trying to impose some kind of discipline on their idle lives: they do nothing all day long but write letters or walk about town twirling their watch-chains; and their evenings are spent at the theatre or at parties, dancing in shoes much too small for them in order to impress the ladies.

There are 900,000 people of low and high estate in this vast city; but it is true that only a small number are dissolute dandies. Compared with other cities, most Londoners are well mannered and sensible; and if there are a few tearaways, they do little harm.

The English are always happy when it rains because it is good for the crops.

At dinner I was served with a vegetable which looked very much like the stalk of one which grows abundantly in Iran. It is plentiful in London as well; here it is called 'asparagus'. One of the English servants seemed surprised when I refused it; he said that in England it is a very expensive delicacy. I told him that, expensive or not, in Iran we do not eat the plants that grow wild in the fields for the animals.

One of the wonders of this city is the cultivation of fruit in winter;

but out-of-season grapes and oranges taste very different from the summer varieties.

The fruit is grown in small gardens surrounded by kilns like those we use to warm our *hammams* in Iran. The gardens are roofed over to keep in the heat. All sorts of fruit may be grown and sold at high prices: four winter oranges sell for one *qurosh*.

Someone who did not sign his name has written me a letter asking me to send to the newspaper a list of all the things I have seen in this country – good and bad – and to swear that what I write is the truth.[2] I told Sir Gore Ouseley I thought I would include among the wonders I have seen – 100-year-old men trying to seduce young girls and 100-year-old ladies flirting with young men at parties so crowded that you cannot move and so hot that you could roast a chicken!

[1] The gentlemen drivers of the Four-in-Hand Club met every Thursday in the spring season to race from Cavendish Square to Salt Hill.

[2] Abul Hassan's letter to *The Morning Post* was published on 29 May.

236

Friday, 18 May

I WENT WITH SIR GORE OUSELEY to that part of Parliament which they call the 'House of Commons'. It looks like a theatre: some 500 members of Parliament sit on three tiers of wooden benches. Members who support the Government sit on one side of the Throne; members who are against the Government sit on the other. The House of Commons is not beautiful. Just two candles in two candlesticks provide light for the two clerks who record the proceedings. The King's representative, who is called the 'Speaker', sits on the Throne; he wears a wig made from the fleece of a sheep. When he wishes to speak, he rises from his Throne and addresses his words to both sides of the House.

This evening two lords were speaking: Lord Castlereagh and Lord Archibald Hamilton.[1] Debating style is important because the man with the better responses gains fame and popularity with the public. The younger man put his questions very well and replied equally well. Everyone said that he had no equal in the art of argument.

The two clerks record everything that is said in the House and it is then published so that the people may be aware of everything that happens in Parliament.

After a debate the members vote, and if the majority approves, the proposal becomes law.

---

[1] Lord Castlereagh, as an Irish peer, and Lord Archibald, as the younger son of a peer, were entitled to sit in the House of Commons. Lord Archibald Hamilton (1770-1827), younger son of the 9th Duke of Hamilton, was MP for Lanarkshire. In 1809 he had moved a motion of censure on Lord Castlereagh for the corrupt disposal of patronage while President of the Board of Control. He had also tried to censure Castlereagh and Perceval for attempting to 'trade' in parliamentary seats. No action had been taken by the House of Commons; on this occasion Hamilton reverted to the issue, despite Castlereagh's protests. See *The Times'* parliamentary report, 19 May.

Sunday, 20 May

EARLY THIS MORNING letters arrived from the great Crown Prince of Iran, Abbas Mirza, the *Naieb os-Soltaneh*. A few lines were addressed to me, his faithful servant, telling me that a representative from the Governor-General in Calcutta had arrived – to convey the Governor-General's conviction that Sir Harford Jones had usurped the prerogatives of the Governor-General and should be dismissed.[1] The Governor-General promised to provide any assistance Iran required on condition that Sir Harford Jones be relieved of his post as envoy and sent home. On this subject the Crown Prince addressed a letter to the exalted King of England. After reading it, I gave it to Sir Gore Ouseley to translate into English and forward to the wise Minister for Foreign Affairs.[2]

I expressed my opinion that the Governor-General should not have sent this man who described himself as Malcolm's deputy and who announced that Malcolm himself would arrive in Iran shortly.

[1] Lord Minto had sent Dr Andrew Jukes from the Residency in Bushire to Tehran to prepare for Malcolm's arrival. See the Introduction, p. 18, and Denis Wright, *The English Amongst the Persians*, p. 8.

[2] Abbas Mirza's letter, in which he praised Sir Harford Jones and expressed concern about the Governor-General's interference, was forwarded to Lord Wellesley on 9 June (PRO FO 60/4).

Tuesday, 22 May

WE WERE INVITED to a 'breakfast' – a form of entertainment which takes place during the day. This breakfast, which they called a 'masquerade', was held at the house of Lady Buckinghamshire. Tables laid with food and drink were beautifully arranged along the paths under the trees of her small garden.

The 500 guests were invited to attend in fancy dress, but Sir Gore Ouseley and I wore our usual clothes. One of the noble ladies was dressed as a lady's maid, and one of the lords came as a sailor. A marchioness appeared as a Roman empress. Everyone wore an amusing costume: Iranians, Turks and Indians paraded in the garden.

One man who said he was dressed as an Iranian wore clothes which looked nothing at all like those we wear. He claimed he could speak Persian and wished to talk to the Iranian Ambassador. He wore a false beard made from the hair of a cat or a goat. When he approached me I asked him why his beard contained so many different colours. The man stuttered and was unable to reply. When it became obvious that he could not speak Persian he disappeared into the garden, snubbed by everyone.

For a laugh, one man had written verses on slips of paper about what the English call 'rouge'. With a great show of politeness, this clown presented his verses to all the ladies with rouged faces. The ladies angrily threw them away. But one lady, after reading the verse, gave her piece of paper to me and told me it was more suited to my beard! I was truly amazed by the antics that I witnessed in that garden!

Garden parties are so much nicer than evening parties; indoors, the odour of perspiration is unpleasant, and the heat makes my head ache.

At the end of the day we returned home.

Wednesday, 23 May

I RODE TO THE KING'S GARDEN to relax for a while. Before returning home I stopped by a jeweller's shop[1] to look at his wares. Gold and silver dishes were neatly arranged on shelves which reached the ceiling: expensive ropes of diamonds, rubies, emeralds, corals and pearls outshone the stars!

I was told that the firm's partners send their representatives to buy stones from mines all over the world. They are then made up into the styles currently popular in London. These jewellers have no equal in Europe; they are famous for mounting stones so that they are visible from all sides and any flaw may be easily detected.

I have heard that the reputation of this shop is so great that the French Emperor has promised it to one of his generals as a reward for victory. But the defeat of England is impossible; the General's hopes are sure to be dashed. I thought of this line from Ferdowsi:

A deer uncaught is not the best of gifts.

I then went to Sir Gore Ouseley's house, where I found a present from the Prince of Wales: a comb for my beard set with diamond chips. It is impossible to describe its beauty! My heart was touched – how can I ennumerate the Prince's many virtues, each one more praiseworthy than the next?

[1] Probably Rundell & Bridges, the eminent firm of silversmiths and jewellers on Ludgate Hill.

PLATE 41

The House of Commons. The chamber shown here,
used by the Commons from the reign of Queen Anne
until the fire of 1834, was the fourteenth-century St
Stephen's Chapel in the Palace of Westminster,
enlarged and panelled by Sir Christopher Wren.
Aquatint by Pugin and Rowlandson for
Ackermann's Microcosm of London, 1808-10.

PLATE 42

The Persian Ambassador (1810), by Sir Thomas Lawrence. This splendid portrait of Abul Hassan was commissioned by Sir Gore Ouseley.

Thursday, 24 May

IN THE MORNING, AFTER praying and giving thanks to the Lord God, I was sitting deep in thought about my journey and departure from London when Lord Keith's daughter, Miss Elphinstone, arrived. She brought me some china which she had painted herself with birds and various other designs. The china was French – apparently it is easier to obtain than English china.

When I wrote to thank that star-kissed girl I expressed the hope that God would provide her with a handsome husband. I know that English girls prefer a husband who is intelligent and might become a member of Parliament, even if he is ugly. But I, like Hafez, pray God to keep the beauties of London from the clutches of the Devil:

> *O Lord God, from our houses the Devil eject,*
> *From the stealer of flowers our gardens protect.*

Friday, 25 May

WE WERE INVITED TO DINNER at the house of Sir Charles Cockerell, who acquired his great wealth in the service of the East India Company. He owns several houses in the country, and in London his house overlooks the Park.[1] Sir Gore Ouseley and I joined the assembly, which included Mrs Perceval, the wife of the Prime Minister, and Lord and Lady Aberdeen.

One of the guests was a very large lady who, so I was told, had been the friend of one of the English commanders whose name was Lord Nelson. Several years ago, in a sea battle against the French, he won a great victory but was killed in the fighting. This lady's name is Lady Hamilton.[2] Her face is pretty, but her figure is fat. Nevertheless, they say that she was sylph-like in her youth and the model for many portraits.

Mrs Perceval told Sir Gore Ouseley that Lady Hamilton sings very well, so he and Lady Cockerell, the wife of our host, persuaded her to sing for us. Indeed she sang most beautifully, but her song was so sad that she wept, and we could feel her inner grief.

---

[1] Sir Charles Cockerell (1755-1837), 1st Baronet, MP for Bletchingley, was head of the East India agency, Cockerell and Co. He married second, in 1808, Harriet Rushout, daughter of the 1st Lord Northwick. His town house was in The Terrace, Hyde Park.

[2] Emma Lyon (1765?-1815) married in 1791 the antiquarian and diplomatist Sir William Hamilton (1730-1803), then British Minister to Naples. Her famous romance with Horatio Nelson began after his arrival at Naples, the victorious hero of the Battle of the Nile (1798).

Saturday, 26 May

I WENT WITH SIR GORE OUSELEY to a looking-glass manufactory; that is, a factory where they make mirrors by
covering the backs of glass sheets with mercury. Sir Gore
Ouseley ordered five pairs.

From there we went to a shop where they sell cloth.[1]

In the evening Lord Aberdeen, Sir Gore Ouseley and several
others came to my house for dinner.

[1] On 28 May Ouseley wrote to the Chairman of the East India Company: 'I have just
found out that the King of Persia is immoderately fond of large mirrors, and that as
his Ambassador has come into the presence of the *Company itself*, it will be expected
that two pair of the largest dimensions ever seen in the East should be sent to
him. . . . Of Cloth there cannot be too great a proportion and after taking the Mirza
into Cloth warehouses, I am able to say that the finest, or first Cloth, such as we wear
in our Coats, is that most eligible for presents . . .' IO L/PS/3/3, Appendix 22, Part 2.

Sunday, 27 May

IN THE MORNING SIR GORE OUSELEY and I went to call on Mrs Perceval. We found Lady Ouseley already there. She is going away for a few days to say goodbye to her father and mother before leaving for Iran with her husband.

Today I was made aware of the great love that exists between Sir Gore and Lady Ouseley. The thought of not seeing Sir Gore for even one day affected her deeply. Among married couples, they can have no equal in the whole world. Such is her affection that she is loth to leave her husband's side for a moment, even though she is not fond of parties. Would that Iranian women valued their husbands' affection as much!

And so ended another day.

Monday, 28 May

IN THE MORNING I rode by myself to the King's Garden. Nobody was there and I sat on a bench reflecting on the journey to Iran and my audience with his Majesty the Shahanshah. An old man came up to me and – thinking that I was one of the Iranian Ambassador's servants – asked me in English: 'What does the Ambassador think of this country?'

I replied: 'He says very good things about it.'

When the old man had asked three times what the Ambassador thought of England, I said: 'Everything in this city is good, except old men who talk too much and prevent one from relaxing in the Park and enjoying the spring flowers.'

Hearing this, he realized that I was annoyed and, laughing, he went on his way.

In the evening we were invited to a music party at the Duchess of Devonshire's house.[1] The ladies were lovely and our hostess in particular was so kind that I became quite embarrassed.

It happened that the Prince of Wales was there, amusing the assembly with his wit. He came up to me and said, with a smile, that he had heard a story about my having taken a woman to my house. 'They say', he continued, 'that you had sex with her eight times, and would have gone on till twenty if a man had not rushed to her rescue with a naked sword!'

'Lies!' I protested. 'It all comes from people having too much leisure and nothing to do but gossip! These rumours must have been started by that shameless woman who writes to me declaring her love and begging to come with me to Iran. Of course I have replied to none of them – and if she continues to write I shall see that she is punished.'

From the Duchess's house I returned home.

---

[1] Devonshire House, Piccadilly (at Berkeley Street).

Tuesday, 29 May

To the Lord, or Gentleman, without name, who lately write Letter to him and ask very much to give Answer.

Sir, My Lord,

When you write to me, some time ago, to give my thought of what I see good and bad in this country, that time I not speak English very well – now I read, I write much little better – now I give to you my think. In this country bad not too much, everything very good – but suppose I not tell something little bad then you say I tell all flattery – therefore I tell most bad thing. I not like such crowd in evening party every night – In cold weather not very good – now in hot weather, much too bad. I very much astonish, every day now much hot than before, evening parties much crowd than before.– Pretty beautiful Ladies come sweat that not very good – I always afraid some old Lady in great crowd come dead, that not very good, and spoil my happiness.– I think old Ladies after 85 years not come to evening party that much better.– Why for take so much trouble? Some other thing little bad.– Very beautiful young Lady, she got ugly fellow for husband, that not very good, very shocking.– I ask Sir Gore why for this.– He says me, perhaps he very good man, not handsome no matter, perhaps he got too much money, perhaps got title – I say I not like that, all very shocking.– This all bad I know – now I say good.– English people all very good People – all very happy – do what they like, say what they like, write in Newspaper what like.– I love English people very much, they very good, very civil to me.– I tell my King English love Persian very much.– English King best man in world – he love his People very good much.– He speak very kind to me, I love him very much.– Queen very best woman I ever saw.– Prince of Wales such a fine elegant beautiful man – I not understand English enough proper to praise him – he is too great for my language – I respect him same as my own King – I love him much better – his manner all the same has talisman and charm.– All the Princes very fine men, very handsome men, very sweet words, very affable. I like all too much.– I think the

Ladies and Gentlemen this country, most high rank, high honour very rich (except two or three) most good, very kind to inferior peoples.— This very good.— I go to see Chelsea — all old men sit on grass, in shade of fine tree, fine river run by — beautiful place, plenty to eat, drink, good coat, every thing good.— Sir Gore he tell me King Charles and King James — I say, Sir Gore, they not Mussulman but I think God love them very much. I think God he love the King very well for keeping up that charity — then I see one small regiment of children go to dinner — one small boy he says thanks to God for eat, for drink, for cloathes — other little boys they all answer Amen, then I cry a little — my heart much pleased. This all very good for two things — one thing God very much please — two things, Soldiers fight much better because see their King take care of old wounded fathers and little children.— Then I go to Greenwich — that too good place — such a fine sight make me a little sick for joy — all old men so happy, eat dinner so well — fine house — fine beds — all very good — This very good country. English Ladies very handsome, very beautiful — I travel great deal; I go Arabia, I go Calcutta, Hyderabad, Poonah, Bombay, Georgia, Armenia, Constantinople, Malta, Gibraltar, I see best Georgian, Circassian, Turkish, Greek Ladies — but nothing not so beautiful as English Ladies — all very clever — speak French, speak English, speak Italian, play music very well, sing very good — very glad for me if Persian Ladies like them; but English Ladies speak such sweet words, I think tell a little story, that not very good. One thing more I see, but I not understand that thing good or bad; last Thursday I see some fine carriages, fine horses; thousand people go to look that carriages; I ask why for, they say me, that Gentlemen on boxes, they drive their own carriage. I say, why for take so much trouble. They say me, he drive very well, that very good thing. It rain very hard, some Lord, some Gentlemen, he get very wet; I say, why he not go inside. They tell me good coachman not mind, get wet every day, will be much ashamed if go inside, that I do not understand.

  Sir, my Lord — Good night —

ABUL HASSAN

*9, Mansfield-street, May 19, 1801 [*sic*].*

(*The Morning Post*, 29 May)

Tuesday, 29 May

BECAUSE SOMEONE UNKNOWN TO ME had written to me asking what I had found good and what bad in this city, I took up my pen and wrote a letter which was printed in the newspaper.

Most people were pleased by what I wrote, but a few asked me why I had bothered to reply. I found so little bad that some people thought I had written only to flatter the English people. But truly, I wrote only what I had seen – both good and bad – without adding or eliminating.

I made some enemies among the old ladies, however – and one can make no worse enemies than that! – because I wrote that ladies over eighty-five years should stay at home in this hot weather and not go to evening parties.

Thursday, 31 May

WE HEARD THE NEWS that during the night one of the valets of the Duke of Cumberland, an Italian, had tried to murder his master by striking several blows to his head and face. The Prince summoned help, but when they went to arrest the valet, they found that he had cut his own throat.[1]

Sir Gore Ouseley and I went to the Prince's house to find out what had happened. Many people were already there: they told us that the Prince had been severely wounded but was expected to recover. I was very distressed for the Prince; he has always been very kind and friendly to me – he calls me 'Mufti'. He is a brave man: he lost an eye in battle.[2] They say that, in spite of his injuries, the Prince intends to provide the valet's family with lodging and a pension.

From there we went to Sir Gore Ouseley's house to look at some muskets and telescopes that he has obtained for me.

Mr Morier returned from two days at Sir Harford Jones's country house. He told us that Lady Jones and all the children were ill. The coach in which Mr Morier returned to London was over-crowded with about twenty people. It broke down and all the passengers fell over. Mr Morier fell on top of a man with a huge grumbling stomach! It seems that travelling by coach is not without its dangers.

---

[1] Although the motive remains a mystery, there is no doubt that in the early morning of 31 May 1810 the Duke of Cumberland's Corsican valet, Joseph Sellis, tried to murder his master and then took his own life. But the Duke was so universally unpopular that it was immediately rumoured that *he* had murdered Sellis, either because he had been caught in bed with Mrs Sellis or because Sellis was blackmailing him for homosexual advances.

[2] At the age of twenty-two, as Major-General commanding a Hanoverian cavalry brigade, Cumberland lost his left eye and was severely wounded in the right arm in hand-to-hand fighting at the Battle of Tournay, 10 May 1794.

JUNE
1810

Friday, 1 June

I SPENT SOME TIME in the King's Garden. When I returned home I was told that one of my Iranian servants had spent the night in a brothel. I ordered that he be brought before me and his head shaved.

There are some 30,000 prostitutes in London, but many of them you would not recognize as such. They dress beautifully; they have nice houses; they keep carriages and horses and servants.

Distinguished gentlemen sometimes engage prostitutes as servants for one or two years at a salary of 5000 *tomans* or more. But if, without marrying, the woman bears his child, the gentleman does not acknowledge himself as the father. If the child is a girl, she may not attend the Queen's Drawing-room until she marries; and if the child is a boy, he may not inherit his father's name or title.

In a brothel, it is usual for one old woman to act as manager for several prostitutes. Some of them earn fifty *tomans* a night, but others earn less, as little as two *quroshes*.

Most prostitutes are pretty and shy. Many of them are ashamed of their profession and if they truly repent, there is a large house, supported by Government and public donations, where they may go for up to one year. It is called Magdalen House. The women spend their time praying in church, day and night. While staying in the House, their expenses are paid and when it is certain they have reformed, they may be found employment as servants.

Saturday, 2 June

THE PERSIAN AMBASSADOR. We are assured that the letter, which recently appeared in this Paper, was actually written in English by his Excellency the Persian Ambassador. Considering the difficulty experienced by foreigners in acquiring, in so short a period, a tolerable knowledge of our language, the proficiency made by his Highness is very creditable to him. His urbanity of manners, conciliating deportment, and genial talents, render it desirable that his Majesty of Persia should again select him for a diplomatic mission to this country, where his conduct has procured him the marked approbation of the Public, and, more especially, in the high circles he has frequented. His Excellency is partial to this country, and has frequently made many judicious remarks on our manners, customs, and amusements. Though he has very politely addressed some of his observations to ladies of a certain age, we think that many still younger may take the hint; and that young ladies, whose beauty and graceful elegance he justly admires, might sometimes give their conversation an interest beyond the fleeting frivolities of the moment. His Excellency is much pleased with the cavalry exercises at Astley's Amphitheatre, and shrewdly said, they ought to be termed – The Equestrian Opera.

(*The Morning Post*, 1 June)

THE ENGLISH ARE VERY KIND to foreigners: a very flattering article has appeared in the newspaper about me. It also expresses pleasure that I have praised the English King and Princes.

The citizens of this city enjoy more freedom than can be imagined and the King's power is strictly limited by the law. Even so, whenever the King's name is spoken, it is with great respect. The English have an anthem – a prayer for blessings on their King – and whenever it is played, they all rise and bow, even at banquets and receptions. In church, the first prayers are for the King's long life.

253

Sunday, 3 June

SIR GORE OUSELEY sent a note asking me to come to his house. As I was leaving with Sir William Ouseley, we encountered a young boy with an old man standing in the doorway. The boy said he had no one in the world and that his one desire was to go with me to Iran! To this I replied that I had quite enough Iranian servants to accompany me and had no need for another. Sir William Ouseley then astonished me by saying that he thought the 'boy' might actually be a girl – the same madwoman who has been writing to me every day. But why, I wondered, if she is a girl, has she cut off her hair and put on boy's clothing?!

We hurried to our carriage and drove to Sir Gore Ouseley's house. He joined us and, after several errands, we went to the house of a handsome young man called Mr Lawrence.[1] Sir Gore Ouseley told me that he is the best portrait painter in London and that he wants him to paint my portrait to take with him to Iran.

When we saw some 500 unfinished portraits of distinguished ladies and gentlemen, I exclaimed that mine would never be finished if we were to leave in ten days' time!

Sir Gore Ouseley made it clear to the artist that if the portrait was not finished by the time we left, he would not be paid! It was finally agreed that he would paint a small portrait – from head to waist – and that I should return in three days' time to sit for him.

---

[1] By 1810 Thomas Lawrence (1769-1830) was the most celebrated portrait painter in London and Principal Portrait-Painter to the King. He was knighted in 1815 and became President of the Royal Academy in 1820.

Monday, 4 June

TODAY WAS THE KING'S BIRTHDAY. The Queen held a Drawing-room and, as usual, the ladies wore Court dress. Sir Gore Ouseley and I also attended. There were many people present and the ladies were very attentive to me.

In the evening I was invited to the house of Lord Wellesley, the Minister for Foreign Affairs. Also present was the Spanish Ambassador,[1] who has recently arrived in London from Spain. He is a Duke and because of his great name the Minister placed him on his right hand and me on his left. I am familiar with English customs; but I know that no other Iranian would have been content with such an arrangement!

Lord Wellesley was in extremely good humour and joked a great deal. His table was arranged with great taste – there was a variety of fruits and ices suitable to the very hot weather.

[1] *The Morning Post*, 23 May, reported the arrival of the new Spanish Ambassador, the Duke d'Albuquerque, at Pulteney's Hotel on 22 May.

Tuesday, 5 June

I WAS INVITED BY SIR SIDNEY SMITH to the house of a Jewish lady named Mrs Goldsmid[1] and I went there in the carriage with Sir Gore Ouseley and Mr Morier. Her house is about two *farsakhs* from London and is set in pleasant gardens of trees and flowers; it looks like many distinguished houses, perhaps even better.

On our way to the entrance, where Mrs Goldsmid was greeting her guests, Mr Morier told me that she was a Jewess who now claims to be a Christian. She is very wealthy and her house and garden alone are said to be worth 100,000 *tomans*. They say she was very handsome in her youth. She has several sons and daughters.

Mrs Goldsmid had arranged this party in my honour and invited the other ambassadors as well. She told me that on the day Sir Harford Jones left for Iran he had been a guest in her house; she hoped that, God willing, he would come here again on the day of his return.

[1] Jessie Goldsmid, née Solomons, was the daughter of a wealthy East India merchant and widow of the Dutch-born banker Benjamin Goldsmid: financial failure had led him to hang himself at their house in Roehampton on 11 April 1808.

PLATE 43

The Daughters of William Wellesley-Pole: Mary Charlotte Anne (Mrs Charles Bagot), Emily Harriet and Priscilla Anne. It is probable that Emily was the 'Miss Pole' of whom Abul Hassan was so enamoured. Chalk drawing by Sir Thomas Lawrence, c 1814.

PLATE 44

*Jane Maryon Wilson, Mrs Spencer Perceval, a
miniature by Andrew Plymer. The Prime
Minister's wife showed much kindness and attention
to Abul Hassan during his stay in London.*

Wednesday, 6 June

I WENT TO A MEETING of the Board of Agriculture at the home of its President, Sir John Sinclair.[1] The meeting was attended by members of the Nobility and distinguished gentlemen.

Every year the Board awards cash prizes for inventions designed to improve productivity and lower costs in agriculture; for example, new agricultural machines or improved fertilizers. Land-owners who profit from these inventions contribute to the cost of the prizes. Sir Gore Ouseley and I inspected several new machines, including a threshing-machine and a plough for use on particularly hard soil.

From there we went to another room where some 100 distinguished gentlemen were seated. One of them held a book from which he read the names of those who had invented or developed something useful during the past year; they were presented with a prize of money and a gold medal inscribed with the King's name.

I went to the house of Mr Lawrence, the portrait painter, so that he could paint my portrait. Sir Gore Ouseley had given him seventy *tomans* to paint a half-length portrait of me – a good painter charges between 150 and 500 *tomans* for a full-length portrait.

---

[1] Sir John Sinclair (1745-1835), 1st Baronet, MP for Buteshire, founded the Board (or Society) of Agriculture in 1793. He lived in New Palace-yard; but this meeting probably took place in the Board's new headquarters at 32 Sackville Street, a mid-eighteenth century house which still stands. *The Morning Herald*, 28 February, reported that, the day before, 'his Excellency the Persian Ambassador was unanimously elected an Honorary Member of the Board of Agriculture'.

Thursday, 7 June

EVERY YEAR IN THE LARGE church known as St Paul's there is a Service of Thanksgiving attended by orphan children, boys and girls up to fifteen years of age, who are supported by the public. I was accompanied to the service by Mr Wellesley, a brother of the Minister for Foreign Affairs, who is a priest of that church.[1]

Some 7,000 boys and girls were seated on wooden benches which had been placed in the middle of the church. Children from the various districts of London were dressed in different colours: red, yellow, green, blue, &c. And one or two children in each group held up an identifying banner. A man stood on a platform raised in one corner and led the children in singing prayers with a baton. They were accompanied on a very large organ. I was deeply affected by their singing and wept copiously.

The congregation also wept: there were about 10,000 people crowded beneath the dome and in the galleries. The intellect is truly unable to comprehend how a dome so high and so wide was constructed without supporting pillars!

[1] The Reverend Gerald Wellesley (1770-1848), the fourth of the Wellesley brothers, was Deacon of St Paul's, later Prebendary of Durham and Chaplain to the Queen. In 1802 he married Emily Mary, eldest daughter of the 1st Earl of Cadogan.

Saturday, 9 June

I WENT WITH SIR GORE OUSELEY and Sir Charles Cockerell to visit the Royal Arsenal at Woolwich, which is several *farsakhs* from London. There are not enough pages in this journal to describe its wonders.

We went first to the house of the General commanding the Arsenal.[1] He and several colonels accompanied us to the brass foundry, where they make brass cannon and shot of various sizes. The foundry operates for twenty-four hours a day. We watched as the necessary ingredients were melted in furnaces and then poured into cannon-shaped moulds which are placed near the furnaces. Twelve cannon are cast at one time. The moulds are slightly larger than the size desired: after cooling, the cannon are lifted from the moulds by a six-horsepower crane; a steam-powered metal drill is used to bore the cannon-mouths and to smooth the barrels. There were ten men each working one of these machines: without steam the work would require 100 men.

In another place they make gun-carriages and other things out of iron. The iron is melted in a large furnace and buckets are used to pour the molten iron into moulds. There are steam-driven circular saws made of iron or steel capable of cutting timber into 100 pieces in one minute. Other machines perform other jobs; for example, a special attachment makes it possible to taper an iron bar as easily as if it were wood. The machines and tools in this workshop were invented only two years ago.

In another place lead is melted in huge cauldrons which hang over constantly burning fires. The lead is used to make shells and bullets. Children are employed to make bullets for firearms. In still another place workers prepare gunpowder and grenades.

In several open fields, cannon made of iron or brass are arranged according to size. There are also two yards for the storage of shot, arranged so that you can tell at a glance how many there are. I asked the General how many cannon balls he had. He said 50,000; but I estimated there were 30,000 in one corner alone.

Cannon captured from the enemy in good condition are stored separately. Only about five per cent of captured cannon are in such poor condition that they must be melted down and used to make new ones.

In another building we saw young men, fifteen years old or more, the sons of distinguished gentlemen, who are sent here to learn to be artillery officers.[2]

There is also a dockyard at Woolwich where one hundred war-ships of all sizes are built yearly to replace ships lost to the enemy or which have become obsolete. Because of the high cost of armaments and machinery, the Government is usually in debt and forced to borrow from the public.

[1] Lieutenant-General William Congreve (died 1814), created 1st Baronet in 1812, was Superintendent of Military Machines at Woolwich.

[2] The Royal Military Academy was established in the Arsenal in 1721.

Monday, 11 June

All the Nobility and Fashionables in or near town are expected to be present at Vauxhall Gardens this evening, in compliment to the Persian Ambassador, who has commanded the Fête, and will go in State.

(*The Morning Post*, 11 June)

A FTER DINNER, ACCOMPANIED BY Sir Charles Cockerell and some of his friends, we went to a garden two miles from the city which they call 'Vauxhall'.[1] Its wonders are impossible to describe, but I shall attempt a short account.

The gardens cover ten *jaribs* of land and are laid out with four broad avenues planted so thickly with tall trees that the sun does not penetrate their branches. The four sides of the garden are lined with wooden arcades covered with painted cloth and hung with coloured lanterns – gold, red and white – filled with sweet-smelling oil. There are cascades of water and in the centre of the garden there is a pavilion which this evening was decorated with illuminations of the King of England and his Royal Crown: the lighting from coloured lanterns gave the impression of enamel-work. In this pavilion beautiful women sang melodious songs to the music of 100 musicians.

Some 10,000 ladies and gentlemen and ordinary folk were there, enjoying themselves; some of them were dancing. Underneath the arcades which line the gardens there were some 1000 tables, each with chairs for ten people, where anyone could sit down to eat or drink wine: a variety of meats and fruits was ready prepared.

On one side of the gardens a scene had been mounted on a raised platform so that it could be seen by people standing at a distance: there appeared to be a small lake with a boat and waterfalls and fountains and a bridge over which people passed from one side to the other on foot, on horseback and in carriages; but I truly do not know if it was real or an illusion.

The avenues were lighted by rows of tall candelabra and by lanterns hung from the trees. In one place there were fireworks: when they did not rise high enough, everyone laughed and said 'Shocking'! The fireworks ended with the name of the Qibleh of the Universe written in Persian letters! Everyone appreciated this display and clapped their hands together. From there we went to a large covered place, beautifully lighted and decorated, like a theatre in the city. It was built to accommodate 5000 people in case of rain. After the fireworks, some people sat down to eat; later they danced.

There is an entrance fee of 2000 *dinars* for each person.

Sir Charles Cockerell had reserved a table for us and a separate table for our servants. We ate a little of everything.

Mr Wellesley-Pole, brother of the Minister for Foreign Affairs, and Sir Gore Ouseley's great friend, Mr Prendergast,[2] came in. Joking, Mr Prendergast said to me: 'Here comes your father-in-law!' (meaning the father of my beloved!). I walked with him for a while in the gardens.

It was early in the morning when we returned home.

[1] Vauxhall Gardens, south of the Thames at Lambeth, were first laid out in 1661. Every summer for two centuries, until the pleasure gardens finally closed in 1859, fashionable Londoners mixed with the *hoi-polloi* who came to watch them promenade, or dine and drink in the elaborately decorated pavilions.

[2] Michael George Prendergast (d. 1834), a former merchant at Lucknow, was elected MP for Saltash in April 1809.

Tuesday, 12 June

FRENCH PAPERS, *Paris June 5. The Persian Ambassador has left Paris, together with his Suite, which is very numerous. Chevalier Amadeus Jaubert, Master of Requests, is appointed to accompany his Excellency to the frontier.*

(*The Times,* 12 June)

I RODE TO SIR GORE OUSELEY'S house. I urged him to speed our departure for Iran because it is reported that Askar Khan, the Iranian Ambassador in Paris, has left for Iran with a French Ambassador appointed to Tehran.[1] The news has disturbed me greatly, because I do not know how this development will affect my mission here.

In the evening I went to the Opera with Sir Gore Ouseley and Mr Prendergast. The Italian woman called Angiolini, who is a good dancer, performed a 'Persian Wedding Dance' which bore no resemblance at all to the real thing. Such novelties are mounted to attract the money of the idle rich who are forever seeking new diversions.

[1] Abul Hassan has misunderstood the report. Jaubert was not an ambassador, merely *mehmandar* to Askar Khan.

263

Wednesday, 13 June

I have the honour to inform your Lordship that the greatest part of the articles for Persia, viz Cut glass, mirrors, Broadcloth, Stationery, Guns and Pistols &c &c are now ready to be sent off – and as they will take some time to send them by the waggon to Portsmouth and get them stowed away on board ship, I purpose commencing the dispatch of them in the course of a day or two. . . .

(Letter from Sir Gore Ouseley to the Marquis Wellesley, 13 June)[1]

I WENT TO THE HOUSE OF Mr Lawrence, the painter. I had a headache and did not feel at all well.

In the evening I was invited to a party. But before I left the house, Sir Gore Ouseley came to tell me that it is not true that a French ambassador is going to Iran. We talked about various things and then I left for the party.

It was late when we returned home.

[1] BL Add.37285, f.235.

Thursday, 14 June

I SPENT SOME TIME riding; and in the evening I went to a meeting of freemasons as the guest of Lord Moira.[1] He was very kind and hospitable. One of the Royal Princes, the Duke of Sussex,[2] was there. I also became a freemason, which was highly gratifying.

Last night the Duchess of Devonshire gave her last grand rout for this season, which was numerously attended by all the distinguished fashionables in the West end of the town.

(The Morning Herald, 15 June)

At midnight Sir Gore Ouseley and I went to a ball at the house of the Duchess of Devonshire, whose husband is a friend of the English Ambassador at Constantinople, Mr Adair. All the grand ladies and gentlemen of London were there, including the Prince of Wales, who was very kind and friendly. He took my arm and praised me to Sir Gore Ouseley. During all the time I have been in London, he has never failed in his courtesy towards me.

It was late when we returned home.

[1] General Francis Rawdon-Hastings (1754-1826), 2nd Earl of Moira (later 1st Marquis of Hastings), Governor-General of India 1812-23, was the eldest son of John Rawdon, 1st Earl of Moira, and Lady Elizabeth Hastings. He added Hastings to his surname of Rawdon under his uncle's will of 1790.

[2] Prince Augustus Frederick (1773-1843), Duke of Sussex, sixth son of George III, succeeded the Prince of Wales as Grand Master of the Freemasons in 1811, when the latter assumed the Regency.

Friday, 15 June

SIR GORE OUSELEY came with me to the painter's house, and then we went to see the carriage which has been built for the Qibleh of the Universe. The carriage is superb – nothing like it has been seen before.[1]

A few days ago Sir Gore Ouseley mentioned that he had proposed that some small presents be given to my servants.[2] He raised the matter again today, indicating that there were difficulties. I told him not to trouble the Council further about it. I thought to myself: 'I do not understand these people. They gave Mohammad Nabi Khan seven *lakhs* of *rupees* (which got him into trouble in Iran) when he went on his mission to Calcutta.[3] But over this trifling amount, not even 500 *tomans*, the Council now raises objections!'

In the afternoon I had a note from Sir Gore Ouseley telling me that there was news from Russia; a French ambassador is in St Petersburg, the capital of Russia, waiting to go to Iran; but the Iranian Government has refused him permission to proceed. I wrote back saying that in any event it would be better if I returned to Iran quickly via Istanbul. It would be a bad thing if this French Ambassador were to meet Askar Khan in Turkey and accompany him to Iran.

But in the evening – we were at a party where our noble hostess offered neither food nor music! – Sir Gore Ouseley repeated his objections to my returning to Iran via Istanbul. He said it would be much better if we travelled together.

[1] The bulk of the presents for the Shah arrived in Tehran from Bushire in May 1812. Sir William Ouseley, *Travels*, III, pp. 370-1, described the Shah's inspection of the carriage: 'The chariot, a beautiful specimen of English workmanship, and one

of the chief presents, had, like most other articles, suffered many injuries on the road; almost every panel was cracked, and many of the silver ornaments broken off and lost. . . . '

[2] In a letter to the Chairman of the EIC on 26 May Ouseley suggested presents of £50 each for Abul Hassan's nine Iranian servants (IO L/PS/3, Appendix 22, ff.265-8).

[3] On p. 48 of his account of his mission to Persia (see Bibliography), Sir Harford Jones refers to the seven lakhs of rupees Mohammad Nabi Khan was able to amass while Persian Ambassador to India in 1807-8; but he makes it clear the money came from commercial speculation and not from the British Government.

Saturday, 16 June

LORD TEIGNMOUTH CAME to say goodbye before leaving for his country house. He showed me much kindness and friendship.

In the afternoon I went riding in the King's Garden. I met Mrs Perceval there, but she left the Garden hurriedly, saying that she had some business to attend to. As soon as I reached home I told Sir Gore Ouseley what had happened. But he assured me that she is my friend and must truly have had an urgent appointment. 'Do not be hurt,' he said. 'Tomorrow I shall ask her about it and let you know what she says.' Nevertheless, I could not sleep all night wondering why she had treated me in this way.

After Sir Gore Ouseley got home he sent me a note to say that the report that a French ambassador had set out for Iran was false.

Monday, 18 June

THE MINISTER FOR THE COMPANY and the Chairman of the Company came to the house to present me with a dagger and a ring as mementos. Sir Gore Ouseley spoke at length about my mission.

This evening there was a 'masquerade' at Mrs Chichester's house.[1] All the nobility and gentry – ladies and gentlemen – came to the party in fancy dress.

Sir Gore Ouseley had told me that he was not going to the masquerade; but, in fact, he came in splendid Iranian dress. He tried to disguise his voice, but I recognized his excellent Persian immediately.

The guests enjoyed themselves until dawn. In the morning, after having something to eat which the English call 'supper', everyone went home.

[1] *The Morning Post*, 18 June, announced that Mrs Chichester's masquerade would take place that evening at her house in Portland Place.

Tuesday, 19 June

AFTER LUNCH I THOUGHT I should take a constitutional and I walked to Portman Square. It is very pleasant in spring when the trees are green; and mornings and afternoons the ladies and gentlemen who live in the houses around the square walk there for pleasure. Because my house is nearby I went there occasionally in the winter; but now I make it a rule to walk there for one hour every afternoon.

My walks are made even more pleasant by the pretty ladies who frequent the square. Today I met the niece of Lord Minto, the Governor-General of India: her name is Miss Elliot. She asked me to write her name – and her sister's as well – in Persian so that they could have their seals engraved in Persian.

Wednesday, 20 June

I RECEIVED A NOTE FROM Sir Gore Ouseley together with some guns which he sent as presents for my servants. I too gave each of them some money so that they can buy presents to take home.

I learned that one of my servants, Mohammad Ali Beik, visited four different taverns in the short space of five hours: he became drunk and visited a brothel. I am disgusted with him because he has given a bad name to all my servants.

Thursday, 21 June

SIR GORE OUSELEY CAME to tell me that today I was invited to the house of the Jew, Mr Goldsmid; he is the brother-in-law of the lady whose party I attended a few days ago.[1] Sir Gore Ouseley asked me to come to his house in my carriage so that we could go together. So later in the afternoon Sir Gore Ouseley, his brother Sir William Ouseley, Mr Morier and I set off for Mr Goldsmid's house, which is about two *farsakhs* from London.[2]

The house stands in a garden crossed by several streams and waterfalls. In the garden there is a building which houses a collection of all sorts of wild animals and birds from India, China, the New World and Europe, as well as flowers and fruit trees.

We were shown all over the house, including the bedrooms, the kitchen, where several sturdy women were busy cooking, and the dairy where they churn cream into butter. We also saw a pleasant marble-tiled room with a fountain in the middle: a statue of a boy pissing provided the water!

Our host has fine collections of glass and gold and silver plate. He boasted so much of his possessions and asked for my approval so constantly that finally I lost patience and assured him that his house was superior to paradise! At last he left me in peace.

Some forty people sat down at the dinner table; after dinner we moved to another table for fruit and wine. We were entertained by a singer – a Jewess who sang beautifully. Some of the ladies also played and sang. My friends Sir Charles Cockerell and his wife were among the guests. Sir Charles Cockerell pronounced himself sick and tired of the endless chatter of our conceited hostess.

Late in the evening we went on to an assembly at the house of the Duchess of St Albans, who is the wife of a Duke.[3] She is a stupid woman, ignorant of protocol: she paid me no attention at all.

The beautifully dressed ladies wilted from the heat.

It was early in the morning when we went home.

¹ Abraham Goldsmid (?1756-1810) was a socially prominent financier; his wife was Ann Eliason of Amsterdam. Like his brother Benjamin, whose widow entertained Abul Hassan on 5 June, Abraham Goldsmid suffered business failures and committed suicide on 28 September 1810.

² Goldsmid's house was by the River Wandle, on the site of the present Morden Lodge, Morden Hall Road.

³ Aubrey Beauclerk (1765-1815), 6th Duke of St Albans, married second in 1802 Grace Louisa Manners (1777-1816), fourth daughter of John Manners and Louisa Countess of Dysart.

PLATE 45

Margaret Mercer Elphinstone as Miranda.
Portrait by John Hoppner.

PLATE 46

*A drawing by James Morier of Sir Gore Ouseley
in Persian Court Dress.*

Friday, 22 June

I WAS WALKING IN THE King's Garden with the Prime Minister's wife when two women came up to me and asked if they could call on me at home. I agreed and in the evening they both came to the house.

One of the women was younger and better looking and I was more attentive to her than to the other. The second woman became jealous and started to make a scene: foolishly, she threatened to break all the mirrors! I was alarmed and fled from the room. I ordered two of my servants to get rid of them; but they were unable to calm them down. Mr Morier, who was asleep in his bedroom, was awakened by the uproar; finally he went into the drawing-room in his white night-shirt (which is what Englishmen wear in bed). The women thought I had shaved my beard to look like an Englishman! They swore and shouted; but, after much persuasion, Mr Morier succeeded in evicting them. Never in all my life have I encountered two such demented females!

Sunday, 24 June

SEVERAL NIGHTS AGO at the masquerade party, a lady unknown to me, who was disguised as a priest, introduced herself to me: the English call such behaviour 'forward'. She later wrote inviting me to a party at her house today. I went there with Sir Gore Ouseley.

The lady's name is Lady William Gordon. Her husband, Lord William Gordon, is responsible for the King's Park where everyone goes to relax. Their very nice house, which is in the middle of the city, belongs to the Government.[1]

From there we went to the Prime Minister's house. Mrs Perceval and her daughters have been extremely kind to me ever since I arrived in London. She presented me with a pen-case as a memento. I only hope God will give me an opportunity to repay her. Lady Ouseley was also there.

In the evening we were invited to the house of Sir Gore Ouseley's special friend, Mr Prendergast. It was Sir Gore Ouseley's birthday[2] and he had invited some thirty ladies and gentlemen. The party was very good-humoured: everyone told stories and jokes. Our host was extremely kind to me – I have not encountered a more sincere or faithful friend in all of London.

When I returned home, late in the evening, my Iranian servants complained to me that the pistols given to them by Sir Gore Ouseley were defective. I wrote him a letter and despatched it.

[1] Lord William Gordon (died 1823), the Deputy Ranger of St James's Park, was the second son of the 3rd Duke of Gordon. In 1781 he married Frances, daughter of Charles, 9th Viscount Irvine. They lived in Piccadilly.

[2] It was Ouseley's fortieth birthday.

Tuesday, 26 June

S IR GORE OUSELEY recently asked me to make him a list of all the gifts I had from the Government. I made the list and despatched it to him about noon.

Mr Prendergast, a true friend, came to the house. We talked about Mr Morier and the fact that he was not paid a salary.[1] Then we went together to the house of Mr Lawrence, the painter.

In the evening I went to the house of Miss Calvert's aunt, Mrs Knox; it is a handsome house, beautifully decorated.[2] Miss Calvert is a charming girl – she has learned a few words of Persian which she pronounced very sweetly.

[1] Morier did not receive a salary in London. In Iran the salaries of the Ambassador and the Secretary to the Embassy were paid by public funds; the East India Company agreed to pay the salary of the Private Secretary (Sir William Ouseley). (Letter from Dundas to the Chairman of the East Indian Company, 18 June. IO L/PS/3/3, ff. 268-73.)

[2] Mrs Warenne Blake, who published Mrs Calvert's journal as *An Irish Beauty of the Regency*, commented, p.159: 'This fiery Eastern potentate showed such warm admiration of the lovely Isabella that we at one time trembled lest he should make proposals for her hand, but matters never seem to have gone quite so far as this.'

Wednesday, 27 June

THAT MADWOMAN WHO KEEPS asking to come with me to Iran – to which I have never agreed – has written to the newspaper claiming that she is going to bear my child! She imagines thus to trick me into taking her with me; but as I swear to God I have never even spoken to her, it is impossible that the child is mine! I am amazed and astonished that the newspapers consent to publish such slander.[1]

In the evening we were invited to Lady Arden's house. Mrs Perceval's daughters were there until late in the evening and showed me much kindness.

I complained a little to Lady Arden and Sir Gore Ouseley that Lord Radstock, who had at first shown me such kindness, had lately – without explanation – withdrawn his friendship. But they assured

276

me of his affection and reminded me that it was because of him that I had so many friends in London.

We left Lady Arden's and went to Mrs Pole's house. Her eldest daughter, Mrs Bagot, was deep in conversation with a young colonel. She urged Sir Gore Ouseley to make certain that he was invited to Mr Prendergast's party the following week. Mrs Bagot's husband is very handsome and I did not in the least approve of her conduct.

Furthermore, she made reference to the newspaper report about my becoming a father and asked me if I would take the child with me to Iran! I was greatly embarrassed by her comments and told her I was grieved that she should hold me in such contempt. God forbid that anyone should believe such slander – the words of a common prostitute.

I was discouraged by dear Miss Pole's indifference this evening. It was late when I returned home.

[1] The British Library holds only those newspapers of the period which paid the required stamp duty. It is likely that only the penny-dreadfuls which avoided paying tax would have printed the 'madwoman's' accusations.

Friday, 29 June

I WENT WITH SIR GORE OUSELEY to the house of the Prince of Wales. We toured the house and garden, the stables and the carriage-house: everything was perfection. The house is furnished with gold and silver plate, mirrors and paintings, huge chandeliers and curtains of brocade. The stables, which are neat and clean, house some sixty carriage and riding horses. One of the horses was being tended by four grooms: in Iran such a horse would fetch fifty *tomans*; but I was told that here it had cost 3500 *tomans*.

In the evening – it was raining – we were invited to the house of Sir Charles Cockerell. He took us on to Sadler's Wells, which I call the 'Water Opera': it is a large building, like other theatres, about one *farsakh* from London.

The performance began with dancing and a pantomime. Finally the curtain rose on an immense lake of real water with a few small boats. A Frenchman and an Englishman stood on a bridge, fighting for the hand of the King of Scotland's daughter. The rivals fell into the water (in this hot weather it could not have been unpleasant!) and continued their combat in one of the small boats. But finally the Frenchman was defeated, and his shrouded corpse was placed on a barge which sank slowly beneath the water.

I enjoyed the performance, but in my opinion the Horse Opera is better.

JULY

1810

Sunday, 1 July

AFTER LUNCH WE SET OFF for Windsor, where the King lives with his family and staff. The Palace, which is about six *farsakhs* from London, is built around a vast open space, like a fortified castle; it must be more than 1000 paces in circumference.

The King travels to London every Wednesday to meet with his ministers; but on Sundays he meets his subjects. Because Sunday is a holiday in England and the people do not work, they come out to Windsor to see their King. To the sound of Royal music, the King walks along the high terrace which surrounds the Castle: he talks to the people and listens to their problems.

The King came up to me and we talked for about an hour. He was very surprised that I spoke English, and he congratulated Sir Gore Ouseley.

It was midnight when we returned home.

Tuesday, 3 July

THE KING'S MASTER OF the Ceremonies came to tell me that my farewell audience of the King has been arranged for one week from tomorrow. This good news cheered me up greatly.

In the evening I received a note from Sir Gore Ouseley to say that the Minister for Foreign Affairs has been taken ill. I replied that I too am at death's door – the result of Lord Wellesley's procrastination over the last eight months!

PLATE 47

The Orchestra Pavilion of Vauxhall Gardens,
decorated with the Royal crown and coat of arms.
Aquatint by Pugin and Rowlandson for
Ackermann's Microcosm of London, *1808-10.*

PLATE 48

PLATE 49

The Wedgwood & Byerley Showroom and a
platter from the Wedgwood service ordered by Abul
Hassan for the Shah of Persia.

PLATE 50

"—AY, HERE'S THE MASCULINE TO THE FEMININE GENDER."

Albinia, Countess of Buckinghamshire, as 'Cowslip'
in 'The Agreeable Surprise'. The caricature is by
James Gilray.

PLATE 51

The Queen's House, St James's Park (Buckingham House) as it must have appeared to Abul Hassan on the day of his farewell audience with the King and Queen on 11 July 1810. Aquatint by Pugin and Rowlandson for Ackermann's Microcosm of London, *1808-10.*

Wednesday, 4 July

SIR GORE OUSELEY came to show me a letter from Sir Harford Jones which left Tabriz three months and four days ago. It concerns Malcolm's arrival in Iran and various other topics. I accompanied him in the carriage to the door of the Foreign Office.

At the door I met Mr Arbuthnot and I teased him a bit: I told him I had heard from Miss Pole that he was to marry her sister. He was not amused!

Sir Gore Ouseley returned and we walked for a while in Parliament Square discussing Malcolm at length: it is clear that Malcolm will refuse to leave Iran until the Qibleh of the Universe receives my letter informing him of the name of the new English Ambassador and making clear the position of Sir Harford Jones.

Thursday, 5 July

ORD RADSTOCK came to see me.

I have received a letter from Mirza Bozorg, enclosed in the one from Sir Harford Jones, saying that he has received no news from me.[1] He reports that Malcolm is constantly trying to make trouble for Sir Harford Jones and that he intends to effect great changes. Mirza Bozorg also complained about the conduct of certain officials of the Government of India.

Because of my close friendship with Sir Gore Ouseley I wrote to him, informing him of these matters, and asking him if he did not think it advisable for me to leave at once, via Istanbul, in order to frustrate the machinations of the Government of India. Sir Gore Ouseley replied that he would come to see me tomorrow.

[1] Mirza Bozorg (Mirza Isa Qaem Maqam, died 1822), Vizir to the Crown Prince Abbas Mirza, Governor of Azerbaijan, was generally sympathetic to the British, but critical of Lord Minto.

Friday, 6 July

IN THE MORNING Sir Gore Ouseley came to the house and I gave him an account of Malcolm's conduct in Iran. Sir Gore Ouseley commented: 'When Malcolm receives the letters from the East India Company and from the Prime Minister clarifying the position of Sir Harford Jones, he will leave Iran immediately.' Then he made a translation of Mirza Bozorg's letter and despatched copies of it to the Minister for Foreign Affairs and to the Chairman of the Company.

In the evening we were invited to Mr Prendergast's house. Among the ladies and gentlemen was Lady Wellington,[1] who is pretty and charming. Although her husband is a lord, the brother of the Minister for Foreign Affairs, and the popular Commander-in-Chief of the army fighting in Spain, she remains modest and unassuming. *'Sobhanallah!'* I thought to myself. 'When compared with those of other countries, the greatest of Englishmen and women are truly without vanity!'

Miss Pole, Mrs Bagot, the third sister[2] and their mother were also at the party. Miss Pole sat next to me and said some things which pleased me very much.

Mr Arbuthnot, who is at the Treasury and formerly served at the Embassy in Constantinople, is also captivated by Miss Pole. This evening I noticed him looking distracted and unhappy. I do not know the reason, but I hazard a guess that she has rejected him! I was content when we left the party and returned home.

---

[1] Arthur Wellesley, Viscount (and future Duke of) Wellington, married in 1806 the Hon. Catherine Packenham, daughter of the 2nd Baron Longford.

[2] It is unclear whether Abul Hassan's 'Miss Pole' was Emily or Priscilla Wellesley-Pole. This reference to the 'third sister' (Priscilla was the third daughter) is a possible clue that it was Emily to whom Abul Hassan was attracted.

Saturday, 7 July

WE WENT TO MR PERCEVAL'S country house,[1] which is about two *farsakhs* from London. The house is indeed wonderful, without equal in elegance and taste.

Mrs Perceval told me that she had purchased the house and garden for 18,000 *tomans*. This is not surprising: most lords spend 1000 *tomans* on their paintings alone. In contrast to the citizens of other countries, who tend to hide their wealth, the English delight in showing off their possessions. The English devote themselves to pleasure and to entertaining each other on a lavish scale.

But at the same time, they do not neglect the education of their children: they take education seriously, with the result that an English child of three is far more courteous and well informed than a ten-year-old from any other country.

Lady Ouseley and Mr Arbuthnot of the Treasury were also there. I strolled in the garden with Mr Arbuthnot; and when I praised Miss Pole, it was quite clear that he is captivated by her.

After dinner Mr Perceval's children politely came to say goodbye to me. They are all very handsome. They were accompanied by their governess and tutor. Even the youngest children of all classes in England are beautifully dressed. The English place great importance on their children's appearance: they are always clean and tidy, for their clothes are changed three times a day!

---

[1] The Percevals bought Elm Grove, on the south-east corner of Ealing Common, seven miles from London, in late 1807. The property consisted of thirty-six acres, ten laid out as formal gardens.

Sunday, 8 July

We have not failed to intimate to the Governor General of India, how highly we are satisfied with your Excellency's conduct, and we have directed him, as proof of our friendship for your Excellency in our behalf a pension of one thousand Rupees per month, which we trust the King your Most illustrious Master will permit you to accept, and which will be regularly paid to your Excellency so long as you shall lend your assistance to the British Ambassador in preserving the friendly relations between Great Britain and Persia.

(The Chairman of the East India Company to Mirza Abul Hassan, 7 July 1810)[1]

THE COMPANY HAS SENT me a letter full of praise for my conduct during the Treaty negotiations. I took it to Sir Gore Ouseley, who studied it and appeared highly gratified by this proof of their absolute confidence in my friendship.

Sir Gore Ouseley presented me with some gifts he had purchased for me on behalf of the Government. He placed them in his carriage and we drove home together.

Mr Morier remarked that the Government had already provided some 1000 *tomans* worth of clothing for me and my servants. I pronounced myself content that the Government had not been negligent in hospitality.

---

[1] PRO FO 60/118.

Monday, 9 July

SOME OF THE GOODS FOR Iran have been sent to the ship. My servants have been given whatever they wished as presents. Never have I known a government to be so considerate and generous in the matter of gifts.

The King's Master of the Ceremonies[1] came to make arrangements for my audience.

Lord Radstock came to the house to give me some books. He is a faithful and considerate friend. After abandoning me for some time, he has resumed his former attentions – *alhamdolillah!*

In the evening I spent some time at Lord Radstock's house. His daughters sang for me. One of the guests was a young lady – she appeared to be about twenty years old – who spoke a little Turkish. Mr Morier told me that she is engaged to a Colonel who is said to be an excellent artist.

---

[1] Sir Stephen Cotterell.

Tuesday, 10 July

THE REST OF THE furniture and other goods for Iran have been sent to the ship.

I wrote some letters for Iran and despatched them. And I wrote to Sir Gore Ouseley about the further delay of two days for our departure from London; we now plan to leave on Saturday.

Then I rode for a while in the King's Garden, where I met Mrs Bagot walking with her small child. I dismounted and said my goodbyes to her. Touched by everyone's kindness, I felt sorry to be leaving England.

In the evening I went to the Opera. Sir Gore Ouseley had sent me a note to tell me that he had spent the day at the East India Company, that all our affairs are in order, and that he would be unable to go to the Opera this evening because he wished to call on the Prime Minister.

At the Opera I noticed that Mrs Bagot had drawn the curtains of her box so that no one could see who was seated there. When the Colonel whom I have mentioned before arrived, they left together. I do not approve! They seem to be madly in love.

Wednesday, 11 July

THE KING'S MASTER of the Ceremonies came in the carriage to take me to my farewell audience with the King.

According to the protocol, the King was standing with his councillors and lords. He spoke to each one in turn and then addressed me. I replied in English and he congratulated me on my cleverness.

The King then took me and the Minister and Sir Gore Ouseley to his private chamber. He expressed much sorrow that I was leaving London and he asked me to convey to the Qibleh of the Universe expressions of his friendship and affection and the satisfaction he derives from the friendship which now exists between our two countries. With his own hand the King fixed to my waist a gold and enamelled dagger set with diamonds, which he asked me to keep as a memento of him. I kissed the King's hand as I took my leave.

Then we went to see the Queen and the princesses. They also expressed sorrow that I was leaving, and the Queen said that she would be very pleased if I were to return to London as ambassador.

When we left the Queen I remarked to Sir Gore Ouseley that the diamond set in the dagger's handle was surely not the same one that I had had the opportunity of examining before. 'Still,' I said, 'whatever they have chosen to give me – may their Royal House flourish forever!'

I returned home in the carriage with the Master of the Ceremonies, but Sir Gore Ouseley and the Minister remained to discuss certain matters with the King. The King told Sir Gore Ouseley that he was pleased that the Shah of Iran had not acceded to the Governor-General's wish to dismiss Sir Harford Jones. He also said that his Government is prepared to assist Iran in every way possible.

In the evening I went with Mr Morier to Vauxhall, even though I was not in the mood. Miss Pole often talked to me of Vauxhall and promised to accompany me there, but she always found an excuse.

Thursday, 12 July

I WROTE A NOTE TO Sir Gore Ouseley to tell him that the diamond in the handle of my dagger is only glass! It is an unpleasant situation, but I told him that when we call on the Prince of Wales to say goodbye, I intend to acquaint him personally with the facts.

Sir Gore Ouseley was with me when some clocks which the Government had purchased for me were delivered to the house. I thought they were of poor quality – a type which is never sent from Europe to Iran. But Sir Gore Ouseley assures me that they are very valuable, so I regret having criticized them.

The Company has sent me a letter agreeing to pay my pension from the date of my arrival in Bombay. I did not expect to receive this pittance and all I want is to reach home quickly and in good health.

Then Sir Gore Ouseley and I went to call on the Prince of Wales. The Duke of Clarence was also there. While we sat talking, mention was made of that woman who has accused me of fathering her child. The Prince of Wales said the woman was mad: last year she claimed to have had children by all the Royal Princes! The Prince showed us an Arab horse which had recently been purchased for him.

When we were taking our leave the Prince of Wales praised me to Sir Gore Ouseley and, taking my hand, he placed a ring on my finger – it has an unusual smooth stone surrounded by diamond chips. Then he bade us farewell and we took our leave.

Friday, 13 July

I HAD NOT YET SAID goodbye to Mrs Perceval – I am extremely grateful to her for her many kindnesses – so I drove out to her country house in the carriage. I spent some time walking with her and her daughters, but it began to rain heavily. After three or four hours I returned home.

In the evening we were invited to the Prime Minister's house. Lord Wellesley, the Minister for Foreign Affairs, spoke at length about the friendship now existing between the Governments of England and Iran and he expressed his great satisfaction with my conduct of affairs. He is extremely intelligent and perspicacious, a wise and witty man. He has no rival in good taste: he dresses beautifully and he drinks in moderation.

I told him I was sorry that in the past I had sometimes pressed him to reply more quickly to my requests. But he said he was pleased that I had been so diligent in the pursuit of my Government's interests. Lord Wellesley wished to see me off at the door, but I would not permit it.

From there we went to a late evening party at the house of the Marquis of Douglas, son of the Duke of Hamilton.[1] He has recently married a lady whose flawless beauty makes other women look like witches. She has a matchless singing voice: the nightingale's song is like a crow's compared to hers! She also plays musical instruments and paints well. And although she is only about twenty years old, she knows several languages. All the guests were conquered by her smiling courtesy, her lovely eyes and her curly hair. We conversed for some time. I asked her why we had not met before; and I lamented that – just on the eve of my departure – I should be ensnared by the curve of a straying lock:

> *It is not only I whom your ringlets ensnare,*
> *There's a captive tied up by each lock of your hair.*

The fourth Royal Prince, the Duke of Kent, was also at the party. After the singing and dancing, I sat next to him for what they call – at the end of an evening – 'supper'. But I had no interest in eating or drinking, so absorbed was I by the beauty of that *peri*-faced girl.

It was almost dawn when we returned home.

My chest has been hurting for two days now.

[1] Alexander Hamilton (1767-1852), Marquis of Douglas (later 10th Duke of Hamilton) married on 26 April 1810 Susan Euphemia, second daughter and co-heir of William Beckford of Fonthill Abbey. They lived at 10 Grosvenor Place.

Saturday, 14 July

Yesterday his Excellency the Persian Ambassador accompanied by Sir Gore Ouseley [sic] and Suite left town for Portsmouth, where they will immediately embark on board the Lion, *64 guns, and proceed on their way to Persia.*

(*The News*, 15 July)

MR MORIER, SIR WILLIAM OUSELEY, Mr Gordon[1] and I in one carriage, and my servants in another, set off for Portsmouth – it is seventy-two miles, about twenty-two *farsakhs*, from London.

We covered the distance in twelve hours, changing the four horses every three *farsakhs*. There is a great deal of traffic on this road. Like the road from Plymouth to London (which covers a distance of sixty *farsakhs*), there are inns every few miles which provide food and drink and rooms for travellers to rest in. A fixed charge is made for food and the hire of horses.

The dockyards at Portsmouth are better equipped than those at Plymouth. There are a fort and an arms depot on the harbour, where many ships of the Royal Navy may be seen sailing in and out.

Sir Gore Ouseley promised to join us in Portsmouth today; but he has not arrived.

My chest was still painful; but the journey had tired me and I slept well.

---

[1] Robert (later Sir Robert) Gordon (1791-1847) was the fifth son of George Gordon, Lord Haddo, and brother of the future Prime Minister, George Hamilton Gordon, 4th Earl of Aberdeen. Aberdeen's friendship with Sir Gore Ouseley secured Robert Gordon's appointment as attaché to the embassy to Persia.

Sunday, 15 July

MR MORIER TOLD ME that he has been invited to a party by two ladies who are sisters. But they have not invited me because they have heard that I am not fond of old ladies! 'Thank God,' I said, 'may He grant them long life for not summoning me to their house!'

I received a letter from Sir Gore Ouseley saying that he had been so busy at the Foreign Office yesterday that he had not been able to leave town. He will come today.

Mr Morier told me that the inn has a bathroom. I asked to take a bath, and I have not enjoyed one more during all my time in London.

Captain Heathcote, Captain of the *Lion* which is to take us to Bushire, came to call on me. He told me that the ship has been ready to leave for some time now. 'When Sir Gore Ouseley arrives, *inshallah*,' I said, 'we shall depart!'

The doctor who was on the ship which brought us from Malta to England recommended bleeding to relieve my chest pains. It made me feel a little better.

I wrote a letter to my dear friend Mrs Perceval.

Captain Heathcote came to see me again – this time with his wife[1] and daughter. His wife begged me not to make any stops on our journey and to send her husband home quickly.

Sir Gore Ouseley arrived at about six o'clock. He gave me a ring from Lord Wellesley, who sent his compliments. Sir Gore Ouseley then left – he is staying elsewhere.

In the evening those travelling to Iran had dinner at my inn and several officers of the Royal Navy came to see me. If the weather is good, we shall board the ship tomorrow. I am not feeling at all well.

---

[1] Captain Heathcote married in 1799 Sarah, daughter of Thomas Guscott; she died in 1845.

Monday, 16 July

MY CHEST WAS VERY PAINFUL this morning. Sir Gore Ouseley and the Lieutenant-Governor of Portsmouth,[1] accompanied by several colonels, came to see me. They invited me to a party tomorrow night.

The weather was very bad, so we could not board the ship today and Sir Gore Ouseley and Mr Morier passed the time telling jokes. Mr Morier told a story about an Englishman living in Istanbul, whose mistress used to shave her pubic hair. This was displeasing to him as it is not an English custom – so he had a little hairpiece made, which he attached before sleeping with her!

The doctor came to see me. He gave me some medicine and left.

Sir Gore Ouseley went to inspect the ship and pronounced himself well pleased. In the evening my travelling companions came to have dinner with me.

---

[1] Major- (later Lieutenant-) General Arthur Whetham (died 1813), was appointed Lieutenant-Governor of Portsmouth in 1809.

Tuesday, 17 July

. . . His Excellency the Persian Ambassador, whilst here, visited the different departments of the Dock-yard, at much of which he seemed astonished, particularly at the Block-machinery. He went on board that fine ship the Hibernia, *she being in dock. On Tuesday he dined with General Whetham, in company with the Commanding Officers of all the Regiments in garrison. His Excellency attracted a great deal of public curiosity: the utmost respect was shown him.*

(*The Hampshire Telegraph*, 23 July)

THIS MORNING I WENT TO Portsmouth Dockyard with Sir Gore Ouseley and the gentleman (whose brother is a lord) who is in charge of shipbuilding and naval research.[1] The yard contains some 100 steam-powered machines, which only two years ago had to be operated by hand. Work formerly done by 100 men can now be done by two. These machines are not yet available in France and other European countries.

The navy gives constant encouragement to inventors: when something new is invented the cost for its development is estimated and the money is provided by the Government. The man who invented a machine to cut wooden planks to different sizes was given a reward of 16,000 *tomans* a year.

In the evening we were invited to the house of General Whetham, who had also invited many of his officers. He is a very sympathetic and generous man, unmarried and advanced in years.

It was late when I returned to the inn. My chest was a little better.

[1] The Commissioner Resident of Portsmouth-Yard was Captain the Hon. (later Sir) George Grey (1767-1828), son of 1st Earl Grey.

Wednesday, 18 July

His excellency Mirza Abduk [sic) Hassan, Ambassador from the King of Persia to this country (on leave), and Sir Gore Ouseley, Bart. the British Ambassador at the Persian Court, with their suites, embarked from the Crown Inn, on Wednesday evening, under the usual salutes, on board the Lion, *64, Captain Heathcote, which sailed immediately to Muscat. The* Lion *will touch at Madeira, the Brazils, and Bombay previously to her going to the Persian Gulph. . . .*

(The Hampshire Telegraph, 23 July)

I WENT WITH SIR GORE OUSELEY and two colonels to see the fortress and the cranes and some of the cannon recently captured from the enemy. Some 500 guns have been taken from Russian ships.

I saw many new inventions, including a wheel and hook for moving big guns on to ships. By turning the wheel, one person can uncoil a very thick rope which attaches itself to the gun automatically and lifts it easily on to the ship.

I received a reply to my letter to Mrs Perceval, and one from Lord Minto's niece, Miss Elliot; but none – alas! – from Miss Pole. She has completely forgotten me!

In the afternoon the sea calmed and Mr Morier and I left the town for the harbour, accompanied by two colonels. (Sir Gore and Lady Ouseley had boarded the ship earlier.) A sixteen-gun salute was fired and many people were out to see us. Another sixteen-gun salute was fired as we boarded the ship – it has a lion's face as a figurehead.

In the evening the sea was still calm. Captain Heathcote weighed anchor and we set sail for Iran.

A GLOSSARY OF PERSIAN AND ARABIC WORDS

Alhamdolillah: Praise be to God!

Alhamdolillah valmena: Praise be to God for his Grace!

Amin od-Doleh (Trustee of the State): a title of the Persian Minister of Finance, Haji Mohammad Hosein Khan.

Araq: a liquor distilled from rice.

Bagh-i Eram: the Moslem equivalent of the Garden of Eden.

Bagh-i Shah: the King's Garden or Park.

Bismallah: in the name of God.

Dinar: see toman.

Div: demon, devil.

Divan: a collection of verse.

Farang: Europe, from 'Frank'.

Farangi: a European, from 'the Franks'.

Farman: a Royal edict or letter.

Farsakh (or farsang): an old Persian measure of length equal to approximately four miles.

Ghazal: a romantic ode.

Haji: the title assumed by a Moslem who has made the pilgrimmage to Mecca.

Hammam: a Persian bathhouse.

Heirat-nameh: a 'Book of Wonders' in the tradition of ancient Eastern histories of the world.

Hind: India.

Houri: a nymph of the Moslem paradise.

Ilchi: the head of a diplomatic mission of whatever rank.

Imam: see Islam.

Inshallah: God willing.

Islam: the religion (meaning submission to God) founded by the Prophet Mohammad (*c.* 570-629 AD). Its adherents (Moslems) are divided into two main sects, the Sunnis and the Shias. The former accept a line of Caliphs descending from Mohammad through a process of election which eliminated his descendants with the exception of his son-in-law Ali. The vast majority of Iranians are Shias, who recognize the Twelve Imams, or spiritual leaders, who were all blood descendants of Ali and the Prophet's daughter Fatimeh.

Isteqbal: An official welcome to a distinguished visitor: dignitaries and other citizens come out of the town to greet him and accompany him back into it.

Iwan: an arch.

Jarib: a Persian acre.

Kamancheh: a violin-like musical instrument.

Khalat: a robe of honour bestowed by the Shah.

Khan: a hereditary or tribal title; but also sometimes bestowed by the Shah for service to the state.

Kurosh: see toman.

Lakh: in 1810 one lakh (100,000 rupees) equalled 12,500 tomans or £11,250.

Mahd-i Olya (Cradle of the Highest): a title of the Shah's principal wife.

Maidan: an open space; a square, arena or parade-ground.

Marhaba: Well done!

Mehmandar: an official assigned as a courtesy to important visitors to act as host, guide and interpreter.

Mirza: used as a suffix it denotes a prince (e.g. Abbas Mirza, Crown Prince of Persia); used as a prefix (e.g. Mirza Abul Hassan) it denotes a scribe, a secretary or an educated man.

Motamad od-Doleh (Trusted of the State): a title of the Persian Prime Minister, Mirza Mohammad Shafi Mazanderani.

298

Naieb os-Soltaneh (Deputy to the Kingdom): a title of the Crown Prince of Persia.

Nastaliq: a style of Persian calligraphy developed from an Arabic script and codified by the end of the fourteenth century.

Padeshah: king.

Peri: fairy.

Qajar: the name of the Persian dynasty from 1796 to 1924.

Qalian: the Persian water tobacco-pipe.

Qibleh: the direction towards which Moslems turn to pray; hence, the focal point.

Qoran: the sacred book of Islam, which Mohammad claimed had been revealed to him as the Word of God.

Qurosh: see toman.

Rum: from its foundation in 330 AD, Constantinople was called the new 'Rome'.

Shah: king.

Shahanshah: King of Kings.

Shia: see Islam.

Sobhanallah: Good God!

Sunni: see Islam.

Tagh-i Khosrow: the Arch of Khosrow (at Ctesiphon).

Takht-i ravan: litter; sedan-chair.

Toman: in 1810 the Persian toman was approximately equal to eighteen shillings. It consisted of ten quroshes or 10,000 dinars.

Vakil: a representative empowered to act for another.

Valiahd: Crown Prince.

Vasalaam: Any may peace be upon you; i.e. 'What more can I say? Farewell.'

Vizir: minister.

BIBLIOGRAPHY

I. MANUSCRIPT DOCUMENTS

British Library (BL): Papers of the Marquis Wellesley, BL Add. 37285.

India Office Library and Records (IO): Home Miscellaneous Series H733; and Correspondence of the Secret Committee of the East India Company May 1807 to September 1810, L/PS/3/3.

National Library of Wales (NLW): Kentchurch Court papers.

Public Record Office (PRO): Foreign Office Series 60/2, 60/4 and 60/118.

II. PUBLISHED DOCUMENTS

Aitchison, C. U. (ed.) *A Collection of Treaties, Engagements, and Sanads relating to India and Neighbouring Countries*, vol. x, Calcutta, 1892.

Aspinall, A. (ed.) *The Later Correspondence of George III*, vol. v, Cambridge, 1970. (Abbreviated *Aspinall/Geo III.*).

III. NEWSPAPERS AND MAGAZINES 1809-10

La Belle Assemblée
The British Press
The Hampshire Telegraph
The London Chronicle
The London Gazette
The Morning Herald
The Morning Post
The News
The Observer
The Statesman
The Sun
The Times

IV. BOOKS AND ARTICLES

A. MIRZA ABUL HASSAN

Anonymous, *'Memoir of the Persian Ambassador'. The London Literary Gazette*, No. 120, 8 May 1819. (This memoir is partially reprinted in Tancoigne.)

Berry, Mary. *Extracts from the Journals and Correspondence of Miss Berry from 1783 to 1852*, ed. Lady Theresa Lewis, Longman, London, 1865.

Blake, Mrs Warenne, *An Irish Beauty of the Regency, compiled from 'Mes Souvenirs', the unpublished Journals of the Hon. Mrs Calvert (1789-1822)*, John Lane, The Bodley Head, London, 1911. (Abbreviated *Mrs Calvert's Journal.*)

Borgomale, H. L. Rabino di, *Diplomatic and Consular Officers of Great Britain and Iran*, London, 1946.

Browne, E. G., Introduction to James Morier's *The Adventures of Hajji Baba of Ispahan*, Methuen, London, 1895.

Busse, Heribert, *History of Persia under Qajar Rule*, translated from the Persian of Hasan-e Fasai's *Farsnama-ye Naseri*, Columbia University Press, New York and London, 1972.

Curzon, George N., Introduction to James Morier's *The Adventures of Hajji Baba of Ispahan*, Macmillan, London, 1895.

Fowler, George, *Three Years in Persia*, 2 vols, H. Colburn, London, 1841.

Fraser, James Bailie, *Narrative of a Journey into Khorasan in the Years 1821 and 1822*, Longman, London, 1825.

Fraser, James Bailie, *A Winter's Journey from Constantinople to Tehran*, 2 vols, Richard Bentley, London, 1838.

Graves, Algernon, *The Royal Academy of Arts, a Complete Dictionary of Contributors and their Work from its Foundation in 1769 to 1904*, 8 vols, London, 1905.

Greville, Charles, *The Greville Memoirs 1814-1860*, Macmillan, London, 1938.

Holmes, William Richard, *Sketches on the Shores of the Caspian*, Richard Bentley, London, 1845.

Johnson, Colonel John, *A Journey from India to England, through Persia, Georgia, Russia, Poland, and Prussia in the Year 1817*, London, 1818.

Jones Brydges, Sir Harford, *An Account of the Transactions of His Majesty's Mission to the Court of Persia, in the Years 1807-1811*, 2 vols, James Bohn, London, 1834.

Kay, John, *A Series of Original Portraits and Caricature Etchings*, vol. II, Hugh Paton, Edinburgh, 1838.

Lamb, Charles, *The Letters of Charles Lamb*, ed. E. V. Lucas, vol. II, Dent and Methuen, London, 1935.

Millard, Charles W., 'A Diplomatic Portrait: Lawrence's "The Persian Ambassador"', *Apollo*, February 1976.

Money, Robert Cotton, *Journal of a Tour in Persia, during the Years 1824 and 1825*, Teape & Son, London, 1828.

Moore, Thomas, *Memoirs, Journal and Correspondence*, vol. II, Longman, Brown, Green & Longman, London, 1853.

Morier, James, *A Journey through Persia, Armenia, and Asia Minor to Constantinople in the Year 1808 and 1809*, Longman, London, 1812. (Abbreviated *Morier I.*)

Morier, James, *A Second Journey through Persia, Armenia, and Asia Minor to Constantinople between the Years 1810 and 1816*, Longman, London, 1818. (Abbreviated *Morier II.*)

Morier, James, *The Adventures of Hajji Baba of Ispahan*, 3 vols, 1st edition, John Murray, London, 1824.

Morier, James, *The Adventures of Hajji Baba of Ispahan in England*, 2 vols, 1st edition, John Murray, London, 1828.

Ouseley, Sir William, *Travels in Various Countries of the East; more particularly Persia*, 3 vols, Rodwell & Martin, London, 1819, 1821, 1823.

Porter, Sir Robert Ker, *Travels in Georgia, Persia, Armenia, Ancient Babylonia, 1817-1820*, 2 vols, Longman, London, 1821 and 1822.

Price, William, *Journal of the British Embassy to Persia*, 2 vols, 2nd edition, Thomas Thorpe, Covent Garden, London, 1832.

Radstock, William Waldegrave, Lord, 'A Slight Sketch of the Character,

Person . . . of Aboul Hassen, Envoy Extraordinary from the King of Persia to the Court of Great Britain, in the Years 1809 and 1810', *The Gentleman's Magazine*, February 1820. (This article took the form of a letter to an unidentified Lady, dated 10 January 1810, and is abbreviated in the text as *Lord Radstock's Letter*.)

Roberts, W., *Sir William Beechey, R.A.*, Duckworth, London, 1907.

Savory, R. M., *'British and French Diplomacy in Persia, 1800-1810'. Iran* (the Journal of the British Institute of Persian Studies), 1972.

Scott, Sir Walter, 'Hajji Baba in England', *The Quarterly Review*, January 1829.

Searight, Sarah, *The British in the Middle East*, Weidenfeld & Nicolson, London, 1969.

Shadman, S. F., 'A Review of Anglo-Persian Relations 1798-1815', *Proceedings of the Iran Society*, 1943.

Stuart, Colonel Charles, *Journal of a Residence in Northern Persia and the Adjacent Provinces of Turkey*, Richard Bentley, London, 1854.

Tancoigne, M., *Narrative of a Journey into Persia, and Residence at Tehran*, William Wright, London, 1820.

Wemyss, Alice, 'The Birth of Hajji Baba as seen through the Letters of James Morier', *Persica VII* (the Journal of the Nederland-Iran Society), 1975-8.

Weston, Revd Stephen, *Persian Recreations, or New Tales with Explanatory Notes on the Original Text, and Curious Details of Two Ambassadors to James I and George III, new edition*, London, 1812.

Williams, D. E., *The Life and Correspondence of Sir Thomas Lawrence, Kt.*, vol. II, London, 1831.

Wright, Denis, *The English Amongst the Persians*, Heinemann, London, 1977.

Wright, Denis, *The Persians Amongst the English*, I. B. Tauris, London, 1985.

B. BIOGRAPHY, HISTORY AND POLITICS

Allardyce, Alexander, *Memoir of the Honourable George Keith Elphinstone K.B., Viscount Keith, Admiral of the Red*, W. Blackwood, Edinburgh and London, 1882.

Anspach, the Margravine of, *Memoirs of the Margravine of Anspach, written by Herself*, H. Colburn, London, 1826.

Boyle's *Court and Country Guide*, April 1810.

Broadley, A. M. and Lewis Melville, *The Beautiful Lady Craven: the Original Memoirs of Elizabeth Baroness Craven afterwards Margravine of Anspach*, 2 vols, John Lane, London, 1914.

Browne, E. G., *Literary History of Persia*, 4 vols, Cambridge University Press, 1969 (first published 1902).

Butler, Iris, *The Eldest Brother: The Marquess Wellesley 1760-1842*, Hodder & Stoughton, London, 1973.

Farmer, Hugh, *A Regency Elopement*, Michael Joseph, London, 1969.

Fulford, Roger, *Royal Dukes*, Collins, revised edition, London, 1973.

Gardane, Le Comte Alfred de, *Mission du General Gardane en Perse sous le Premier Empire: Documents Historiques Publiés par son Fils*, Librairie Ad. Laine, Paris, 1865.

Gray, Denis, *Spencer Percival: The Evangelical Prime Minister 1762-1812*, Manchester University Press, 1963.

Hedley, Olwen, *Queen Charlotte*, John Murray, London, 1975.

Hibbert, Christopher, *George IV, 2 vols, Longman, London, 1972.*

Holme, Thea, Prinny's Daughter, Hamish Hamilton, London, 1976.

Holme, Thea, *Caroline: A Biography of Caroline of Brunswick*, Hamish Hamilton, London, 1979.

Kaye, J. W. *The Life and Correspondence of Major-General Sir John Malcolm*, 2 vols, Smith, Elder, London, 1856.

Malcolm, Sir John, *The History of Persia*, 2 vols, John Murray, London, 1815.

Minto: *Lord Minto in India: Life and Letters of Gilbert Elliot, first Earl of Minto, from 1807 to 1814*, ed. Countess of Minto, Longman, London, 1880.

Morris, Henry, *Charles Grant*, John Murray, London, 1904.

Philips, C. H., *The East India Company 1784-1834*, Manchester University Press, revised 1968.

Ramm, Agatha, *Sir Robert Morier*, Clarendon Press, Oxford, 1973.

Reynolds, Revd James, 'Memoir of the Rt Hon Sir Gore Ouseley, Bart.', prefixed to Sir Gore Ouseley's *Biographical Notices of Persian Poets*, W. H. Allen, London, 1846.

Royal Kalendar 1810, The

Stevens, Roger, *The Land of the Great Sophy*, Methuen, London, second edition, 1971.

Sykes, Sir Percy, *A History of Persia*, 2 vols, Macmillan, London, 1930.

Watson, Steven, *The Reign of George III, 1760-1815*, The Oxford History of England, 1960.

Woodruff, Philip, *The Men Who Ruled India*, 2 vols, Jonathan Cape, London, 1953.

INDEX

Asaf od-Dowleh, Vizir of
Oude, 86
Askar Khan, envoy to France,
263, 266
Astell, William, Dpty. Chmn.
EIC, 55-6, 56n., 115;
Chmn. EIC, 200, 226, 269
Astell, Mrs William, 226, 226n.
Astley's Amphitheatre, 232, *38*
Astley, Philip, 232n.
Augusta, Princess (sister of
Geo. III), 201, 201n.
Augusta, Princess (dau. of Geo.
III), 138

Baba, Mirza, artist, 75n.
Bacon, John Jr, sculptor, 183,
183n., 193
Bagot, (later Sir) Charles, 148,
148n., 157-8, 277
Bagot, Mrs Charles, 148,
148n., 277, 287, *43*
Bank of England, 84, *10*
Bath, 32-34
Beechey, Sir William, artist,
121, 121n., 162, 163n., 217
Book of Wonders, The, 7, 9
Bozorg, Mirza, Vizir of
Azerbaijan, 282-3, 282n.
Brandenburg House,
Hammersmith, 178, 227-8,
234
Brownlow, John Cust, 2nd
Baron (later 1st Earl), 216,
216n.
Brunswick, Duke of (nephew

of Geo. III), 103, 105n.
Buckingham House (Palace),
59-60, 103-4, 184-5, 288,
12, 18, 47
Buckinghamshire, Albinia,
Dowager Countess of,
98-100, 100n., 239, *51*
Burdett, Sir Francis, 196,
197n., 199

Calvert, Mrs Nicolson, 109n.,
222
Calvert, Isabella, 109, 110n.,
275, 275n.
Cambridge, Prince Adolphus
Frederick, Duke of (son of
Geo. III), 57, 103, 105n.,
171, 201, 203, 204n.
Canning, George, MP, 141,
141n.
Carlton House, 104, 112-3,
130-1, 278, *21*
Carneiro, Chevalier,
Portuguese Amb., 231
Castlereagh, Robert Stewart,
Viscount, MP, (later 2nd
Marquis of Londonderry),
141, 141n., 237, 237n.
Catalani, Angelica, soprano,
165, 165n., 166, 231, *34*
Cecil, Lady Emily, 99, 100n.
Charlotte, Queen, 89, 102-4,
106, 136-8, 255, 288, *11*
Chester, Robert, Dpty. Master
of Ceremonies, 39, 39n.,
59, 138, 175

289; plate presented to (1819), *20*

East India Docks, 209, 209n.

East India House, 74-5, 75n., 90-1, *6*

Eldon, John Scott, 1st Earl of, Lord Chancellor, 181, 182n., 184

Elgin, Thomas Bruce, 7th Earl of, 192, 192n.

Elizabeth I, Queen, 7, *225*

Elizabeth, Princess (dau. of Geo. III), 138

Elliot, Miss, 111n., 270, 296

Elm Grove, Ealing, 284, 284n.

Elphinstone, Margaret Mercer, 139, 140n., 157, 197, 206, 212, 241, *45*

Fanshaw, Robert, 30, 31n.

Farabi, Hakim, 94, 94n.

Fath Ali Shah Qajar, Shah of Iran, 15, 50, 55, 67, 69, 83n., 122, 144; gifts for, 233, 266, 266n., letter to Geo. III, 40-1, 44, 53, 60, 126, 145; portrait of, 74, 90, *8, 37*

Fayerman, Captain Francis, 24-7, 30, 32

Fayerman, Mrs Francis, 30

'fire-worshippers', 108, 115

'Firouz, Mirza', 8, *17*

Formidable, HMS, 24

Four-in-Hand Club, 235, 236n.

Freemasons, 17, *265*

Gardane, Brig-Gen. Claude Matthieu, French Amb. to Iran, 16, 95, 96n., 144

George III, King, 8, 50-1, 58-61, 167, 184-5, *255*, 280, 288, *3*

Gloucester, Duke of (nephew of Geo. III), 171

Goldsmid, Abraham, 271, 272n.

Goldsmid, Mrs Abraham, 271, 272n.

Goldsmid, Mrs Benjamin, 256, 256n.

Gordon, (later Sir) Robert, 292, 292n.

Gordon, Lord William, 274, 274n.

Gordon, Lady William, 274, 274n.

Grant, Charles, Chmn. EIC, 55-6, 74-5, 90, 107, 146, 200

Grey, Captain (later Sir) George, 295, 295n.

Grimaldi, Joseph, clown, 92-3, 93n.

Hafez, poet, 54, 54n., 241

Hajji Baba novels, 8-9, 13

Hamilton, Lord Archibald, MP, 237, 237n.

Hamilton, Lady (Emma), 242, 242n.

Hamilton, William Richard, 192, 192n.

Morier, The Misses, 73, 196
Morier, William, 196, 197n.
Morning Post, MAH's letter to,
   236, 246-8, 253
Motamad od-Doleh, First Vizir
   of Iran, 44, 49, *55*, 144,
   164, *23*
Mountnorris, Arthur Annesley,
   1st Earl of, 189, 189n.

Naeb os-Soltaneh: see Abbas
   Mirza.
Napoleon I, 14, 126
Naqd Ali Beg, portrait of, *75*
Nasir ud-Din of Tus, 107n.
Nelson, Horatio, Lord, 242,
   242n.

Opera: see King's Theatre.
Ouseley, Sir Gore, *passim*;
   biog. info. 39n.; appt. as
   Amb. to Iran 139, 140n.,
   147-8, *159*, 162, 167, *46*, *5*
Ouseley, Lady (Gore), 18, 66,
   66n., 94, 194, 244, 274,
   284, 296
Ouseley, Mary Jane (Janie),
   18, 66
Ouseley, Sir William, *159*,
   160n., 189, 192, 224, 227,
   254, 271, 275n., 292
Ouseley, Lady (William), 192,
   192n. 227

Panorama, The, 222, 222n.
Parks, Royal, 61, 73, 78-9,

114, 188, 206, 222, 231,
   234, 240, 245, 252, 268,
   273, 287, *7*
Perceval, Frances (Fanny),
   139, 140n., 226, 276
Perceval, Helena, 188
Perceval, Spencer, Prime
   Min., 43, 50-2, 52n.,
   58-60, 85, 97, 128, 130,
   139, 175, 198, 226, 284,
   287, *25*
Perceval, Mrs Spencer, 8,
   97-8, 100n., 102, 128, 139,
   149, 177, 180, 198, 201,
   222, 226, 242, 244, 268,
   273-4, 284, 293, 296, *44*
Perceval, Spencer, Jr, 208
Plymouth, 24-32
Pole: see Wellesley-Pole.
Portman Square, 88, 151, 270
Portsmouth, 292-6
Portuguese Ambassador, 231
Powis, Edward Clive, 1st Earl
   of, 85, 85n.
Prendergast, Michael, MP,
   262, 262n., 263, 274-5,
   277, 283

Queen's House (Palace): see
   Buckingham House.

Radstock, Adm. William
   Waldegrave, 1st Baron, 37,
   39n., 43, 54, 57, 64-5, 119,
   122, 133, 135, 139, 156,
   277, 286, *15*, *31*

Richmond, Surrey, 218, 219n.
Royal Academy, 162, 217, 217n.
Royal Arsenal, Woolwich, 259-60
Royal Hospital, Chelsea, 204, 204n.
Royal Hospital, Greenwich, 208, 209n.
Royal Italian Opera House: see King's Theatre.
Royal Menagerie, 225, 225n.
Royal Military Academy, Woolwich, 260, 260n.
Royal Military Asylum, Chelsea, (Duke of York's School), 204, 205n.
Rundell, Bridge & Rundell, Crown Jewellers, 240, 240n.
Russia (see also Tiflis), 15-18, 56, 64, 68, 91, 94, 117, 119, 266
Ryder, Richard, Home Scty., 51-2, 52n.

Saadat Ali Khan, Vizir of Oude, 86, 87n.
Saadi, poet, 130, 131n., 169
Sadler's Wells Theatre, 278
Sadri Effendi, Turkish Amb., 41, 67, 132-4
St Albans, Duchess of, 271, 272n.
St James's Palace, 136-8, 180, 255, 26

St Paul's Cathedral, 224, 225n., 258
Salisbury, James Cecil, 1st Marquis of, 154, 155n., 181
Saltoun, Dowager Lady, 199, 199n.
Sellis, Joseph, 249, 249n.
Serpentine, The, 108, 146
Shafi, Mirza Mohammad: see *Motamad od-Doleh*.
Sheridan, Richard Brinsley, MP, 177, 177n.
Shir Khan of Afghanistan, 118
Sinclair, Sir John, MP, 257, 257n.
Sligo, Howe Peter Browne, 2nd Marquis of, 49, 50n.
Smirke, Robert, artist, 193n.
Smith, Lady Anne Culling, 151, 152n.
Smith, Mrs Nicolas Hankey, 54, 54n., 73, 74
Smith, Adm. Sir (William) Sidney, 128, 129n., 256
Smith, Lady (Sidney), 128, 129n.
Smith, Thomas, Lord Mayor of London, 210-12, 212n.
Smith, Miss, Lady Mayoress, 210-12
Society for Promoting Christian Knowledge (SPCK), 176
Somerset House, 217, 217n.
Sophia, Princess (dau. of Geo. III), 138
Spanish Ambassador, 255, 255n.

ILLUSTRATION ACKNOWLEDGEMENTS

The illustrations appear by kind permission of the following:
Plate 1 Author's Collection; 2 British Library/India Office
Library and Records; 3 Crown Estate Commissioners/Bridgeman
Art Library; 4 Guildhall Library/ Bridgeman Art Library; 5
Mansell Collection; 6 and 7 Guildhall Library/Bridgeman Art
Library; 8 British Library/India Office Library and Records; 9
Private Collection; 10 Guildhall Library/Bridgeman Art Library;
11 Crown Estate Commissioners/Bridgeman Art Library; 12
Mansell Collection; 13 Guildhall Library/Bridgeman Art
Library; 14 Ahuan Islamic Art Gallery, London; 15 Private
Collection; 16 Private Collection; 17 Private Collection; 18
Mansell Collection; 19 Reproduced by Gracious Permission of
H. M. The Queen; 20 Victoria & Albert Museum; 21
Bridgeman Art Library; 22 John Lucas-Scudamore, Kentchurch
Court; 23 Private Collection; 24 Stratfield Saye/Courtauld
Institute of Art; 25 National Portrait Gallery; 26 and 27 Mansell
Collection; 28 Author's Collection; 29 John Lucas-Scudamore;
30 Mansell Collection; 31 Private Collection; 32 Mansell
Collection; 33 Hertfordshire County Library; 34 Victoria &
Albert Museum; 35 Guildhall Library/Bridgeman Art Library;
36 Victoria & Albert Museum; 37 John Lucas-Scudamore; 38
Wedgwood Museum, Barlaston; 39 and 40 Guildhall Library/
Bridgeman Art Library; 41 Private Collection; 42 Harvard
University Art Museums Fogg Art Museum (Bequest William
M. Chadbourne); 43 Stratfield Saye/Courtauld Institute of Art;
44 Private Collection; 45 Private Collection/Courtauld Institute
of Art; 46 Private Collection; 47 Mansell Collection; 48
Guildhall Library/Bridgeman Art Library; 49 Wedgwood
Museum, Barlaston; 50 Fotomas.